BOOKS, BYTES AND BUSINESS

Books, Bytes and Business
The Promise of Digital Publishing

BILL MARTIN and XUEMEI TIAN

*Swinburne University of Technology,
Melbourne, Australia*

Routledge
Taylor & Francis Group

LONDON AND NEW YORK

First published 2010 by Ashgate Publishing

Published 2016 by Routledge
2 Park Square, Milton Park, Abingdon, Oxon OX14 4RN
711 Third Avenue, New York, NY 10017, USA

Routledge is an imprint of the Taylor & Francis Group, an informa business

British Library Cataloguing in Publication Data
Martin, William J., 1938-
  Books, bytes and business : the promise of digital publishing.
  1. Electronic publishing. 2. Publishers and publishing--
  Technological innovations. 3. Knowledge management--
  Technological innovations.
  I. Title II. Tian, Xuemei.
  070.5'0285-dc22

Library of Congress Cataloging-in-Publication Data
Martin, William J., 1938-
  Books, bytes, and business : the promise of digital publishing / by Bill Martin and Xuemei Tian.
      p. cm.
  Includes bibliographical references and index.
  ISBN 978-0-7546-7837-3
1. Electronic publishing. 2. Book industries and trade--Technological innovations. 3. Publishers and publishing--Forecasting. 4. Publishers and publishing--Case studies. 5. Information society--Economic aspects. I. Tian, Xuemei. II. Title.
  Z286.E43M37 2010
  070.5'797--dc22

2010010562

ISBN: 9780754678373 (hbk)

Contents

List of Figures

List of Tables

List of Case Studies

List of Abbreviations

ABC	Australian Broadcasting Corporation
B2B	business to business
CAL	The Copyright Agency
CGML	Common Ground Markup Language
CMS	content management system
CRM	customer relationship management
DOI	Digital Object Identifier
DRM	digital rights management
eBooks	electronic books
ePub	electronic publication
HTTP	Hypertext Transfer Protocol
ICTs	information and communication technologies
JSON	JavaScript Object Notation
MMOGs	Massively Multiplayer Online Games
MMORPGs	Massively Multiplayer Online Role-Playing Games
MOB	Mobile & Online Business Innovation Lab
NAICS	North American Industrial Classification System
OECD	Organization for Economic Cooperation and Development
ONIX	Online Information Exchange
PDA	personal digital assistant
PDF	Portable Document Format
PC	personal computer
POD	printing on demand
R&D	research and development
RDF	Resource Description Framework
REST	The Representational State Transfer
RSS	Really Simple Syndication, Rich Site Summary
SaaS	software as a service
SMS	Short Message Service
URL	Uniform Resource Locator
W3C	World Wide Web Consortium
XML	eXtensible Markup Language
XML-RPC	XML Remote Procedure Call

Preface and Acknowledgements

This book is about business in the knowledge-based economy. It is concerned with how businesses are affected by and are responding to global changes in markets impacted upon and frequently driven by changes in technology. Whatever the industry, the trends are familiar and include globalization and the rise of industrial conglomerates, and the continuing incidence of mergers and acquisitions. They also include the networking of businesses and markets, the growing practice of outsourcing and shifts in the distribution of resources and production. These trends are all reflected in the emergence of new players, new products and services and new forms of competition.

As arguably the first such manifestation of the categorization, book publishing provides an ideal setting for the study of challenge and opportunity in knowledge-intensive business. As one of the oldest industries in the world, and based upon the first of the great technological breakthroughs, the invention of movable type, book publishing is currently experiencing fierce levels of competition, extreme financial pressures, restructuring and the threat of technology-induced obsolescence. When to these are added the challenges posed by new and potential entrants to the market, the emergence of new products and services, of new ways of doing business, including trading in virtual markets, and the vulnerability of traditional business models, the suitability of book publishing as a context for researching the emergence of knowledge-intensive business becomes all too apparent.

This book had its genesis in a three-year government-funded research project into digitization in the Australian book publishing sector which was completed in December 2008. The findings of this original research were then applied to an examination of the book publishing industry as a whole, based upon an analysis of the relevant global literature as contained in hard copy and electronic sources.

Structure of the Book

The book begins with an introduction and is followed by three parts entitled respectively 'Books', 'Bytes' and 'Business'.

Chapter 1: Introduction

This chapter provides an overview of the book publishing industry, its structure, the major players involved and key trends and innovations, not least in value chains and business models.

Part I: Books

This first part looks at key trends in book publishing. In particular it focuses upon the restructuring of markets and organizations, and on those radical shifts in consumer behaviour that are calling into question the very survival of the book as we have known it. It is comprised of two chapters:

Chapter 2: The Business of Book Publishing
Chapter 3: Book Publishing in the Digital Age

Part II: Bytes

This part looks at the role of technology in book publishing and the resulting implications for the industry. These implications range from production and editorial-type activities through to the emergence of electronic formats and a new generation of reading devices. The spectrum of technologies covered includes the familiar, such as the internet and World Wide Web, and the perhaps less familiar in the form of a set of potentially disruptive semantic technologies. The current stage of technological development in book publishing (as in knowledge-intensive industries in general) can be captured conveniently and succinctly in the term 'digitization'. Although clearly a label which is open to a wide range of perceptions, digitization now permeates the argot of business in much the same way as other terms such as globalization, disintermediation, niche and virtual. As employed here, it signifies not only advances in digital technologies and their applications, but also their impact on industry and society. This part contains the following chapters:

Chapter 4: Digital Technologies and Book Publishing
Chapter 5: Web 2.0 Applications and Book Publishing

Part III: Business

This part focuses on the nexus between recent developments in book publishing and the trend towards knowledge-intensive business. The impact of knowledge and related intangibles and of the potentially transformative power of digital technologies has resulted in new perspectives on the nature and focus of value in organizations, with particular implications for value and supply chains and business models. Earlier predictions of, for example, the widespread disintermediation of value and supply chains, have proved to be somewhat wide of the mark. Changes have occurred, however, including a shift in organizational structure from the lateral towards the networked form. Likewise there have been changes to the spectrum of business models, ranging from the traditional to the hybrid and, to a much lesser extent, the purely digital.

Experience has shown that, despite their undoubted enabling characteristics, digital technologies are only one piece of the organizational jigsaw. The key to business success continues to lie in the delivery of viable value propositions to customers who are currently enjoying an unprecedented range of choice and degree of market power, while harnessing the power of technology where appropriate. Increasingly, these value propositions are grounded in the ability to convert information into knowledge and/or to combine the two in the search for competitive advantage, for market differentiation and for the creation of new products and services. In other words, there is real potential in the pursuit of knowledge-intensive business.

This part seeks to capture and synthesize this trend towards knowledge-intensive business by examining the changes and continuing trends in book publishing and the players, categories and niche markets involved. It will shed light on the sources of value in organizations, on effective responses to challenges and opportunities in terms of policies, processes, technologies and strategies and the possibilities in terms of value chains, supply chains and business models. Drawing heavily on in-depth interviews with book publishers in Australia and on the analysis of secondary data on the global publishing industry, it presents a set of generic models of book publishing at industry and sector levels. These models will be useful in an academic context, as well as in industry domains beyond that of book publishing. The part is comprised of the following five chapters:

Chapter 6: Knowledge-intensive Organizations
Chapter 7: Supply Chains and Value Chains in Knowledge-intensive Organizations
Chapter 8: Business Models in Knowledge-intensive Organizations
Chapter 9: Business Models for Book Publishing in Australia
Chapter 10: The Future of Book Publishing

Why Read This Book?

- The book is research related and, as it complements existing books in the knowledge-intensive business and business model fields, it is a useful addition to the literature.
- The detailed treatment of knowledge-intensive organizations and business models is set in the contexts both of our primary research into the Australian book publishing sector and of secondary research into the global book publishing sector and changes in markets and technology.
- Starting from our original research, the book contains a plentiful supply of business cases which have application across the management disciplines as well as within publishing.
- For anybody interested in business models, this book effectively combines the theoretical background with the practicalities of analysing and building models in a way that is applicable to a range of industries and disciplines.
- The book is written in a style likely to prove attractive to a wider audience, including academics, practising managers and students in such disciplines as business and management, publishing, information and knowledge management and information systems.

Acknowledgements

Special thanks are due to Dr Bill Cope, CEO of Common Grand Publishing, for agreeing to our use of Common Ground Publishing as a case study, and to those other publishers who, while requesting anonymity, gave of their time and knowledge during our original research. Thanks are also due to Dr Carmine Sellitto, Victoria University, Melbourne and Dr Marianne Gloet, Higher Colleges of Technology, United Arab Emirates for taking the time to read and suggest improvements to the original proposal. We must also record our appreciation of the contribution made by Rob Manson of the Mobile & Online Business Innovation Lab (MOB) in Sydney. He not only helped us with a valuable critique of the drafts of Chapter 4 and Chapter 5 but more generally was a stimulating and effective source of feedback and ideas.

Special thanks are owed to our families, who provided understanding and support during a process that inevitably meant long hours spent away from them.

Chapter 1
Introduction

Introduction

The idea for this book emerged from a three-year research project into the implications of digital technologies for book publishing in Australia (Martin and Tian 2008). In the event we realized that any such volume would be more meaningful if set in a wider context than that of Australian book publishing. Consequently, our treatment of the process of digitization in book publishing is set within the context of a global networked economy in which knowledge-intensive organizations have acquired an increasingly significant profile. Within the global markets that characterize this networked economy, the interplay between books, bytes and business is growing in both scale and complexity.

Book Publishing

The North American Industrial Classification System (NAICS) describes the publishing industry as a whole as one that produces a variety of publications, including magazines, books, newspapers and directories (NAICS 2007). It also produces greeting cards, databases, calendars and other publishing material, excluding software. The production of printed material continues to dominate the industry, although the marketplace now reflects the emergence of material in other formats, such as audio, CD-ROM, or other electronic media. Book publishing is different from other media sectors such as magazines, newspapers and journals. In dynamic markets characterized by great multiplicity in output, books are uncertain products that are also dependent on a high degree of creativity and individual attention. Understanding today's book publishing industry involves acknowledging the growing concentration of resources, the effects of globalization, the changing structure of markets and of channels to these markets and the potential impact of new technologies (Thompson 2005).

Industry structure

The structure of book publishing can be variously perceived depending on the number and type of categories into which it is divided. Cheng (2004) categorized production according to consumer (or general) book publishing, covering a wide range of general interests; educational book publishing, covering schools and higher education; and professional book publishing, covering the areas of finance, legal, medical, scientific and technical publishing. All categories are dominated by large conglomerates that are responsible for a significant proportion of sales (*Encyclopaedia of Global Industries* 2007). At the time of writing (late 2009) there are 20 global publishing companies with revenues of over US$ 250 million. Allowing for various alliances and interconnections, some two-thirds of these conglomerates are located in Europe and the United States, with the remaining (Asian) third comprised mainly of three Japanese publishers (Wischenbart 2009).

Although the power and significance of such conglomerations are facts of life, this is not quite the whole story so far as book publishing is concerned. Even at the global level, there is still a place for numerous smaller and independent publishers that survive and, indeed, remain profitable by focusing their efforts on niche markets (IBISWorld 2010, Pira International 2002). An excellent example is the Lonely Planet Company, founded in Australia but now owned by the British Broadcasting Corporation, and which in many ways has set the benchmark for publishing guidebooks for travellers.

The nature of book publishing

In order to understand what is happening in book publishing today, it is important to take account both of change and of continuity. The effects of change are all around us and are exemplified by conglomeration, the restructuring of markets and channels, rising costs and competition and the all-pervasive impact of technology. Continuity can be seen in the continued role and perception of book publishing as being somehow different from the general run of commerce and, notably, as regards the cultural significance of its products and services (Thompson 2005).

In seeking to fund and profit from the production of these cultural artefacts, book publishers are especially vulnerable to changes in the demographics of the customer base and to increasing competition for time between the activity of reading and other, mainly electronic-based activities. To some, the sheer social and cultural significance of books, another dimension to their special status among consumer goods, renders their demise unthinkable. However, it is clear that books and the practice of reading face serious and immediate challenges, and it is less clear that the industry is capable of responding in the necessary manner.

One area of concern involves the perceived tardiness of the industry's response to change in general, and to change involving digital technologies in particular. While it may still be too early to gauge the impact of the so-called 'digital revolution' on book publishing, it is also the case that much of the industry is involved to some degree with digital processes, whether the content is hard copy or electronic. There is, however, no substantial uniformity in approach, as each individual publisher has different requirements, characteristics and target markets, and hence they exhibit various levels of take-up of and involvement with digitization. What is clear, however, is that in the emerging digital environment, traditional ways of doing things will no longer be appropriate and radical changes will be required to ensure a viable, ongoing competitive future. Above all, publishers must now accept that theirs is an industry dependent upon the ability to produce what the end-user wants rather than what the publisher can give to them.

The role of publishers

Book publishing is the process of commissioning, producing and distributing books for sale. Traditionally the key players in the production channel have been authors, agents, publishers and printers. The key players in the distribution channel can be separated into distributors (sometimes the publishers), wholesalers, retail stores and book clubs, libraries and printers (Keh 1998). The range of players in both channels has increased even in the context of traditional print-based publishing, and it continues to expand with the onset of digitization. In both these channels, the publishing company still serves as the centre of gravity and plays a pivotal role in moulding the process. This is despite continued predictions that the uptake of digital technologies would result in disintermediation of the value chain for book publishing, given that authors could potentially perform all the roles involved, from creating the content to marketing and selling the finished product. In other words, authors would have the ability to become publishers. As with many technology-related predictions however, this one has not eventuated to any serious extent, and for good reason.

With their long experience of and considerable expertise in the book trade, publishers continue to add a considerable amount of value to the book publishing business. Publishers are not just another partner in the process. Rather, they are the major risk takers in what not infrequently can turn out to be extremely marginal ventures. They are responsible for everything from commissioning the book, to its design and production, marketing, sales and customer service. Over time the structures of the industry and the relationships between the players have changed as the result of a range of both internal and external forces, which will be explored in Chapter 2.

Key Trends in Book Publishing

Over the past decade, the global book publishing industry has been on a kind of roller-coaster ride, frequently alternating between turmoil and stability. This has brought change and disruption to markets and distribution channels, to products and formats and to business processes and practices. Traditional publishing markets have expanded to include opportunities in niche and specialist areas, such as those involving professional, educational and scholarly communities. New distribution channels and supply chains have emerged with the advent of the internet, and book publishers are using their web pages to communicate with authors and to provide a growing range of products and services directly to end-users.

Internet sales of print books continue to rise, as do sales of eBooks, albeit at a slower pace. Inevitably, such developments will add to fears of channel conflict and potential damage to conventional markets. Over the nine-week-long holiday sales period around Christmas 2009, in-store sales at Barnes & Noble fell by some 5.4 per cent to $1.1 billion, as compared with the same period in 2008. However, over the same time frame, online sales at BN.com increased by 17 per cent, peaking at $134 million. For the same period in 2008, Barnes & Noble had online sales of $114 million. Analysts agree that the increased figures for 2009 were a direct reflection of the launch of the nook reading device in November that year, estimating that nook revenues came to somewhere between $10 million and $20 million (B&N Press release 2010). The experience at Amazon.com was not dissimilar, with the company announcing that over Christmas 2009 customers bought more eBooks than hard copy books, again largely owing to the popularity of the Kindle (Amazon News Release 2010a). The subject of eBooks will be discussed in detail in Chapter 4.

The technology dimension

The most visible technologies in book publishing over the past decade have been the internet and the World Wide Web. However, at the core of technological change is the digitization of everything from content creation and editorial, to printing and distribution. At the most basic level, digitization involves the conversion of images, characters or sounds into digital codes so that the information may be processed or stored by a computer system. In this book, however, the use of the term 'digitization' goes beyond consideration of the functionality of individual technologies, to embrace their collective impact on organizational missions, structures, processes, cultures and behaviours. So far as book publishing is concerned, by enabling the conversion of data and information to electronic form, these digital technologies have the potential to transform the entire industry, from the creation of the book in digital form to its marketing, sale and even its use through a range of digital devices.

Today, organizations, including book publishers, typically employ a variety of digital technologies and applications, ranging from document management, workflow and collaborative systems, to enterprise resource planning systems and corporate portals. Digital technology has the capacity to act as an enabler in terms of production and distribution options, and of new products such as eBooks. It is impacting directly upon publishing costs through the provision of viable options in outsourcing and the subcontracting of specific business processes. Further, it is enabling the restructuring of firms and the industry as a whole, and is already transforming everyday marketing and communication practices. Not for the first time, however, there are at least two sides to this story, with technology retaining the capacity to be something of a two-edged sword. Hence, while undoubtedly helping book publishers with regard to competitiveness, costs and strategy, digital technology can also be a source of disintermediation, with the potential to increase the power of authors and readers and to disrupt industry and company value chains. In seeking to address such issues, the successful firms will be those that succeed in balancing the enabling power of technology, on the one hand, with the ability to exploit its potential to leverage the value of intangible resources, on the other.

The importance of intangibles

Within the global networked economy there have been fundamental changes to the organizational resource mix, with a high priority now afforded to acquiring, creating and capturing value from a broad range of intangibles. The acquisition of information and knowledge and their coordination and redeployment while learning from past experience is fundamental not just to continuous innovation, but also to competitive capacity and survival itself. It is obvious that technologies are undoubtedly an enabling force when it comes to facilitating the capture and transfer of information, here defined as data organized to characterize a particular situation, condition, context, challenge or opportunity. However, they are much less effective when it comes to the capture, codification and transfer of knowledge. For present purposes, knowledge is understood to consist of facts, perspectives and concepts, mental reference models, truths and beliefs, judgements and expectations, methodologies and know-how. Critically, it also includes an understanding of how to juxtapose and integrate seemingly isolated information items in order to develop new meaning and create new insights (Wiig 2004).

With knowledge now the predominant business resource, much of the emphasis in strategy today is on the acquisition and maintenance of the knowledge competencies and capabilities that are embedded in the social and physical structure of organizations across the spectrum from for-profit to not-for-profit operations. Whether viewed in terms of disciplinary domains, such as those of strategy or knowledge management, or of theories including, for example, resource-based or organizational learning theories, these developments constitute a significant shift in market and organizational dynamics.

Although information and knowledge have always been important to organizations, the recent shift in resource requirements, emphasizing the value residing in intangible assets, has produced a virtual step change in the level of this importance. The shift in emphasis from information to knowledge has been closely associated with the acquisition of the ability to connect information on networks. This connectivity, and its implications for interactivity, customization and learning, has extended not just to products and processes, but also to organizations, their structure and operations. It has also made a major contribution to the emergence of knowledge-intensive organizations.

Knowledge-intensive organizations

The rise of knowledge-based economies, and their links to innovation and rapid technological change, continue to have extremely significant implications for all kinds of organizations and their management. Furthermore, in what is a dynamic and often turbulent business environment, concepts such as industries, firms, suppliers, competitors and clients are all much less clearly demarcated than had previously been the case, with flux and fluidity apparent in both meaning and context. As a result, traditional command and control structures and classic bureaucracies are giving way to decentralized structures and to the employment of more flexible, fluid and integrated business processes.

Although the term 'knowledge-intensive organization' is socially constructed, there is more at work here than just simple perception. The concept relates to the kind of work performed in organizations and to the characteristics of the people who perform it. It embraces aspects of organizational infrastructure, of technology and human resource systems and structures, and involves a search for crucial synergies between people and work, innovation and creativity (Newell et al. 2002). As with many such popular terms, 'knowledge-intensive organization' comes with a level of intuitive plausibility, the most obvious examples coming from within the services sector. This plausibility was reflected in a notable description of service companies as being 'brain rich' and 'asset poor' (Quinn 1992). Nevertheless, it would be wrong to think of knowledge-intensive organizations as residing entirely in the services sector. Much of the early research into knowledge management occurred in the context of Japanese manufacturing industry, and also in the oil and agricultural chemistry businesses, involving companies such as BP Amoco and the then Buckman Pharmaceuticals (now Bulabs). Later, Heineken NV, the major multinational brewery, underwent a major organizational transformation by recognizing the value of strategic and operational knowledge. The goal was to leverage this knowledge within a horizontal, team-based structure based on soft networks of people, supported by hard networks comprised of personal productivity tools, communication tools and knowledge tools (Tissen, Andriessen and Deprez 2001).

However, within both hard and soft networks, the capture and transfer of knowledge is by no means a straightforward or routine affair. For example, although there are circumstances in which knowledge can be codified through embedding it in systems and structures, this not infrequently results in its becoming 'sticky', which is to say, resistant to transfer (Brown and Duguid 2001). In any case, simply codifying knowledge into a system does not necessarily make it usable for people working in a different time and space context (Swan, Robertson and Newell 2002). Consequently, there are other infrastructure elements at play within knowledge-intensive organizations, and specifically, structural and behavioural elements.

The need to create, develop and capture value from knowledge has had a significant impact both upon organizational architectures and on human resource management practices. So far as architectures are concerned, this can be seen in the emergence of everything from flat, flexible and competency-based organizational structures to those that are networked and virtual. To some extent these changes are a reaction to the perceived restrictions imposed by traditional bureaucratic arrangements, and a shift in the direction of structures where control based on professionalism and shared organizational values supplants that based on direct supervision and adherence to rules and procedures, thus providing the necessary environment for employees to enjoy autonomy and engage in creative and innovative behaviour (Newell et al. 2002).

In the sphere of human resource management, there are implications for new roles, accountabilities and relationships, with senior management increasingly readjusting to a role that largely involves supporting and coaching teams of staff newly empowered to be proactive and creative. The basic objective of such adjustments to human resource management practices is to instil in staff the kinds of attitudes and patterns of behaviour that are perceived to be more suitable to the circumstances of knowledge-intensive organizations. These relate largely to recognition of the value of knowledge, and the inculcation of habits of collegiality and openness, leading to expected improvements in organizational climate and, especially, in conditions for the creation and sharing of knowledge. Put differently, this involves a search for organizational cultures that are knowledge based. This wider cultural dimension is captured in Figure 1.1, which presents an overall picture of the nature of knowledge-intensive organizations.

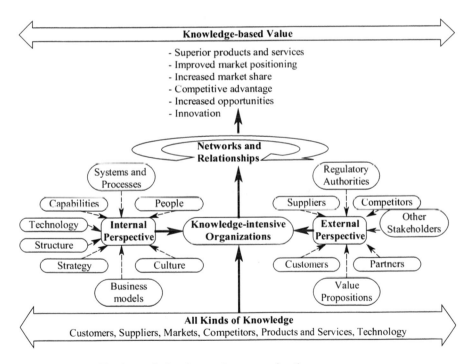

Figure 1.1   The knowledge-intensive organization

Two types of knowledge-intensive organization

Whatever their particular characteristics, or the industries and markets in which they operate, knowledge-intensive organizations can be divided into those for which knowledge is itself a product or service, and those for which it is a key business resource. Those in the former category make money either from creating knowledge and embodying it in new products and services (Nonaka and Takeuchi 1995) or from repackaging and reselling existing knowledge (Botkin 1999). Those in the latter category are skilled at acquiring and transferring knowledge, and at modifying their behaviour to reflect new knowledge and insights (Choo 2005). To some extent, therefore, all these knowledge-intensive organizations also engage in the practice of knowledge management, which for present purposes is understood as the process of creating, capturing and using knowledge to enhance organizational performance.

The rationale for knowledge-intensive organizations is that they are the logical response to a series of almost seismic commercial, regulatory and technological transformations that have taken place around the globe. These include radical shifts in the nature and composition of markets, in the locus of value and production, in the kinds of goods and services involved, and in organizational arrangements by way of response. Across the industry spectrum today, companies are faced with the same kinds of challenges and opportunities involved in the necessity of having to capture and exploit internal and external knowledge resources. Not surprisingly, there will be considerable variation in the response of different kinds of organizations, even among those operating in the same sectors and markets. Nonetheless, they will have in common an appreciation of the need for change and for creative and innovative responses based on recognition of the value that resides in intangibles. This is as true of the book publishing industry as any other, and it is to that industry that the focus now turns.

The cultural dimension to knowledge-intensive organizations   The fact that the culture of organizations is shaped by many factors results in considerable variation in the perceptions of organizational culture, whether in terms of assumptions, beliefs and ideologies, artefacts, symbols and practices (Hatch 1993, Schein 1985), or in the extent to which organizational cultures should be regarded as being homogeneous or diverse (Hofstede 2001, Deal and Kennedy 2000). Organizational culture emerges from the social construction of reality by generations of leaders and individuals within organizations, in order to reduce the equivocality and uncertainty of events (Erez and Gati 2004). It represents the essential qualities of human groups transmitted as a common worldview from one generation to the next, an enduring set of values, beliefs and assumptions that characterize organizations and their members (Cameron and Quinn 1999, Schein 1999).

In the specific context of knowledge-intensive organizations, culture is central to the shaping of assumptions about what knowledge is worth exchanging, or converting from tacit to explicit, or from individual to corporate levels. Culture also defines relationships between individual and corporate knowledge, creates the context for that social interaction between individuals and groups that determines how knowledge will be shared in particular situations, and shapes the processes by which new knowledge is created, legitimized and distributed in organizations (Karlsen and Gottschalk 2004, Gold, Malhotra and Segars 2001). Put more succinctly, culture influences behaviour and the role of leaders, the selection of technology, the evolution of knowledge management and its expected outcomes (Alavi, Kayworth and Leidner 2006). Consequently, organizations with more open and supportive values, such as those of trust, collaboration and learning, are more likely to engage in effective knowledge creation and sharing practices, as well as to be more innovative and flexible in responding rapidly to the needs of changing markets (Barrett et al. 2004).

Supply Chains, Value Chains and Business Models in Knowledge-intensive Organizations

In engaging in such practices, knowledge-intensive enterprises recognize that the key to business success continues to lie in the delivery of viable value propositions grounded in the ability to convert information into knowledge and/or to combine the two in the search for competitive advantage, for market differentiation and for the creation of new products and services. As this increasingly involves selling to customers enjoying an unprecedented range of choice and enhanced market power, it is important that firms pay sufficient attention to the currency of their value and supply chains and business models. Although earlier predictions of the widespread disintermediation of value and supply chains in technology-enabled markets have proved to be somewhat wide of the mark, changes have occurred in both cases, entailing a shift in chain structure from the lateral towards the networked. Likewise, change has resulted in a spectrum of models ranging from the traditional to the hybrid and, much less common, the purely digital business model. It seems likely that further changes can be expected as the knowledge-intensive business sector continues to expand.

Whatever the business concerned, a business model is the same. It is a representation of how an organization makes (or intends to make) money. Furthermore, it is an architecture for product, service and information flows, a pattern of organizing exchanges and allocating various costs and revenue streams so that the production and exchange of goods or services becomes viable (Brousseau and Penard 2007). The widespread changes in resource status, markets and technologies already identified have mandated changes to business models as existing competitors strive for increased market share and as newcomers enter the market. This clearly includes the onset of digital business models, but as many activities are inter-modal – that is, have both digital dimensions and significant links with physical products, infrastructures and related services – combined or hybrid versions are popular. The search for innovation has also resulted in the emergence of open business models designed to enable companies to be effective not only in creating value, but also in acquiring it or sharing it with others, either through partnerships or on a commercial basis (Chesbrough 2007). A major concern of this book is with the impact of digitization on business models for book publishing, at both industry and firm level, and the relationship of these models to value chains and supply chains.

Book Publishing and Knowledge-intensive Business

Although for centuries engaged in the production of physical objects, by virtue of its involvement in the creation and transfer of knowledge, the book publishing industry has always had a claim to be knowledge intensive. In responding to the pressures of recent commercial and technological change, it has enhanced this claim through structural and market reorganization and the adoption of leading edge technologies. It has also enhanced its knowledge-intensive status through recognition of the potential value inherent in being able to separate the (increasingly digital) content of its products from the carrier or codex format.

Clearly, both through the ages and in a current context, book publishing can boast very strong credentials as a knowledge-intensive business. However, because few such attributions are likely to remain either absolute or immutable, this innate plausibility is subject to critical scrutiny on a number of grounds. In Part III of this book, we examine the nature of knowledge-intensive business by comparing book publishing with a range of benchmarks commonly applied to such organizations. This will include comparisons which take account of changes in products and services, in customer and partner relationships, in value and supply chains and in business processes. In particular, we will assess the impact of digitization on book publishing and look at how an industry largely associated with the manufacture of physical products has begun the transition to the world of electronic and virtual markets, and hence to knowledge-intensive status.

At the firm level, and using case-based research, we will assess how individual book publishers are making the transition to operations based not only on the sale of knowledge in its traditional containers, namely books, but also on the exploitation and management of knowledge for everyday operational purposes and, more strategically, as the basis of new products and services based on intangibles and embedded in new forms of container. As much as anything else, this will entail an assessment of attitudes and mindsets among book publishers, looking for signs of an ability to define the enterprise in terms of the knowledge it has, be this a knowledge of products, competitors, processes, finance or people.

PART I
Books

Chapter 2
The Business of Book Publishing

Introduction

This book is appearing at a time when book publishing, like many other industries, is facing perhaps the most difficult set of circumstances in its long history. These circumstances were thrown into relief in 2007 by the onset of the most unfavourable economic environment since that of the Great Depression in the 1930s. However, so far as book publishing is concerned, the present difficulties, while clearly attributable to those depressed conditions evidenced in receding demand in falling markets can also be explained by factors much more specific to the industry. Prominent among these would be its collective response to a set of challenges and opportunities that became evident to industry watchers at least a decade ago. This in turn has led to a lack of flexibility, and of innovation and market focus, and to a widespread faltering and, in some cases, the outright failure of business models. Admittedly all such things are much clearer after the event, and some sort of defence might be mounted along the lines of 'if it ain't broke don't fix it'. Nonetheless it is a key role of management to anticipate future developments, not least when things are going well, and forward thinking seems to have been in short supply. It is hard not to see at least some connection between this conclusion and those perceptions of obsolescence in trade publishing raised at the Digital Book World conference in New York in January 2010 (Ginna 2010).

A case in point is the revolution in information and communications technologies that has been a constant feature of the last two decades. Clearly, technology is no panacea for the ailments of any business, and its adoption must align firmly with organizational missions and value propositions. Moreover, publishers could be forgiven to some extent if hard-learned lessons from previous failed technology-based ventures inclined them to caution in relation to the evident opportunities in such areas as eBooks and digital content. Markets however, are notoriously unforgiving, and a seeming inability to perceive and respond to changes in the nature of competition and the consumer base and, not least, to appreciate the changing relationship between carrier and content, all contributed to the vulnerability of book publishers when recession hit in 2007.

Not that the industry had lacked for change in the previous 20 years and indeed, therein lay at least some of the roots of its later difficulties. The spate of mergers and acquisitions in the early years of this century that saw the involvement of major media and entertainment corporations in publishing and led to the emergence of global publishing conglomerates left its mark in cultural as much as in structural terms. The impact, however, was soon to be felt in the business models, cost structures, revenue and profit performance of the entire industry. But what do we mean when we talk about the book publishing industry?

Book Publishing

Book publishing forms part of a wider industry involving the production and distribution of a diverse range of products ranging from books, newspapers and magazines to electronic media. Extracted from this wider context, book publishing itself is much less of a unitary activity than might be expected. It can usefully be regarded as being not one, but several industries that are joined by the common distribution medium of the book (Daniels 2006). Although there are an estimated 10,000 book publishers operating in some 180 countries, what matters is not such raw numbers but the market shares enjoyed by the major players. In national terms these can still be identified as the United States, Japan, Germany, the United Kingdom, the Netherlands and France (*Encyclopaedia of Global Industries* 2007), although such descriptions are complicated by the global make-up of the industry and the emergence of conglomerates built upon different industries in different countries. Hence, whereas the United States remains the world's largest market for book publishing, it is also a market where foreign-owned multinationals such as Bertelsmann, the world's largest English- and German-language publisher, play a major role. In this turbulent environment, moreover, it is difficult to estimate future market positions. For example, in the Asia-Pacific region, Japan is still the biggest player, although its market share fell from 51 per cent in 2006 to 49.6 per cent in 2008. By this time China had become the fastest-growing book market in the world, with a growth rate of 24.5 per cent in 2008 (Datamonitor 2009).

During a long and often turbulent history, book publishing has frequently been at the forefront of social and technological change. This continues to be the case today, with the industry seemingly poised somewhere between decline and extinction on the one hand, and revival and radical reinvention on the other. As a business, book publishing has always been a risky enterprise on account of the levels of investment and competition involved and owing to the fickleness of its markets. In striving to sell their product, publishers have accepted as a fact of life that many books will fail to find an audience, and that only a small percentage of titles will make it to their backlists (Thompson 2005).

Publishers have long occupied the high ground in this business. Functioning both as venture capitalists and as gatekeepers, they have traditionally exercised considerable influence over who and what is published. Today, however, things are no longer quite so simple. The digitization of content and of distribution channels, combined with market and demographic change, have seen the dissolution and reconstitution of book publishing value chains, along with the increasing liberation of aspiring authors and the empowerment of their readers. Accordingly, long-established book publishers now face market competition that is different both in degree and in kind. This competition has acquired a digital dimension in everything from the acquisition and creation of content to rights management. It is as likely to come from new industry entrants, including self-publishing services, online aggregators and bookshops, and search engines, as from established book publishers. Consequently the entire fabric and structure of the industry is in a state of flux.

Structure of the Book Publishing Industry

Traditionally, book publishing has operated on the basis of specific interests and markets. This has led to its categorization broadly into general-interest books and educational and professional books (Cheng 2004) or, in somewhat more detail, trade books, textbooks, scientific, technical and professional (STP), mass-market paperbacks and all others (*Encyclopaedia of Global Industries* 2007, Greco 2005). In this book we employ a fivefold categorization, used during our recent research into the Australian book publishing industry. This includes:

- trade publishing: focusing on adult fiction and non-fiction books, children's books and young adult titles;
- educational publishing: involved in the production of a wide range of textbooks to cover all levels of the education process;
- professional publishing: refers to material relevant to specific occupations and industries and is commonly comprised of five categories: financial, legal, science, technology and medicine;
- specialist publishing: involves operation in different niche markets, with their products orientated towards areas such as technology, travel, cooking and feminist publications;
- university press publishing: predominantly focusing on higher educational publications.

There is considerable variation in levels of sales and profitability among these different categories. Traditionally, the most profitable segments have been trade, which includes consumer books, education and professional and technical (*Encyclopaedia of Global Industries* 2007). An earlier estimate for the United States market found that sales of textbooks and technical, scientific and professional books accounted for nearly half of the revenue of the book publishing industry, with general adult books making up the rest (Straubhaar and LaRose 2006). Perhaps more relevant in the near future will be the question not so much of the absolute performance of various publishing segments, as of their performance when compared to that of other media. In this context, it is sobering to find predictions that over the period 2009 to 2013 not only will there be sectoral differences in market performance, but also revenues in consumer, educational and business publishing will all fall in absolute terms. To make matters worse, revenues in internet access, TV and advertising are all expected to grow at around 9.2 per cent annually, representing a growth rate of three times that of the entertainment and media market as a whole (PriceWaterhouseCoopers 2009). Such predictions aside, however, the viability of such market categorizations as trade and educational is questionable, owing both to the power of a relatively small group of multinational media conglomerates and to wider and deeper-seated changes in technology, in market structures and in author–publisher–consumer relationships.

Inevitably much of the focus remains upon the major players and on the seemingly endless process of mergers and acquisitions both within and between market segments. Just as inevitable is the constant effort to separate the marketing hype and some of the wilder predictions from reality and what is actually happening within publishing. Hence, despite recurring predictions that the six leading trade publishers could reduce to three within the next five years, the list of the biggest trade publishers in the United States did not change between 2000 and 2009. This said, few commentators are predicting that the picture will be the same in 2020 (Publishers Lunch Deluxe News 2010a).

So far as educational publishing is concerned, there are similar contradictions between prediction and performance. The London-based Pearson plc remains the leading educational publisher, with Reed Elsevier, the Anglo-Dutch joint venture, another major player. Indeed, the previous success of Pearson Education in selling and distributing content on a global scale precipitated a series of mergers and acquisitions in the sector. These involved such leading players as Harcourt, Houghton Mifflin, Bertelsmann, Springer, Blackwell, Thomson Learning and Wolters Kluwer (Publishers Lunch Deluxe News 2010a). Unfortunately, the outcome for many of these companies was the accumulation of massive debts in the absence of few sustainable business models. There could be further bad news ahead with the emergence into the vibrant Asian educational market of Korean and Chinese publishers possessed of critical advantages in terms of costs and cultural fit (Wischenbart 2009).

When it comes to the prospects for smaller publishers, the predictions tend to become more optimistic. Hence, argues Hunter (2009a), independent publishers with low overheads, small staffs and narrower missions are better suited than their larger counterparts to an age where profits are smaller and audiences are fragmented. However, rather than attempting to compete in mainstream markets, their best policy could be to raise consumer awareness and create or leverage online platforms to reach the kind of specialist audiences largely ignored by the major publishers. Indeed, it could be the biggest publishers who are the most challenged, because almost by definition, they are the least vertical, whereas the smaller, more nimble houses are focused on targeted communities of readers (Ross 2010).

For over a decade now, book publishing has been a stable rather than an expanding activity. Consumer interest in both reading and buying books has declined, while at the same time the use of the internet and electronic formats has increased dramatically. These developments are related both to demographic change within the consumer base and to the impact of new technology on both users and producers (Kovac 2008). Side by side with such developments is the widespread perception that the book publishing industry has been relatively staid in its acknowledgment of and response to change. It is further argued that this prevailing attitude has hindered the implementation of progressive procedures and practices such as, for example, those associated with digital publishing (*Encyclopaedia of Global Industries* 2007). The impact of digitization on the book publishing industry is the subject of Chapter 3, and here it will suffice to point out that such developments are best viewed in the context of specific publishing categories, and even of individual publishers. More immediately, any understanding of today's book publishing industry involves acknowledging that combination of external and internal forces which provides both impetus and background to current events.

External and Internal Forces

Among the many external forces which can impact on the book publishing industry, the following are the most significant:

- the globalization of markets and publishing firms
- government policy
- mergers and acquisitions
- technological change
- shifts in consumer demand and behaviour
- competition.

Internal forces are largely comprised of the activities of owners and management faced with the pressure of external forces. This has resulted in a series of strategic decisions with implications for markets, products and services, and organizational strategies. The most significant of these internal forces have been:

- organizational structure
- organizational strategy
- organizational culture
- ICT strategies
- knowledge management
- outsourcing
- niche markets
- relationship building.

These forces, individually or in combination, will affect the book publishing industry either directly or indirectly via value chains and supply chains, leading inevitably to a rejuvenation of business models. Figure 2.1 illustrates these interrelationships. They will now be considered in more detail, beginning with external forces.

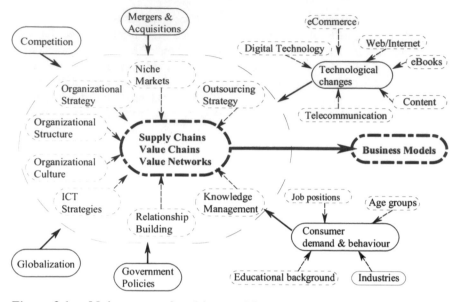

Figure 2.1   Major external and internal forces

External forces

The globalization of markets and publishing firms   A defining characteristic of our modern world, globalization has been described not as a single event, but as a process in which products, people, companies, money, and information are able to move freely and quickly around that world, unimpeded by national borders or other territorial limitations (Morrison 2006). It has also been portrayed as an ideology whose function is to reduce resistance to the process by making it seem both highly beneficial and unstoppable (Herman 1999).

In its totality, globalization combines the social and economic and the emotive and political. It can be perceived as providing a technological platform for progress with wide ranging benefits to the global population. Alternatively, it can be viewed as a force for the erosion of national identities, with the influx of foreign influences impacting upon national cultures (Cope and Gollings 2001). Although in many instances they are often seen as being under siege from such developments, there remains an important role in all this for national and for international governments.

Government policy   Governments and, increasingly, international agencies continue to exercise a significant influence on the book publishing industry. Even in a globalized world, national governments continue to have responsibility for ensuring that the appropriate legal and social environment exists to support the operation of viable book publishing industries. This can involve the need for action and oversight across the board, from the protection of copyright and intellectual property to freedom to publish and to access material; to fiscal policies ranging from taxation to industry or wider book trade subsidies (Thompson 2005). At the international level, agencies such as the World International Property Organization and forums such as the World Trade Organization have an important role to play in ensuring the operation of efficient and transparent markets and supportive environments for book publishing.

It is scarcely surprising that the complex of issues around globalization should be of direct concern to the book publishing industry, which, like others, has proved vulnerable to technological change, a growing concentration of resources, the changing structure of markets and channels to these markets (Thompson 2005). Most of these issues are subsumed in the successive waves of merger and acquisition activity that have occurred within the book publishing industry.

Mergers and acquisitions   Mergers can be defined as a consolidation of two or more entities into a single unit, whilst acquisitions are the outright purchase of either the assets or the equity of the target company (Keh 1998). Companies become involved in mergers and acquisitions for a variety of reasons, including:

- risk reduction and diversification
- competitive reaction
- perception of underutilized or undervalued assets
- anticipated synergies in markets, finances, operations or human resources
- legal and tax benefits
- access to new technologies or processes
- ego-emotional or psychological motivations (McCann and Gilkey 1988).

Book publishing has a long history of merger and acquisition activities. However, during the years 1990–2002, the book publishing industry in the United States was exposed to a frenzied period of activity ascribed to a combination of strategic marketing considerations, globalization and the emergence of global markets (Greco 2005). In fact, by 2002 merger and acquisition activity was a global phenomenon and had significantly altered the structure of the book publishing industry. This development was greeted with alarm in many circles, with fears that it might result in the further limiting of competition and the demise of smaller, often more innovative publishing houses (Keh 1998).

Technological change   Since the 1980s, the book publishing industry has engaged in a continuous debate about the impact of new technologies on its working practices, management systems and supply chains. All areas of the industry have been affected by computerization and digitization. The emergence of online selling and of eBooks provides a visible demonstration of how such developments have impacted upon the book publishing industry at every level of the value chain (Thompson 2005). As Chapters 4 and 5 are devoted entirely to the subject of technological change and its implications for book publishing, this section is intended only to capture the essence and wider implications of the current stage of technology development.

In order to understand such developments, it is necessary to get behind the specific technologies and look for the reasons why they might be important to publishing. Clearly, the adoption of any kind of technology can have a direct link to issues of cost and efficiency, and to productivity and profit. In somewhat more abstract terms, but specifically relevant to book publishing, however, are the key themes of content, convergence and communication. Technology can aid and, indeed, advance the processes and practices involved in the acquisition, creation, use and reuse of content. The convergence of different kinds of technology, including computing, telecommunications and, in particular, that family of networking technologies emerging from the internet and the World Wide Web, can enable the repackaging and mixing of different kinds of content in existing and nascent businesses. Communications technologies, ranging from the World Wide Web and the use of blogs and emails to the ever-growing range of social networking technologies, are already embedded in the book publishing life cycle from content acquisition and creation through to publicity, marketing and selling. Whilst computerization in all its aspects now pervades the printing and physical production of books, the wider focus in book publishing has been on technologies that have impacted upon it in more incremental fashion. However, although their adoption can prove to be more risky, the major breakthroughs in publishing, as anywhere else, are more likely to come from those technologies which can be described as being disruptive.

Disruptive technologies are just that. They have the potential to introduce new combinations of media, to erode existing revenue models and to force content companies to formulate new business models and work out new relationships with consumers. The internet and the World Wide Web were the major disruptive technologies of the 1990s (European Commission 2003). Currently the major candidates for the designation of disruptive technologies would be those related to the Semantic Web and the next generation of social networking technologies. Advances in technology inevitably present challenging options with regard, for example, either to early adoption or to waiting for signs of maturity, with business opportunities and risks either way. Book publishing has had its share of both experiences, and in the final analysis the most effective decisions will be those that combine vision and understanding of technological potential with the needs and capabilities of individual businesses.

Shifts in consumer behaviour and demand   There can be few issues more pressing for book publishers than those to do with the retention of existing customers and the attraction of new ones. There is no point to the production of books unless there are people in the market wishing to buy them. Just as evident is concern in the book trade over both the current and future behaviour of consumers and perhaps, more important, the identity of those consumers and their interests. Even today and as regards existing readers, both the book reading experience and the role of readers within the publishing process have changed remarkably. For book publishers, the challenge is no longer simply one of producing and selling books, but rather to sell a whole range of things, including consumer flexibility, answers, entertainment, enlightenment and learning (Lichtenberg 2000). Today book industry consumers want not only products, but also personal attention from and contact with publishers and authors, as well as with other like-minded readers (Davis and Walter 2004). Moreover, not only are readers embracing technology to access and read content, but also they are increasingly becoming creators of content. As new niche markets emerge on the basis of numerous communities of readers, the readers themselves will become players who will engage in rating, appending and tagging activities, and who will in effect play key roles in the editorial and marketing functions (Shatzkin 2007). The adoption of new technologies can facilitate such developments, but the need for improved knowledge and understanding of current and potential future consumer behaviour is absolutely paramount in book publishing.

Perhaps of even greater concern to publishers is the behaviour of those people who either are defecting from the book reading community or never have really been part of it (Phillips 2007). A 20-year study of reading habits in the United States (National Endowment for the Arts 2004) detailed a long-term decline in the role of reading in national culture. Worse still, this trend was set against a very liberal interpretation of the term 'literature', with reading as an activity described as being in significant decline among adults and in freefall so far as young people were concerned. Nor should this decline be viewed as a matter of concern for book publishing alone, with large-scale defections from all forms of print media regarded as being inevitable in face of the increasing dominance of the internet and of a growing range of electronic alternatives, from websites to games (Gomez 2008).

Competition Although competition is fundamental to the functioning of the market economy and has ever been present, it is particularly intensive in book publishing today. This is the result of various factors, including technological change and globalization, increasingly sophisticated consumer demands and competition from both within and outside the industry, as well as from new forms of digital media. The new media provide users with exciting options based on the convergence of technologies, not least the facility for interactivity and content generation through Weblogs or blogs, and social networking sites such as Myspace, YouTube and Facebook (Straubhaar and LaRose 2006). Publishers must compete both for content and for the attention and purchasing power of readers, not only with other publishers and, to some extent, self-publishers, but also with professional services firms, government-funded agencies and broadcasters and a myriad of internet-based portals.

Included within the orbit of new media would be alternative book formats and, most notably, eBooks. Although their record has been unimpressive to date, eBooks are still widely predicted to become a significant if not dominant presence in book publishing (Sorenson 2009). So far as competition is concerned, eBooks are already a source of concern, not least when linked to the activities of companies such as Amazon.com. With its global brand and unparalleled market reach Amazon.com has gained a virtually unassailable position in the markets not just for new, but for used and rare books also. Armed with the third internationally compatible version of its Kindle reader, it is currently the market leader in sales of eBooks (Pilkington 2009). Indeed, with its Print-on-Demand (POD) facility in BookSurge, Amazon.com already has the capability to offer a complete publishing service, a capability which, as will be seen in Chapter 10, it has already begun to exploit.

The abiding power of external market forces in a global, networked economy is there for all to see, but unless firms get their internal focus right, they are unlikely to be sustainably competitive within that economy. For book publishers, this presents a series of challenges to decision makers with regard to previously discussed issues such as mergers and acquisitions, and organizational structure, organizational strategy (both general and in relation to specific activities) and organizational culture.

Internal forces

Organizational structure   Organizational structures play a significant role in the responses of book publishers to the challenges and opportunities of changing markets and technologies. Structural change has of course been a prominent feature of conglomeration within book publishing, but it has not always found favour with those sitting remote from the decision to restructure. Indeed, whether the removal of the alleged inflexibilities commonly associated with, for example, family-owned firms has merely succeeded in replacing one form of hierarchy with another remains a moot point. A less controversial but important structural consideration has to do with the organizational and staffing implications of the uptake of digital technologies. This is because it is not just new technologies that are needed, but a new approach to the hiring and training of staff that will reflect their innate value to companies while recognizing the need for new mixes of skill, qualifications and experience. Issues of appropriate structures, both at organizational level and in relation to the management of technologies, and especially people, will continue to challenge book publishers in the coming decades.

Organizational strategy   A major advance in the understanding of competitive strategy occurred in the 1990s, when the value of internal as well as external resources and capabilities was formally acknowledged (Grant 1997, Barney 1996). Henceforth, not just the ability to respond to external market forces, but also a facility to generate and develop dynamic capabilities was deemed essential for any company that sought to be competitive (Wang and Ahmed 2007). Strategy can be described succinctly as a projection or plan which enables a firm to achieve a specific set of goals. In more detail, it describes the direction and scope of an organization over the long term, and a search for advantage through the configuration of resources within a changing environment to meet the needs of markets and fulfil stakeholder expectations (Johnson et al. 2007). Another important distinction to be made is that between the formulation of strategy based on environmental analysis and the selection of an appropriate response, and its implementation based on structures and systems (Hill et al. 2007).

Strategy can be based on a search for competitive advantage by competing on cost, differentiation, scale or scope, or on some combination of all of these (Porter 1996). Today, however, strategic planning is at once a more complex and less linear affair than in the relatively recent past. Where once companies could plan for long time horizons, it is now essential that their strategies can exhibit flexibility and responsiveness in the face of unanticipated events. These include short- to medium-term decisions on markets, competitors and collaborators, on technology, on structures and resource management (Mintzberg and Lampel 1999) and on the acquisition of knowledge and the management of human capital (Prahalad and Krishnan 2008). One obvious example of disruptive change and its impact upon strategy is that of the internet, which is relevant to almost any strategy. By levelling the competitive playing field between companies, the internet has put a considerable premium on differentiation in order to create and deliver value to customers, frequently on the basis of entirely new business models (Porter 2001). This all carries implications for strategy at the corporate, business and functional levels (De Wit and Meyer 2005).

Of particular interest at present are issues to do with the impact of conglomeration on book publishing strategies. There is specific concern over whether, in the perceived quest for high returns on investment, the new owners and managers of book publishing companies are responding to earlier external market stimuli rather than making the most of their internal resources in an economy based on knowledge and capabilities. While such scrutiny applies in overall terms to strategies for imprint acquisition and control, and for organizational structures and human resource management, it also applies to specific areas such as investment, the management of information and communications technology (ICT), knowledge management, outsourcing, operation in niche markets and relationship building.

Organizational culture   In publishing, as elsewhere, however, it is important to bear in mind that what is most important is not the adoption of the latest technologies. What matter are the potential connections between the culture of those organizations that implement the technology and the outcomes that eventuate, outcomes such as enhanced relationships with customers (Li and Bernoff 2009). As is only too clear amidst the current turbulence in book publishing, culture both organizational and national is a significant force for and against change. Culture is the sum of social patterns characteristic of a group, including behaviours and qualities that are valued (Schein 1999). Although Hofstede and Hofstede (2004) distinguished between national cultures, which differed at the level of values, and organizational cultures, which differed at the level of practices, in the event there are overlaps between the two, with, for example, national cultural differences being reflected in organizations. Furthermore, while cultural change is an extremely difficult task, cultures do evolve, and indeed, such evolution is critical to the process of change (Pool 2000, Silvester and Anderson 1999).

The effects of cultural change and, indeed, resistance to it have been particularly noticeable in book publishing, an industry where entrenched attitudes have frequently been seen to impede progress (Thompson 2005). On the one hand, book publishing continues to be one of the great cultural icons of our society, founded on respect for knowledge and learning, and viewed as responsible for maintaining the cultural record. On the other hand, in global markets driven by issues of cost and scale, a harder-edged, commercially driven culture based unashamedly on turnover and profits has emerged. The result is seen by many as a battle not only for the future, but also for the very soul of the book publishing industry.

Investment strategies   For at least a decade, the balance between costs, revenues and profits has been a matter of particularly serious concern for book publishers. Accordingly, investment decisions, whether for new initiatives or for existing projects, are, if anything, even more critical than ever. Much has been made in trade circles and in the popular press about the dangerous skewing of trade publishing investment in the hunt for best-selling novels. In straight 'return-on-investment' terms such strategies seem unlikely to last. Meanwhile, in a different category, the publishers of academic textbooks seem to be doing very nicely, with the likely inference that so far as investment strategies are concerned, the answer would be more of the same. Nevertheless, the digitization of content and the means of its delivery are already having a significant effect on academic publishing. This is clear, for example, through the growth of printing-on-demand (POD) and, more significantly, of open source learning projects in the United States, where collaboration in content creation and sharing has gained considerable momentum (Baranuik 2006). Clearly, no publisher can choose to ignore the potential of digital publishing. However, making choices as to which investments are likely to be most effective is by no means a trivial consideration in the context of new kinds of products and services, markets and technologies, customers and competitors.

ICT strategies   Like any strategy, that for ICT must be comprehensive, aligned with the firm's objectives, easy to comprehend and forward looking (Savin 2004). In the case of book publishing, this requires the incorporation of factors such as operating systems, content management and manipulation, marketing and service provision and content delivery (Thompson 2005). In all of these areas the strategic implications of digitization loom large, whether in relation to content creation and digital rights management, to workflows, warehousing and distribution or to supply chains and business models. The need for a viable and coherent ICT strategy for book publishers is easily illustrated in the context of the key themes of content, convergence and communications. None of these areas is attainable in the absence of an ICT infrastructure, while this and the strategies upon which its construction is founded must relate to other strategies, and in particular to production and human resource strategies.

Knowledge management   As both information and the technology for handling it became ubiquitous in the closing decades of the last century, organizations began to focus on acquiring and managing knowledge. Knowledge exists both as a stock and as a flow. It is dynamic and is resident in people, artefacts and practices. There are clear connections between the ability of organizations to develop and compete, and their ability to learn and to transform knowledge and experience into new or improved products and processes (Nidumolu, Subramani and Aldrich 2001). Knowledge management has both supply side and demand side dimensions. The former (also dubbed the First Generation of knowledge management) involves the capture, codification, reuse and sharing of already existing knowledge. The latter (or Second Generation) is marked by the creation of new knowledge through enhancing the conditions in which innovation and organizational creativity can flourish (McElroy 2003). In more specific terms, it involves critical issues of organizational survival in a context of structural and environmental change, and the search for synergies between the creative and innovative capacities of people and the communication and learning potentials of ICT (Jansen, Steenbakkers and Jagers 2007).

   Knowledge management is as important for book publishing as for any other business, not least within the current eBusiness environment, where it is essential that organizations have knowledge of their markets, customers, products and services, methods and processes, competitors, employee skills and the regulatory regime. Particularly important for publishing, however, is that knowledge management principles and practices are applied in the spheres of content and customer relationship management.

Content management   generally refers to the management of digital content and can cover everything from text to multimedia. Content management systems (CMS) support the creation, management, distribution, publishing and discovery of this digital content. The functionality of these systems can be broken down into the major categories of content creation, content management, publishing and presentation (Robertson 2003). Within these systems, documents are disassembled into their individual parts, such as chapters, photos, tables, graphs and charts for storage and reuse as separate components and are tagged and indexed for the purpose (Kleper 2001). There is also a relationship between CMS and other information systems within an organization, including systems for document management, records management and digital asset management (Robertson 2003). In publishing, digital rights management (DRM) systems continue to be a significant and, to some extent, controversial element of content management. Another important component of content management is customer relationship management.

Customer relationship management (CRM) is defined by the Gartner Group (Thompson 2009) as a business strategy whose outcomes optimize profitability, revenue and customer satisfaction by organizing around customer segments, fostering customer-satisfying behaviours and implementing customer-centric processes. More specifically, it comprises the activities that companies carry out in order to develop relations with loyal and profitable customers by delivering them exactly what they want, when they want it and through the most appropriate channel (Galbreath 1999). CRM systems consist of databases of customers and their purchasing patterns which can be exploited through sophisticated techniques such as data mining. Although often equated with the use of software, the underlying purpose of CRM essentially involves a series of customer-focused business strategies and processes implemented by an organization to unify its customer interactions and provide a means to track customer information. In essence, the aim is to build a different kind of relationship with customers, a long-term and dynamic partnership based on the two-way exchange of information.

CRM leverages, that is takes advantage of, strategic and proprietary customer information in order to personalize the content of advertising messages to customer or potential customers, seeking as far as possible to address their unique needs. Although the channels by which such relationships might be created are themselves multiplying and fragmenting, the basic concept is likely to survive within the web-based marketing context. Within the book trade, Amazon has made somewhat of a science of user engagement and, with user participation at virtually an order of magnitude greater than its competitors', it continues to set the benchmark (O'Reilly 2007).

Outsourcing Knowing what to produce and how to achieve this are key areas of strategic decision making. Almost as important nowadays is the issue of where to produce the goods in question, and to an ever-increasing extent this happens offshore. For book publishing, outsourcing can provide the opportunity to reduce costs, or at least to maintain them at a stable level, while also providing access to a greater knowledge pool, including to the most advanced technology available (Kasdorf 2003).

Outsourcing is a common practice across the range of publishing functions, from digital composition to editorial activities. Outsourcing provides cost benefits and flexibility, along with access to a diverse range of technology and associated skills. Currently outsourcing within the book publishing industry extends not just to arrangements with traditional trading partners, but also to networks involving new partners and, where circumstances dictate, competitors.

There are, however, potentially negative aspects that need to be considered prior to committing to outsourcing. These include the potential loss of coordination and control, exploitation by opportunistic suppliers, and employee concerns regarding job security (Thompson 2005, Kumar and Snavely 2004). It is generally agreed that outsourcing something, be it a process or a function, makes sense when the operation can be performed more efficiently and more cheaply elsewhere. It is also generally understood that the outsourcing of key strategic functions is not to be recommended. However, with even editorial functions no longer immune from such treatment, outsourcing will remain a topic of interest to book publishing in the foreseeable future. So will decisions on markets, and not least on niche markets.

Niche markets   Kotler (2003) defines niche markets as a more narrowly defined customer base seeking a distinct mix of benefits. Niche markets are small, specialist markets consisting of an individual customer or a small group of customers with similar characteristics or needs (Dalgic and Leeuw 1994) that can be met within a segment (Michaelson 1988). As they offer prospects for growth and good returns in the absence of serious competition (Kotler 2003), niche markets have been embraced by publishers, as a means not only of diversification but also of survival in the face of industry conglomeration (Straubhaar and LaRose 2006). This practice need not necessarily be confined to smaller companies, but often such companies can be better focused and equipped to serve those specific markets than can their larger competitors (Dalgic and Leeuw 1994). Niche markets are, if anything, likely to grow in importance as book publishing continues to face the challenges of conglomeration and limited resources.

Relationship building   As with most businesses today, an integral activity within the book publishing industry is the establishment of successful relationships (Parrish, Cassill and Oxenham 2006). Whereas once the mix of relationships involved was largely a matter of those between authors and publishers, on the one hand, and booksellers and the reading public, on the other, today in what has been described as the *Attention Economy* (Davenport and Beck 2001) the configuration is much more complex. Today the technologies employed range from email and blogs to RSS feeds, and communication is at once an individual, group and community affair. The result is networks of authors, reviewers, publishers, agents and readers, many of them playing multiple roles, and all engaged in building those relationships which are not only critical in themselves but which may well help to shape the future of book publishing. For book publishers this has implications across the spectrum of strategies from content acquisition to marketing to sales.

All these external and internal forces continue to have significant bearing on the book publishing industry. However, in one way or another they can best be seen at work in that massive restructuring of the industry that has resulted in the creation of those transnational publishing conglomerates that are currently the focus of so much attention.

The Rise of Conglomerates

The origin of today's vast publishing conglomerates is to be found in successive waves of mergers and acquisitions that occurred in the 1960s, from the mid-1970s to the late 1980s and again in the mid-1990s. During the last quarter of the 20th century, the book publishing industry was transformed from a privately owned and independently run small-scale industry to one dominated by global media conglomerates. These waves of mergers and acquisitions occurred in a series of overlapping stages:

- Changes in the nature of ownership during the 1960s: through a series of share market flotations and mergers and acquisitions – the latter including the entry into book publishing of firms from outside the industry and including the likes of IBM and Xerox. However, when neither the content–technology synergies nor the profits anticipated materialized, most of these earlier alliances dissolved in the 1980s (Luey 2007).
- The acquisition of trade book publishers by media corporations such as RCA, CBS and Gulf & Western: these conglomerates typically had holdings in film, broadcasting, music, newspaper and magazine publishing as well as in books. They too saw prospects for synergy, hoping that the content they acquired could be reproduced across a variety of media, using cross-promotional strategies and the convergence of technologies including computing, telecommunications and the internet (Wirten 2007). A distinguishing feature of this wave of mergers and acquisitions was that it involved corporations from around the world and not just the United States (Miller, L.J. 2007).
- Consolidation of conglomeration in the 1990s: by the mid-1990s, book publishing was firmly integrated into the domain of transnational media conglomerates such as NewsCorp in the United States and Bertelsmann in Europe. Between 1996 and mid-1998, three US publishing houses were sold to overseas conglomerates. Although the most spectacular of these sales was that involving Bertelsmann's purchase of Random House, the world's largest English-language trade publisher, the purchase of Houghton Mifflin by Vivendi of France in 2001 briefly made the latter the third largest publisher in the world and the second largest educational publisher, before it sold its publishing assets to the Lagardere Group a year later (*Encyclopaedia of Global Industries* 2007).

At the peak of conglomeration in the mid-1990s, book publishing was very much the poor relation in such entities, typically generating a minor share of total revenues (Wirten 2007). Even before then, however, the attractions of conglomeration had begun to fade as anticipated profits failed to materialize and the search began for new, more lucrative investment strategies (Miller, L.J. 2007) or, as Epstein (2002) puts it:

> One-by-one, the mighty media conglomerates such as CBS, ABC, RCA, and MCA Universal that acquired such distinguished houses as Henry Holt,

G.P. Putnam and Random House deluded by the false promise of synergy, eventually found them a burden on their balance sheets and disgorged them.

Not that this by any means meant the end of conglomeration, but simply a reshuffling of the major players involved.

The state of play in global book publishing in 2009 is reflected in Table 2.1, compiled by Rudiger Wischenbart. It lists the top 20 global publishing companies with revenues of over US$ 250 million.

Of the top 10 global publishing groups, five have a significant presence in trade books: the UK's Pearson (with its Penguin group), Germany's Bertelsmann (with Random House), France's Hachette Livres (which is also a strong player in education), Spain's Planeta and Italy's De Agostini. All these publishers are headquartered in Europe, although North America still features prominently.

The outcome of this transformation

In economic terms, this transformation in book publishing was just part of a wider industrial phenomenon, leading to the global expansion of the book market while concentrating control in the hands of a relatively few conglomerates. In socio-cultural terms, however, many viewed it as evidence of the once-genteel world of book publishing and retailing being forced to accommodate to the market-oriented and profit-driven ethos of the mass entertainment industries (Kovac 2008). Both these issues continue to resonate within the book publishing world. Let us first consider the cultural dimension.

A cultural tragedy? In the opinion of some observers, the impact of conglomeration and consolidation upon book publishing and the book trade in general has been little short of disastrous. At its most extreme, it is represented as a struggle between culture and its associated values of quality and integrity, on the one hand, and of crass commercialism, on the other. A business that had overtones of a vocation run by enlightened owners and committed editors had been suborned and overwhelmed by indifferent and remote transnational media corporations controlled by investors and accountants. There are other points of view, however, and in particular, that which while accepting the existence of a long-established culture within book publishing, nevertheless attributes many of the industry's current ills to its essentially insular and non-entrepreneurial culture (Nash 2010a). Whatever the case, and with advocates for both viewpoints more than capable of fighting their corner, cultural and business issues are seldom far apart in the book publishing industry.

Furthermore, it seems safe to say that the structural shift from private to public ownership did have an impact both upon decisions over title selection and upon relations between authors and editors (Luey 2007). However, this is not to argue that such developments necessarily resulted in fatal damage to the culture and values of book publishing. Nor did it necessarily signal the end of a benign and

Table 2.1   Ranking of the world's largest publishing companies

Rank 2008	Rank 2007	Company name	Parent company	Nationality	Revenues 2008 £m	Revenues 2007 £m	Revenues 2006 £m
1	2	Pearson	Pearson	UK	5,044	4,812	5,616
2	4	Reed Elsevier	Reed Elsevier	UK/NL/US	4,586	4,217	5,851
3	1	ThomsonReuters	The Woodbridge Company Ltd	Canada	3,485	49,998	
4	5	Wolters Kluwer	Wolters Kluwer	NL	3,374	3,413	3,693
5	3	Bertelsmann	Bertelsmann	Germany	2,980	4,392	4,612
6	6	Hachette Livres	Lagardere	France	2,159	2,130	1,975
7	7	McGraw-Hill Education	McGraw-Hill	US	1,794	1,853	
8	13	Grupo Planeta	Group Planeta	Spain	1,760	1,000	1,015
9	10	De Agostini Editors	Gruppo De Agostini	Italy			1,668
10	11	Scholastic	Scholastic Corp	US	1,499	1,493	
11	9	Houghton Mifflin Harcourt	Education Media and Publishing Group	US/Cayman Islands	1,712		
12	12	Holtzbrinck	Verlagsgruppe Georg von Holtzbrinck	Germany			1,324
13	15	Cengage Learning	Apax Partners et al.	UK	1,172	968	
14	21	Wiley	John Wiley & Sons	US	1,139	846	
15	14	Informa	Informa	UK	1,028	997	978
16	16	HarperCollins	News Corp	US/AUS	944	923	
17	18	Shogakukan	Shogakukan	Japan	927	901	
18	20	Shueisha	Shueisha	Japan	902	852	
19	19	Kodansha	Kodansha	Japan	886	885	908
20	17	Springer Science and Business Media	Cinven and Candover	UK/Germany/ Italy/France	880	906	924

Source: Wischenbart (2009)

progressive culture and its replacement by one that was opportunistic and ultimately destructive of the central ethos of book publishing. Indeed, Kovac (2008) found little empirical evidence in either the European Union or the United States for the homogenization of book cultures or a lack of diversity in titles, possibly owing to an unexpectedly relaxed and plural dimension to conglomeration. Nevertheless, the view that somehow or other a golden age had come and gone persists in certain quarters.

The pessimistic view of conglomeration is to some extent grounded in an assumption that somehow or other culture and commerce are innately opposed, or at the least are uneasy bedfellows. As L.J. Miller (2007) pointed out, however, these two forces actually coexist in society, with commerce modified by cultural contexts, while in turn affecting the development of cultural ideas. This analysis will perhaps cut little ice with those who would lament what they see as the reduction of books to the status of less exalted commodities such as shoes or soap powder, but it is arguably more realistic than the proponents of a lost age would admit. It must also be remembered that those waves of mergers and acquisitions that launched the subsequent transformation of the book publishing industry were driven by a need for the capital deemed necessary to expansion and the pursuit of greater profits. This represented rational, commercial behaviour by the book publishing industry at the time, whatever its acknowledged cultural status and credentials.

The picture is somewhat more complex when it comes to the issue of trade publishers and the search for best-selling titles. The so-called blockbuster strategy, based on the payment of spectacular and inflationary advances to celebrity authors, can work, as in the case of Dan Brown's successful novel *The Lost Symbol*. As Nash (2010a) points out, however, like all winners of auctions (in this case those involving competing bids for the signature of celebrity authors), the book publishers concerned are more likely to be losers in that they will almost certainly have paid more than they ought to for the privilege. Worse still, this pursuit of blockbuster sales is essentially a short-term response that almost inevitably will involve opportunity costs in terms of reduced investment capital for other categories, while doing little to address more fundamental issues of organizational structure and strategy.

Nash (2010a) attributes such strategies to the limited time horizons of publishing executives whose positions customarily depend upon performance. Although it is plausible to infer that people acting in pursuit of short-term targets will almost inevitably respond with short-term solutions, there is rather more to it than that. Even more critical could be the absence of that entrepreneurial culture deemed necessary to taking the long-term view and, in the process, difficult decisions about organizational structures and employment levels. Time and the market will ultimately resolve this issue, but clearly the ongoing interplay between market forces and cultural milieu has by no means spelt the end of book publishing culture per se.

The commercial impact of restructuring   It is indisputable that the growth of conglomerates led to a radical restructuring of the book publishing industry around the world. At the end of the 1990s, 60–80 per cent of the respective book markets in the European Union and the United States were controlled by 5 to 10 of the world's biggest publishing houses (Kovac 2008). This structural reorganization reflected the rise of a new knowledge-based economy, and the onset of technological breakthroughs in everything from book production to the tracking of sales around the world. Concern mounted throughout the book trade as publishers feared the onset of further consolidation and restructuring, and authors and agents anticipated a loss of influence and earnings (Wirten 2007). Although to some extent these fears were all realized, the anticipated impact of restructuring has turned out to be different in both nature and extent. Arguably, this has been owing to a continuation of the symbiotic relationship between culture and commerce in the book trade.

On the minus side of the ledger it has become more difficult for authors to find publishers for first novels and for mid-list books, that is, those expected to sell fewer than 10,000 copies (Luey 2007). Nevertheless, at the height of conglomeration, with the book undergoing a shift in status from being a cultural icon to becoming a marketable mass-market product, title production in most developed countries grew almost sixfold (Kovac 2008). Furthermore, independent family controlled publishing houses such as Wiley and McGraw Hill continue to flourish, and new medium and even large publishing houses have emerged, many serving niche markets and fostered by the internet (Wirten 2007).

So, while clearly there has not been much to cheer about for those corporate and individual casualties of a reorganizational process which has still to run its course today, the more pessimistic predictions for the book trade have turned out to be both premature and inaccurate. Statistics for 2009, for example, show that sales held steady, with only a 3 per cent fall from the previous year, although profit margins came under pressure. So far as eBooks were concerned, on the other hand, sales attained a level whereby concerns were expressed as to their potentially adverse effects on the sale of print books. Over the Christmas period in 2009, Amazon sold more eBooks than hard-copy versions, while Hachette Livres sold more eBooks in the United States during December 2009 than in the whole of 2008. This latter performance was deemed sufficiently significant for Hachette to convene with other leading publishers in France to devise a single digital book platform for the country in anticipation of an explosion of eBook sales across Europe as a whole (Casassus 2010).

For book publishing in general, 2009 was a difficult year, although books are said to have performed very creditably in comparison with other media (Flamm 2009). Therefore, while there is no denying the existence of conglomeration, there remain issues to do with its overall impact on levels of competition and diversity within book publishing. Furthermore, while further restructuring is likely, this could involve more than the simple expansion of conglomeration. Potential outcomes could include the devolution of some of the largest companies or their reorganization into vertically focused businesses. Just as likely, however, could be the emergence of alliances between trade publishers with rich backlists and those based on the internet or focused on ePublishing (Publishers Lunch Deluxe News 2010b). In the meantime, as industry structures, staffing levels and organizational cultures respond in varying degrees to the pressures of change, fears of current and continuing hard times persist. It remains to be seen whether these turn out to be justified or are simply the opinions of latter-day Luddites unable to accept the inevitability of progress and to see its benefits?

A Crisis in Book Publishing?

For almost a decade now, people have been lamenting a crisis, not just in book publishing per se but across the entire book trade. In bookselling, for example, the growth of huge chains, operating first in shopping malls and then as separate superstores, has reached its seemingly inevitable logic in the form of internet behemoths such as Amazon.com and Barnes & Noble.com. In the process, there have been massive reductions in the numbers of independent bookstores (Miller, L.J. 2007). As if such developments were not bad enough, there is the added complication of the likelihood that these conglomerates are themselves far from bullet proof. In this context, the wider significance of the failure of both the massive Time Warner/America Online and the Vivendi Universal conglomerates in 2002 should not be overlooked. Furthermore, these business failures were no more than what industry insiders like Jason Epstein had predicted as managers faced the realities of trying to control a complex of imprints within a single firm, with all the attendant risks and inefficiencies (Epstein 2002). It could be argued that 2002 was a particularly bad year for book publishing, as confidence in convergence evaporated and the once-hoped-for synergies failed to materialize (Wirten 2007), but this might not turn out to be the whole story.

Currently, as the world struggles to escape the clutches of global recession, the book trade is suffering its fair share of pain. Some, such as Engelhardt (2008), have argued that a combination of declining readership and the effects of the internet and overinvestment spells the end of the road for the massive publishing conglomerates. However, it must be said that within these conglomerates and elsewhere in the industry, the capacity to make money remains, and, as the experience of textbook publishers has demonstrated, this is not only a matter of bestselling novels. Nevertheless, there is a strong tendency to view book publishing in a binary context: as an industry similar to Hollywood (and in fact controlled by the same conglomerates), and as a much larger yet more marginal industry that is similar to YouTube (Christensen 2007).

Anderson (2006) explains this latter, more marginal element of the industry in terms of a new economics of publishing, based on a long tail of niches rather than as hitherto, on a big head of hits. Whereas previously the head of the book sales curve (bestsellers) was big and the tail was short, in the long tail the aggregation of low-selling titles amounts to quite respectable sales for books which previously would have had difficulty reaching the shelves of bookshops. Furthermore, thanks to technological developments that enable almost anybody to publish, sell or buy any book, it has proved possible to bypass the conglomerates and their profit-driven publishing policies (Kovac 2008).

It would seem both overly pessimistic and somewhat premature to accept the binary perspective on the book publishing industry. Indeed, the positions adopted by various groups and individuals on the current state of book publishing seem to a considerable extent to depend on their standing in the culture-versus-conglomeration argument. The continued emergence of small and niche publishers would suggest that the long tail could indeed be wagging into the foreseeable future. So far as the conglomerates are concerned, some may lose patience with unacceptable rates of return on their investment and withdraw to find pastures new, while others may continue to turn a profit on the basis of one or two bestsellers a year. Should the bestseller phenomenon continue to flourish – and there is little reason to suggest it would not – the current trend among blockbuster authors to move away from publishers and operate through business managers could well accelerate. However, on balance perhaps there is more room for optimism in the book publishing industry than might be thought from reading the more lurid headlines.

Perhaps, but there remain concerns over the combined impacts of conglomeration in book publishing and bookselling upon the options available to customers, and no less to authors and publishers. Just as worrying is what appears to be the steady decline in the popularity of reading since the closing decades of the 20th century. Increasingly, books must compete with a variety of other forms of entertainment for the time and attention of consumers, particularly those young consumers enthralled by or perhaps even in thrall to the charms of dynamic, interactive and, it seems, liberating electronic media. Indeed, to an increasing extent, this freedom extends to removal of the need to pay for content. Time alone will tell, but clearly, when trying to interpret the future of book publishing, issues such as the nature of books and, indeed, of reading are moot. These are taken up in the next chapter.

Chapter 3
Book Publishing in the Digital Age

Introduction

The 'culture wars' in book publishing is one example of the continued complexity of the industry. Another related example is the contrast between the continuing popularity of traditional print formats and the thorough digitization of the book publishing process, involving everything from the delivery of text from authors on disk or by email, through to page design on computer and the electronic delivery of files to the printer (Phillips 2007). In seeking to understand these contrasts and, indeed, the apparent contradictions, it is important first to address the wider aspects of digitization.

Digitization: A Socio-Economic Perspective

Digitization is a truly global phenomenon, incorporating developments in the social, commercial and technological spheres. In technical terms, digitization is the process of converting analogue information: letters, print, photographs, maps, audio, film, video, ephemera and three-dimensional objects into digital form for access, transmission and archiving electronically (Hurst-Wall 2007). Additionally, digitization has been described as the transformation of any signal, whatever its form (voice, image, text) or nature (content or algorithm), into a set of digits for processing and transmission, or alternatively as the integration and interoperability of digital sequences and digital information-processing devices (Brousseau and Penard 2007).

Commercially and economically, digitization has made possible the structural coupling between the internet and the World Wide Web (Qvortrup 2003), and the convergence of formats, functions and industries that has powered the emergence of the global networked or knowledge-based economy.

The Role of Digitization in the Knowledge-based Economy

The concept of the knowledge-based economy was created 40 years ago by the late Peter Drucker (1969). More recently it has been defined in terms of trends within advanced economies towards greater dependence on knowledge, information and high skill levels, and the increasing need for ready access to all of these by the business and public sectors (OECD 2005). These are clearly matters of immediate interest to book publishing, given that it deals in the creation and dissemination of knowledge, and with the evidence for such relevance all around us in the form of infrastructure and new markets and of products and services. Underlying such developments, however, have been a number of fundamental reassessments of such core concepts as value, resources and competition. Here, these are reviewed within the specific context of book publishing under the themes of richness and reach, disintermediation, collaboration and social capital.

Richness and reach

Although long a feature of markets, the concepts of richness and reach gained maximum attention with the advent of electronic commerce. Hitherto, a basic tenet of information economics was the need for a trade-off in information transmission – a trade-off between the richness of a message and its reach. Although the precise meaning of 'richness' varies from one context to another, it generally means the quality of information as defined by the user. This includes characteristics such as accuracy, bandwidth, currency, customization, interactivity, relevance and security. 'Reach', on the other hand, refers to the number of people who participate in the sharing of the information (Evans and Wurster 2000). Today, the need for this trade-off has been removed by a combination of technological and economic change, and specifically by the new-found ability to unbundle (or separate) the information from its physical carrier.

This separation of content and carrier has already resulted in radical changes in book trade practices, from production to sales. It offers well-nigh universal access to content and an enriched reading experience in terms of formats and delivery platforms, including access by mobile reading devices. Within the book trade, Amazon.com is in many ways the most comprehensive example of richness and reach, combining 'anytime anywhere' content delivery with reader input and feedback, reviews and reader–author interaction. As will be seen later, these concepts of richness and reach have practical implications for the structure and composition of value chains. This is particularly the case where value chains start to deconstruct as businesses are disintermediated or where new ones emerge on the basis of scarce knowledge.

Disintermediation

Although a feature of markets for some time, interest in disintermediation accelerated in the late 1990s. It refers to the removal of an intermediary, or middleman, from a business transaction or process, often involving companies bypassing traditional retail chains to sell directly to customers (Atkinson 2001). Before long this phenomenon morphed into 'cybermediation', with the emergence of entirely new kinds of intermediaries in categories such as search, logistics and trust. These were players that could not have existed prior to the advent of eBusiness and the internet (Giaglis, Klein and O'Keefe 1999).

Although the combination of the internet and electronic commerce was expected to, and indeed did, result in considerable levels of disintermediation, the outcome has been more complicated than anticipated. For example, initial cost savings accruing from disintermediation were often negated by increased costs in other areas, notably in customer handling and the expense of maintaining websites. Perhaps inevitably, businesses began to reassess the value of intermediaries, not only through the direct services they provided, but also as indirect channels to entirely different customer segments. One outcome of this reassessment was a process of reintermediation, involving the introduction of a new step or steps to the value chain as new players found fresh ways to add value to the process.

There is ample evidence for the operation of disintermediation in the book trade with, for example, bookshops becoming publishers, publishers operating virtual shop fronts and authors becoming publishers by selling directly to their readers. As both sources and types of content continue to proliferate, this is likely to be no more than the tip of the iceberg, with both disintermediation and reintermediation continuing and necessary features of the market (Vaknin 2003). Alongside such developments there are likely to be related changes in the spheres of competition and capital accumulation.

Collaboration and social capital

In the knowledge-based economy not only has there been a shift in focus from tangible to intangible resources, but also there have also been radical changes to the way that firms compete. Some of the most effective strategies today are based upon collaboration, and indeed, illogical and counterintuitive as it might seem, this includes collaboration with competitors. The reasons for such collaboration include a search for access to markets and scarce resources, especially resources such as organizational capabilities and human competences, and to achieve economics of both scale and scope (Hamel and Prahalad 1994). Collaboration is present in virtually every form of business activity from R&D to manufacturing, to marketing, to sales and service. Collaboration also takes place in the context of various communities, involving not just businesses and their trading partners and suppliers but also, increasingly, their customers.

By providing consumers with the ability to interact with each other and with suppliers of goods and services, the advent of the World Wide Web has helped to generate real business value for all concerned. A significant element of such value occurs in the form of social capital. The idea behind social capital is that by operating in networks people can embed commercial interactions within social relations. Through social exchanges, people build webs of trust and norms of behaviour, including a willingness to cooperate and to share knowledge (Cohen and Prusak 2001). Although hitherto much of this social interaction has taken place within company and inter-company-based communities of practice, it is clear that web-based communities are the future for this kind of socio-commercial initiative.

Book publishing has not been entirely lacking in collaborative efforts, notably in respect of the adoption of standards, from ISBNs to ONIX (Online Information Exchange) and, increasingly, ePub, and in concerted responses to perceived threats from sources such as Google. At the same time, collaboration has not always been as effective as it might be, with, for example, continuing disparities over adoption of the ePub file format and even to do with so-called electronic versions of ISBNs (Weissberg 2008). However, where such collaboration has really been found wanting has been in the realm of strategic development. One example of a lost opportunity in this regard is that of an earlier proposal for a publisher-led consortium to sell direct to consumers on the basis of a combined annotated catalogue and a network of warehouses (Epstein 2002). This proposal ultimately failed not just on the grounds of anticipated concerns about channel conflict, but also, it is claimed, owing a perceived failure of executives from non-publishing backgrounds to comprehend the point. While perhaps slightly ahead of its time, this would seem to be an idea whose time will inevitably come. Just who will implement it of course remains moot. Finally, so far as membership of communities is concerned, the evidence is that book publishers, while already involved, are likely to become more so. This is because of their need for social capital which, whether in the form of consumer recognition and trust or in terms of access to content and skills, will abound in such communities. This point and the issues that surround it will be taken up later in the book. Now the attention turns to some of the more specific implications of digitization for book publishing.

Digitization and Book Publishing

It is scarcely surprising that, given the current and growing impact of digitization upon society as a whole, there has been talk of a digital revolution in book publishing. So far as actual book production is concerned, the onset of digital printing has been hailed as marking a paradigm shift, with positive implications for productivity, for flexibility in print runs and for both production and distribution costs (Breede 2006). When it comes to digital publishing, however, opinions differ as to exactly how revolutionary these changes have been (Thompson 2006), with talk of both overestimation and underestimation of their impact (Kasdorf 2008). Hence, while Phillips (2007) has pointed to a transformation in the range and numbers of published titles available, both in terrestrial bookshops and via the web, and to the virtual demise of the 'out-of-print' problem, others are less impressed. Cope and Kalantzis (2006) for instance, argue that even the internet is not so revolutionary when viewed in the context of that truly epochal invention, the printed book, a format that has long offered the same kind of information architecture for search and interconnection as happens with hypertext links. They do, however, see a revolutionary dimension to digital technology in that, by bridging the gap between text and image, it has succeeded in putting an end to the

Gutenberg logic of mass production, making the smallest of print runs viable, with attendant economic and social implications (Cope and Kalantzis 2006).

Despite different interpretations of the potency of its impact, and the likelihood that this will vary from one category of publisher to another, digitization is already changing the way that book publishers do business. Whether this is in regard to the digitization of frontlists and backlists, of internal workflow processes and supply chains or the management of digital storage and distribution (often involving third-party specialists) the industry is clearly responding to the challenges and opportunities of digitization. Consequently, publishing today has been described as reinventing its traditional purpose of understanding what matters, then gathering the necessary information and disseminating it to those who need it (O'Reilly 2008).

Digital Publishing

In seeking to define digital publishing it is important to bear in mind that ultimately we are still talking about publishing. Furthermore, practices that might appear to be radical and revolutionary today could before long appear simply as 'business-as-usual' (Daniels 2006). With this caveat, digital publishing is defined here as the production and distribution of digital content using the World Wide Web as a communication channel, with provision for the establishment of digital database facilities for future reuse. Based on customer requirements, the product (information) can be produced and provided in various formats, such as online, web, TV, CD-ROM, audio, paper, print-on-demand (POD) and video-on-demand (Liu and Rao 2005). Put differently, true digital publishing means creating, producing and delivering content that may never appear on a printed page, or which will be offered to customers as a variety of options, including that of POD (O'Reilly 2009).

The digital publishing production and supply chain incorporates authors, publishers, aggregators, technology providers, databases, web distributors and end-users. The extended nature and more complex composition of this supply chain is indicative of the kinds of impact that digital publishing is likely to have on the book publishing industry. Not the least of these impacts will be upon the nature and features of books themselves.

What's in a name?

Well before the end of the previous century people were confidently predicting the demise of books. This of course meant printed books, those familiar and much-loved objects that contain all manner of content between two covers, and which can be read more or less anywhere, as and when the reader chooses. Today, the very concept of what constitutes a book is extremely elastic, embracing everything from printed books, through audio and CD-ROM formats, to eBooks. eBooks will be discussed in detail in the next chapter, and here all that is necessary is to clarify their purpose in the current digital environment. The first and most obvious point to be made is that, despite all predictions to the contrary, books as they have been known for centuries continue to exist, giving pleasure and serving as information sources to millions of readers. However, even if the digital environment continues to coexist with print, both in distinct and in hybrid forms, it is important to recognize the existence and characteristics of alternative book formats. Cope and Phillips (2006) have no problem with this, asserting that books are no longer physical things, but rather are information architectures, structured renditions of text and images. In similar vein, Kelly (2006) has invoked the prospect of digitization enabling books to seep out of their bindings and weave themselves together, something that John Updike was later to deride as a 'grisly scenario' (Thompson 2006).

More recently, there have been calls for a redefinition of books as places where readers, and sometimes authors, congregate. There have also been predictions that the individual dimension to both authoring and reading books will be replaced by collaboration involving authors and readers engaged in what would become a communal rather than a solitary activity (Nawotka 2009a). Although perhaps to some extent in tune with wider developments in society and the media, this vision of the future is far from universally popular. Hence, rather than the perceived joys of togetherness, others interpret such developments as signalling the replacement of a way of life where, for example, time could be spent in quiet reflection with a book by one marked by permanent distraction and a constant need to hit the search button (Morozov 2009). To traditional book readers and publishers alike, this is a challenging scenario. It is rendered all the more intimidating in that the true source of danger lies not in the technological but in the social and organizational domains. This immediately raises issues to do with the nature of the reading audience and the role of book publishing in satisfying its needs.

The audience factor

The same mix of optimism and pessimism that characterizes opinion on the prospects for book publishing in general is to be found when it comes to the issue of reading and readers. There is certainly plenty of evidence to suggest that the audience for book reading is changing, and that in many cases reading is in decline, owing to increased competition from a growing range of new media, games and interactive television (Phillips 2007). This is as true for adult readers raised in a largely print-dominated culture as it is for the so-called 'digital natives' or Generation Y, those young people that have grown up during the computer age. Gomez (2008) perceptively expands this perspective on Generation Y to include a distinction between what he calls, respectively, Generation Download and Generation Upload. The former was the first generation to grow up with the web. It is characterized by a need for interaction with the sources of content, and for exposure to a constant stream of digital stimulation. However, Generation

Upload has moved beyond being part of the audience, towards creating its own audience through participation and sharing. Needing an audience rather than just being part of one, it is engaged in content creation and the formation of myriad online communities. Where Generation Download was characterized by the revolutionary means of experiencing internet content, Generation Upload is making its mark through activities such as mixing and combining the disparate information elements pulled from the internet, changing it into something else and uploading it for the world to see (Gomez 2008).

Although not nearly so extensive or as well documented, there is however, another point of view on the issue of reading and readers. Hence, argues Rose (2009), people have not actually stopped reading. Rather, they have found more ways to read the printed word. Whether or not one accepts this assertion, it is to some extent still part of an argument about the future, and more specifically about the future of the book. On this hardy perennial of a topic, some authorities are predicting that by the year 2020, far from having further declined, the percentage of the population engaged in reading will be roughly the same as it is in 2010. More to the point, these people will be reading immersive text-only, long-form narratives, or printed books as we currently know them, despite the by-then proliferation of multi-model forms (Nash 2010b). Others, while agreeing that this is a debate that is less about whether or not people will read as about how and in what format they might do so, are more cautious with regard to the prospects for print editions. Hence, it has been predicted that, while reading will still thrive in 2020, the majority of people will be using portable reading devices, with the reading of print on paper confined to POD versions (Shatzkin 2009a).

For book readers and publishers alike, these and other developments in the current environment throw up many more questions than answers. For publishers in particular, however, a failure to answer these questions could have severe consequences. Two questions in particular are of pressing importance. As the range of alternatives to book reading becomes wider and even more exciting, will books as we know them come to exist only as objects of curiosity, the purview of an eccentric minority of older people? If so, what will replace them and for what purposes will these replacements be used?

Although to a degree futuristic, these questions already apply to the context of a book publishing industry widely pervaded by digital formats and devices, and where social and cultural disruption is taking place at a rate that may, if anything, exceed that of the pace of technological change. The growing practice whereby everything from classic literature to adult comics is being read on handheld devices poses serious questions about the survival of the book as we have known it. Hence the possibility has been raised that, as people are increasingly exposed to web-based publishing and to phenomena such as Twitter, they will begin to lose sight of the values of the traditional book format (Morozov 2009).

In the meantime, the challenge for book publishers is twofold. First, they must come up with the kinds of products and services that are likely to appeal to the changing needs and demands of consumers. Second, they have to develop new roles for those existing and emerging contexts in which they can remain significant players. These are quite fundamental issues that touch upon the essential rationale for and contribution of book publishing, or on what would be termed more formally as its value proposition.

The value proposition for book publishing

Value propositions are distilled from organizational missions and strategies. They tell the market and potential customers what a company is and what it can do for them. It is value propositions that persuade customers to buy goods and services from one company rather than from another, while explaining the benefits of making that choice. Until quite recently, the value proposition for book publishing was both clear and succinct. Publishers could effectively and efficiently combine that mix of functions from content acquisition to editorial and design, to marketing and distribution that met the demands of a wide range of readers in the book market. Within this market, different publishers would offer different value propositions based on specific publishing categories, market niches, capabilities and competencies. It should be added that matters of supply and demand and the gate-keeping function of publishers and booksellers inevitably meant that not every author could find a publisher, and that prices were often higher than consumers would have liked, especially for mid-list titles. In general, however, book publishers have been able to offer a powerful combination of skills in the development of ideas, in linking content to markets and in managing the vast amount of scale involved in the publishing process (Shatzkin 2009a).

Today there are clearly opportunities for publishers to refine and re-apply these skills in, for example, exploiting the reusability of content, both in the production of eBooks and by working with competing media providers to repackage content into other, non-textual formats (Murray 2007). This will be complicated by, among other things, struggles over copyright and contracts, and decisions in such areas as technology adoption, partnering and alliances. However, the current and likely future challenges facing book publishers will require much more than adjustments to well-established processes and models. Indeed, talk of paradigm shift is not too far off the mark in a context of Web 2.0, social networking and the active participation of readers in the publishing process (Kasdorf 2008). Not unexpectedly in such an environment, book publishing value propositions are already beginning to change, with a shift in focus from content and markets to publishing in databases and networks (Shatzkin 2009a). Put differently, the entire fabric of book publishing is currently subject to a bewildering and all-enveloping complex of change. Critically, this includes changes in the relationship between content and context and in the mix of stakeholders concerned. It also includes changes in stakeholder roles and positions in value and supply chains, in publishing channels and in branding and marketing. Not all of these changes are occurring at the same pace, at the same time or in the same place, but they are happening in what appears to be an unstoppable process. Equally unstoppable would appear to be the trend by which consumers are seeking to gain greater control over content and a better return for their own investment of time and money (PriceWaterhouseCoopers 2009).

Content and context

Until very recently both in the media industries and more generally in eCommerce, the view that 'content is king' was unlikely to face a serious challenge. Today, things are not nearly so straightforward, and the statement might well need amending to read 'great content is king'. Perhaps more important, however, is the fact that new mobile technologies and online delivery channels within the book publishing supply chain have enabled new choices for consumers to discover, access, purchase and consume book content (Weissberg 2008). Today, the challenge is not so much one of a shortage of content as of a surfeit of content and, accordingly, of the significant change that has occurred in the relationship between content and context.

The adage that 'content is king' may well have had more relevance to the economics of scarcity that characterized the economy before digitization, than with the current economics of abundance (Anderson 2006). Increasingly, all manner of content is available free of charge, with the wholesale removal of paid restrictions on access (Reed 2009). The resulting abundance has brought its own costs in terms of information overload and the increased costs of searching for quality content. Nonetheless, aside from issues of quality and provenance in relation to free content and, indeed, its often limited and highly circumscribed nature, there is much more at work here than simply giving intellectual property away for nothing. For example, rather than dealing a death blow to traditional markets, free content can, along the lines of loss leadership in other industries, be used to attract consumers to buy more expensive paid content (O'Reilly 2008).

Nevertheless, for publishers this is only going to be one issue in an industry that is moving in a direction that is light years away from its traditional customs and practices, and where the days of the delivery of top-down, pre-packaged content to customers through familiar advertising channels are over (Reed 2009). In such an environment, neither content nor the means for its delivery will be scarce (Shatzkin 2009a) and, arguably, context rather than content will be king. Furthermore, book content must be made available in smaller chunks and be taggable, accessible and available (Kasdorf 2008).

Stakeholders and their roles

Before the advent of digital publishing there was a clear demarcation between those responsible for authoring, producing, distributing and selling a book, and those who purchased it or read it. Today such distinctions, while still in existence, are no longer either so clear cut or so absolute. With both self-publishing software and services available, the route from author to publisher is, at least in theory, open to all. Likewise books can find a market through individual websites and those of the mega-online book retailers as well as through traditional independent or chain bookshops. And whereas there is room for individuals at every stage in the supply chain, the concept of reader as end-user of the finished product has fragmented to accommodate diverse levels of involvement as creator and co-creator of content and as communal and collaborative consumer. Although still in their early stages, these changes in the role and status of readers have tremendous implications for the activities and, indeed, the future of book publishers.

In seeing an element of 'back to the future' in all of this O'Reilly (2009) argues that the way ahead for publishers is to do what they have always done, that is, seek to bring information and readers together, albeit in different ways. One option available lies in the realm of curation, that is, in providing a service that entails locating, editing and packaging high-value and relevant content from the mass that is available. As the number of available resources that writers and readers could consult rises dramatically, it seems obvious that people would begin to place increasing value on the process of synthesizing rather than simply aggregating information (Morozov 2009). Linking this idea to the potentially vast reservoir of free content on the web, Collingridge (2009) observes that in the web-based environment content would be free but context, filtered by trusted curators, would be sacred. Although publishers are already engaged in the practice of curation, this has largely occurred within such content silos as those of legal or educational publishing, although recently specialist companies have emerged to circumvent and extend such silos and exploit the growing opportunities in this field (Cairns 2009). This has led to the emergence of another option for book publishers in a changing industry environment.

This option involves the exploitation of verticals, that is, niche markets comprised of numerous vertical channels focused around very specific subjects (Shatzkin 2008a). This verticality, as opposed to the horizontal nature of traditional publishing markets, offers an additional advantage. This accrues from the fact that because what is involved is an exchange of files, verticals are in effect format agnostic. This means that files comprised of text, art, photographs or other graphics, animation, moving images, sound, games or code, can be combined, sorted or tagged (Shatzkin 2008a). This is still a work in progress and the horizontal, format-specific media continue to dominate, but it presages serious reductions in publishing costs, along with further potential to exploit the long tail. The increased importance of verticals is connected to another major shift in the book publishing paradigm, in this case involving the emergence of collaborative communities.

Communities

The book trade as a whole has always reflected an element of community. However, the onset of digitization has given this an entirely new meaning, one to do with dealing with what O'Reilly (2009) calls the 'slush pile'. In similar vein, Shatzkin (2009a) envisages a point in time when much of the work of publishing will involve what he terms 'the crowd'. The crowd in this case will comprise myriad different communities, the members of which will be engaged in social networking. The arrival of social networking sites in the early 2000s added a much more personal dimension to web page content. Simple tools on popular sites such as Facebook and MySpace enabled people to share their lives with others in virtual communities by building personal profiles, including text, photos, videos and blogs, and in linking to others by sending messages and comments. However, in seeking to exploit these new channels publishers must be careful not to overlook the proven value of traditional reading groups for stimulating connections and conversations between authors, publishers and readers, while also addressing reader needs for communication and connection (Nash 2010b).

As long-established market and organizational structures re-adjust to developments in the networked economy, book publishers are searching for content and ideas in different ways, and notably they are doing this among these emerging communities. These community gateways and portals are opening the way to new kinds of markets for books. These markets consist not simply of niches of readers interested in very specific subjects or genres, but also of nuggets within niches, groupings that are more granular than niches but that can end up in many niches. Publishers will be active inside and outside niches and nuggets, some owned by them, and some by others, and engaged in the business of generating, curating and aggregating content (Shatzkin 2009a). It is increasingly common for content which first saw the light of day in a blog to re-emerge as a book, either though a self-publishing channel or through an established or emerging publishing imprint. Already these forms of community collaboration in authoring, with comments going back and forth in what in many ways is a variant of beta testing, are increasingly common.

As these community-based information platforms targeted at specialized groups of readers continue to present opportunities for publishers, it is important for publishers to exercise as much influence as possible within them. In seeking to do this, it is essential to bring a changing perspective to the task, one informed by the insight that the key dimension to the book publishing business today lies not in physical objects, nor in elevating one set of objects over and above the others. Rather, the business is in the readers (Calder 2008). In addressing and seeking to influence readers and communities, the concepts of branding and marketing continue to be important, although like just about everything else they are subject to ongoing change.

Branding and marketing

Over the years, for book publishing as for other industries, the brand, if not quite everything, has remained a matter of the utmost importance. Brands distinguish one product, service or concept from another and can be easily communicated to potential customers. They embody the mission of a company and deliver value in terms of name recognition, profits and consumer loyalty. The challenge facing publishers today is that in an increasingly web-based marketing environment in which vertical niches play such an important function, the horizontal approach of selling the brand to clearly defined and recognized readership categories is unlikely to be effective. Hence, with relationships between content providers, marketers and consumers in a continuous state of flux, the role of brands in particular has come in for considerable scrutiny.

Moreover, in those vertical markets that offer such promise today, the output of a single publisher may not be sufficient to make the targeted niches viable. Also, as the answer probably lies in collaboration between multiple publishers in the matter of niches, this could result in the emergence of issues to do with relationships, including potential conflicts between individual brands. More important, however, is that in a marketing environment dominated by completely new channels such as blogs and social networks, the targets for those brands, the people most likely to be influenced by them, are going to be unclear and elusive. Increasingly, the goal will no longer be to inform a clearly recognizable and, to some extent, definable market segment about the latest titles from individual imprints. Rather, it will be to catch the attention of elusive and dynamic niches and nuggets wherever they happen to be, and in a mix of contexts and formats (Shatzkin 2009a). That this will by no means be either easy or routine can be grasped from the continuing criticism of publishers' websites. Much of this criticism is directed at their limited vertical and community dimensions, including perceived weaknesses in promoting discussion and attracting user-generated content and in fostering partnerships with non-publishing brands (Shatzkin 2008a).

In striving to improve their web presence, the overall aim of publishers is to expand their current sphere of influence from one comprised of a relatively small set of influence points, to one made of up thousands of truly influential points of information and recommendation (Calder 2008). Nor is this state of affairs by any means confined to the sphere of book publishing. The value of pursuing consumer contact through channels such as blogs, SMS or major social networking sites such as Facebook or MySpace is very much the accepted wisdom in overall marketing circles (Digital Outlook Report 2009). Clearly, however, the mix of social, demographic and technological change that characterizes the current digital environment is as relevant to book publishing as it is to other industries.

Nevertheless, it is important that, in pursuing community-oriented strategies, the marketers involved really seek to understand the communities at which they are aiming, and not least the purposes for which they have formed. Social networking and commerce can coexist but, with signs that consumers are in many cases lukewarm about overlapping domains (Digital Outlook Report 2009), a degree of subtlety on the part of marketers is required. By way of example, Shatzkin (2009a) relates a cautionary tale about the need for publishers to avoid mentioning their books on social network sites, on the grounds that the users of such sites are, above all, interested in themselves and not in books. This is not to say that social websites are unlikely to be effective venues for the promotion of books, but rather that it is important that such promotion appears in the context of broader discussions of themes and ideas by other than the publisher. Hence, Hunter (2009a) suggests that a well-placed fact or a quote compelling enough to induce followers to share it with their friends can result in much greater marketing potential for the titles concerned.

Accepting that the attraction of social websites remains strong, it is important, on the one hand, that publishers find ways of bringing content and context together by placing content where the potential users are located. On the other hand, it is necessary that such activities align with customer expectations as regards the positioning of content and its nature and purpose. Currently, major emphasis is being placed on the necessity of pitching marketing programmes at digital natives, the so-called Generation Y. However, that this is likely to involve more than just demographics is suggested by recent research conducted in the United States (Della Penna 2009). This research revealed that whereas up to 90 per cent of young people surveyed had created profiles on social networking sites, only just over 20 per cent had joined Twitter, a site of which much is expected as a marketing vehicle. Moreover, of the 84 per cent that actually noticed advertisements on social networks, only 19 per cent said they found these advertisements to be relevant, while 51 per cent would have preferred a separate social network to manage their brand interactions (Della Penna 2009).

So while there is considerable promise in the use of social networking sites for book promotion, marketers still have work to do in understanding what drives member participation and engagement within social networks. This will most likely involve building or accessing sites which contain a broad mix of content, not least that in the form of video and music. Furthermore, because people will more and more want to consume content where and when they want it, mobile devices are emerging as particularly important. Hence, when the iPhone first appeared on the market in 2007, it was hailed by some in marketing circles as the pivotal event of the year (Digital Outlook Report 2009). Finally on the subject of networking, it is important to remember that what matters is not simply putting content onto sites. What is really important is active engagement on the web and in the blogosphere, both to gain insights into the minds of community members and to solidify and strengthen one's own ideas (Collier 2009). So what do all these developments say to us in terms of the future of books and book publishing?

A Look into the Near Future?

In a sense, there is perhaps more reason than ever to be pessimistic about the future prospects for both books and book publishing. For starters, there are the effects of disruptive technologies, the potential threat of eBooks, the disintermediation of markets and the defection of once-loyal readers to contend with. And as if these were not enough, there is the reminder that anyone who writes a blog, records a podcast, uploads a website, films a YouTube video or uploads an eBook, a video or some music to Lulu, Yudu or Createspace, is also a publisher whose content is available anywhere through social networks in both aggregated and disaggregated form (Reed 2009). On the other hand, there is a sense that the future is now. It is actually happening and, as such, may be less cause for concern than the pessimists would have us believe. Book publishers are already engaged in using new technologies and their related services, from those of semantic search to Scribd. Equally it can be argued that, amidst all the excitement and complexity of digital publishing, the essential editorial skills of publishers will still be required, albeit supplemented by expertise in discovery and digital content, in digital rights and metadata management (European Commission 2008). This is likely to be the case because, notwithstanding the disappearance of the original container, namely the printed book, the knowledge contained in electronic texts will be more important than ever, and with it the skills of book publishers in finding and acquiring content and advising and nurturing authors (Gomez 2008).

So far as eBooks are concerned, the jury has still far from returned to the room. On the one hand, eBooks are continuing to grow in influence and numbers, owing to developments in both hardware and software and the adoption of the new ePub standard (Shatzkin 2008a). On the other hand, eBook sales continue to languish in a segment that represents less than 4 per cent of the market share of printed books and, for all their portability and convenience, there is little sign that this will improve in the foreseeable future (Reed 2009). In any case, the most pressing issues facing book publishing are more likely to be commercial and organizational than technological in nature.

For all their proclaimed focus on new technology, on social networking and the changing role and status of consumers, publishers still have a long way to go in understanding the implications of ongoing change in both readers and their needs. In this connected age, readers want to be noticed and, above all, to be heard and involved. They want access to authors and to other readers and to information that is meaningful in context. For publishers seeking to make contact with such audiences, success will lie not so much in what they have to say and to sell, but in what they can do to solve readers' problems or to present them with opportunities (Calder 2008). It is clearly well within the capabilities of publishers to respond to such challenges, but their ability to do so is likely to be constrained to a greater or lesser degree by a range of factors, some of them strategic and cultural, others to do with technology. The nature and implications of current technological developments are considered in the next chapter.

PART II
Bytes

Chapter 4
Digital Technologies and Book Publishing

Introduction

Any attempt to use the book format to write about current, let alone future, technologies faces the risk of instant obsolescence. To make matters worse, it is increasingly difficult to separate technological developments from those in the wider social domain, with the groundswell of technology take-up among ordinary citizens predicated as a threat to the future of all kinds of businesses (Li and Bernoff 2009). While it would be folly to dismiss these and other predictions out of hand, experience shows that technology alone is unlikely to result in the solving of business problems unless its adoption aligns with organizational missions and strategies. Experience also shows that, to have a realistic chance of success, strategies involving the adoption of technology should aim for a user-centred focus.

Furthermore, not only are the outcomes often far less revolutionary than expected, but also concerns are already emerging that social networking, a flagship new technology, may not deliver the kinds of innovation expected, owing to insufficient diversity and conflict within networks (Mayer-Schonberger 2009). With these caveats in mind, we will track current changes in technology as of early 2010 and will assess their implications for book publishing. Logically, this would include social networking, but in our opinion this technology is of sufficient importance to merit a separate chapter. The developments covered in this chapter include:

- services computing
- the internet and the World Wide Web, which includes: Web 1.0, Web 2.0, the Semantic Web and the future of the web
- mobile technology (pervasive computing), which includes: screen resolution, user interface and interaction, and smartphones
- eBooks
- digitization of content.

Services Computing

The provision of computing software as an application hosted by vendors on a remote server and accessible by clients over the internet first gained traction in the form of SaaS (Software as a Service). There are two broad classes of SaaS:

- first, there are business solutions for enterprises, such as supply chain or enterprise management systems, which are accessed following the payment of a subscription;
- second, is a range of services to the general public usually provided free and supported by advertising, notably web-based email systems such as Microsoft Hotmail or Google Gmail.

In both categories, a vendor hosts the programs, logic and data in a central location, with users downloading what they want over the web. The advantages that SaaS offers to clients include savings in the cost of software licences and data storage, and in staffing and maintenance, with the vendor responsible for handling service maintenance and the updating of software. For vendors there are the attractions of a steady stream of income and mitigation of the risks of piracy and the unlicensed use of software. Critics of SaaS have expressed concern about the risk to clients of having their data under the control of somebody else. A move from closed source to open source software has been proposed as one solution (Blankenhorn 2008).

Such issues notwithstanding, the move towards networked services has continued inexorably. This is not to say that the transition is complete or that is has been entirely smooth in operation. Hence, the most recent innovation in networked services, cloud computing, has attracted its share of controversy, not least over the alleged loss of control over data. Opinions are divided on the merits of this technology, however. On the one hand, the CEO of Oracle, Larry Ellison, has dismissed cloud computing as being simply the latest fashion (Farber 2008), while on the other hand, senior executives at HP are reported as having welcomed it as a generational change that will allow the internet to solve new kinds of problems (Lawson 2009). Basically, the idea behind cloud computing is of a future scenario where all the computing resources and application developments that companies need can be obtained like a public utility on the web. There would be no need for packaged software or licences, with networks of distributed computing power and limitless data storage being available on demand 'out there' in the cloud (Funk 2009). One authoritative source, the Berkeley University R&D lab, has described the characteristics of cloud computing in terms of:

- the availability of massive computing resources upon demand, thus facilitating a range of highly agile and scalable applications;
- computing services immediately available for use without the need to commit to ongoing or long-term agreements;
- payment only for the computing resources actually used, with no further payment required once these resources are released (Golden 2008).

This technology can also operate at the internal organizational level, with private clouds providing the same functionality as public clouds, but only to the one enterprise. These private clouds have the additional advantage of leveraging current infrastructure by placing the cloud in existing data centres while avoiding the risk of external data exposure (Brodkin 2009).

Allowing for differences of opinion and the fact that technology breakthroughs can frequently take longer from inception to widespread adoption than anticipated, there are clear benefits that can be attributed to cloud computing:

- First, it delivers cheap and easily available infrastructure provided by a third party which specializes in managing computing resources.
- Second, these resources as managed by the provider are always available and will be ready to scale in the event of increased demand.
- Third, this easy availability enables quick response to business demands, both for start-up firms and for established enterprises whose own IT departments are either unresponsive or costly (Golden 2009a).

Gilberto (2009) suggests the following additional reasons why cloud computing is the wave of the future:

- Increased scalability: users need not worry about hard-drive space and can apply for additional resources from their service provider as required.
- Environmentally friendly, with the server located at the provider's premises: clients need not have their own, thus making a significant communal contribution to reduction of the carbon footprint.
- Matches current computing trends: as cloud computing matures and an increased volume of processing is shifted to the cloud, computers will require less processing power and will have basic functionality.
- Versionless software: users can always access new versions, thus keeping at the cutting edge of technology.

The excitement generated by cloud computing has yet to solidify into any substantial level of market presence. As recently as 2008, there were promising signs in the response of start-up companies, many of whom had taken advantage of Amazon's EC2 and S3 services (Golden 2008). However, this was more than balanced by estimates that only around 20 per cent of established enterprises had adopted or were planning to adopt cloud computing (Brodkin 2009). Nonetheless, with a 2009 Forrester Research survey reporting that more than one-third of both large and medium enterprise companies were ready to invest in external clouds and a further 20 per cent were ready to commit to an internal version (Golden 2009b), this technology may at last be gaining real momentum. In the United Kingdom, for example, there are plans for an internal cloud that will provide a shared utility service to some 80 per cent of central government desktops by 2015, offering predicted savings of £2.5 billion a year (Arthur 2010). However, as a podcast on the Australian Broadcasting Corporation (ABC) on 2008 made clear (ABC Podcast 2008), significant issues remain to be addressed, including:

- Trust and privacy: can service providers be trusted? Do companies know who is handling and managing their data?
- Data centre malfunctions: in the event of these happening, companies could experience difficulty retrieving their data and everything could come to a halt.
- The market power of major firms: as the business is likely to be dominated by big players such as Google, Microsoft, Amazon and Yahoo, if customers are unhappy with a service provider there may not be much choice should they decide to change to another. Even where customers decide to change providers there could be difficulties involved in transferring historical data.
- Expense: the use of the provider's software on a pay-as-you-go basis could turn out to be an expensive option.

However, despite these difficulties, we believe that cloud computing has a future. Figure 4.1 illustrates the operation of a typical cloud containing a wide range of user data types.

As Funk (2009) points out, there is no fundamental difference between cloud computing and the SaaS model, except in its scope. In both cases, what is important is to see the wider implications for how people will interact in both their business and their social lives, with most software being delivered on demand.

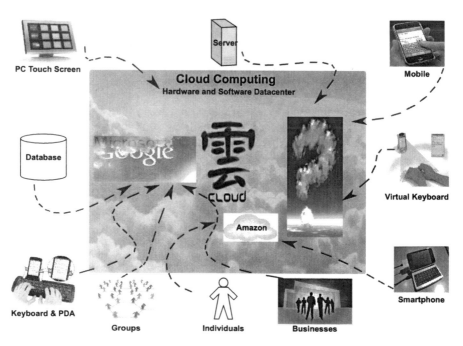

Figure 4.1   Cloud computing

Nor need all of these services involve payment, with, for example, the Google vision for cloud computing envisaging the free provision of services underwritten by targeted advertising (Funk 2009). This would be just one element in a gift economy, a visible underground of valuable creations – text, music, film, software, tools and services – all given away for free, fuelling an abundance of choices, mass participation and the conversion of consumers into producers (ABC Podcast 2008).

Cloud computing is already a growing feature of corporate and academic life. Given its potential for widespread application, it is hardly surprising that people outside book publishing could see a use for it in that industry. Among these is Hewlett Packard, which is engaged in a cloud initiative involving connections between content creators, sellers and readers aimed at overcoming the constraints of specific software applications, taking data outside application silos and eliminating the need for application integration work (Lawson 2009). Seen from the viewpoint of the end-user, this plethora of silos is akin to that proliferation of handheld mobile devices from phones to PDAs, to eBook readers that is such a feature of the digital technology landscape. Just as the emerging solution to such proliferation lies in the field of multifunctional devices, there is clearly a case for looking to clouds to bring a less-cluttered functionality to their application within book publishing (Ross 2010). Already, moreover, publishing experts acknowledge that, with content files and software applications stored and provided as an outsourced service by aggregators such as Google, Amazon and Microsoft, as well as by smaller targeted outsourcers, a key change is on the way for book publishing (Schwartz 2009).

Current expectations also are that when everything is stored in and accessed from the cloud it should be easier for rules about content access to be enforced, with the focus of concern shifting from piracy and rights management to issues of potential system (Shatzkin 2008b). This could all happen within a decade, which in terms of technology uptake might be a little too soon for an industry not actually renowned for its speed of response to technology, with the possibility that publishers might risk losing out to competitors from other industries (Lawson 2009). Of course there is always the possibility that publishers might be overestimating the power of technology in such matters, and hence that issues such as piracy and rights management could continue to be a problem for much longer than predicted.

The Internet and the World Wide Web

In terms of their influence and recognition factor, the internet and the World Wide Web must be among the most influential technologies of all time, enjoying truly global influence and popularity. Writing about these topics is akin to introducing that proverbial person 'who needs no introduction', but nonetheless having to say something by way of entrée. Suffice it to say that together these technologies have provided the disruptive force that has succeeded in transforming industries and economies, along with the social and personal lives of millions of people around the world. While commonly treated as a single technology, they are of course quite distinct in nature. The internet is a data communications system, a combined hardware and software infrastructure that provides connectivity within a global system of computer networks that uses the standardized Internet Protocol Suite (TCP/IP). It is a network of networks that supports an ever-growing range of facilities, from the infrastructure to support markets and business activities, including electronic mail, Voice over Internet Protocol telephony, podcasts and video, to popular services such as online chat and social networking, file sharing and gaming.

When it comes to talking or writing about the World Wide Web, it is important to bear in mind that it too has been subject to continual change, resulting in different versions or generations of this technology. These changes are considered here under the rubrics of Web 1.0, Web 2.0 and the Semantic Web, followed by a brief look at the future of the web.

Web 1.0

The term Web 1.0 was closely associated with the rise of eBusiness and essentially involved a read-only interface as compared with the read-write interface that characterizes Web 2.0 (Stephen 2009). The World Wide Web (hereafter the web) is an internet-based service which uses the HTTP (Hypertext Transfer Protocol) standard to connect documents and other resources using hyperlinks and Uniform Resource Locators (URLs). Web services also use HTTP to allow software systems or user agents to access web pages, and to enable users to navigate from one to another. Web documents may contain almost any combination of computer data, including graphics, sound, text, video, multimedia and interactive content including games, office applications and scientific demonstrations. Under the guidance and governance of the World Wide Web Consortium (W3C) the web is based on royalty-free technology standards in order to enable universal access.

This is all the more impressive in that, before the arrival of the Netscape browser in 1995, the internet was very much a minority interest. Since then the internet and the web have established an all-pervasive presence, to the point where it is hard to imagine a world where they did not exist. That this presence transcends the mere technological is explained by commentators such as Kelly (2006), to whom the world, in effect, has become a giant flea market, a gift economy where much of the value is generated by users rather than corporate interests, and where corporate webs such as those of Amazon, Google and eBay interact with the public commons to produce an abundance of choices. Indeed, a mere seven years after the development of Netscape, the world was coming to terms with a much more complex phenomenon, namely Web 2.0.

Web 2.0

Despite reportedly being dismissed by Tim Berners-Lee as a 'nonsense of a term' (Laningham 2006), the concept of Web 2.0 has resonated around the world. To most people Web 2.0 probably calls to mind such phenomena as blogs, wikis and mash-ups and, perhaps above all, of social networking. In fact, this is not too far off the mark, because, based on earlier technologies such as Ajax, these services are transforming the user experience and, along with it, the face of the web. Not only has Web 2.0 transformed relationships between users, content providers and enterprises, but also it has ushered in an era of networked computing in which any number of devices from smartphones to music players can function as information terminals (Wolcott 2007).

Elsewhere, Web 2.0 has been described as a landscape where users control their online experience and influence the experiences of others, and where success comes from harnessing the power of a range of social, computing, media and opinion and advertising networks (Funk 2009). Creation of the term Web 2.0 is widely attributed to Tim O'Reilly. Since its emergence in 2004 it has continued to develop, with some commentators already talking about Web 3.0. Be that as it may, the major features of Web 2.0 (as shown in Figure 4.2) can currently be categorized as follows:

- User experiences: the quality and range of software and services available, not least those that enable user interaction and immersion through architectures of participation have resulted in greatly enriched user experiences.
- Data and information management: data and information have become as important as, or more important than, software, which has rapidly become commoditized. Data management and the harnessing of collective intelligence acquired through network effects and feedback loops have become core competencies.
- Business models: there has been tremendous growth in lightweight business models designed for the mass servicing of micromarkets in the long tail.
- Innovation in assembly: the web has become a massive source of small pieces of data and services, loosely joined, increasing the recombinant possibilities and unintended uses of systems and information.
- Software and services: the most notable features here include:
    - a basic shift from the position of software as an artefact to one of software as a service, with continuous updating and the employment of users as co-developers in a context of perpetual beta-testing;
    - deployment of lightweight web services such as XML-RPC, JSON and REST that are designed for syndication rather than for coordination and for innovation in assembly;
    - emergence of lightweight software models with cost-effective scalability and fundamental implications for the economics of software development and the industry;

  – software design that increasingly occurs above the level of a single device
    to accommodate vertical and horizontal markets in which a diverse
    collection of players employ an increasingly rich array of platforms,
    from PCs to servers to handheld devices (Hinchcliffe 2006).

Since its inception the web, in whatever version, has, in a sense, appeared to
book publishers as two very different sides of the same coin. On the one hand,
it has offered an exponential expansion of customer contacts on the principle
that the bigger the network, the greater the potential client base. On the other,
by making information easily searchable, accessible from anywhere and capable
of combination in micropackages, it has threatened to disintermediate publishers
(Karp 2007). To date and on balance, this latter threat has proved less potent than
many had feared, and in the final analysis it will be business acumen and foresight
that will decide this issue. This and other issues facing publishing, including those
related to Web 2.0 and social networking are considered in some detail in the next
chapter.

The Semantic Web

Overlapping with Web 2.0 are developments in a range of technologies that are
pointing to the development of a semantic version of the web. The Semantic

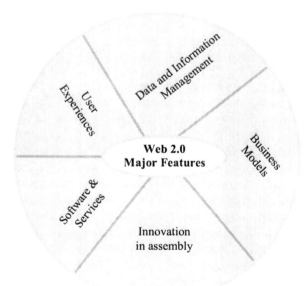

Figure 4.2   The major features of Web 2.0

Web means different things to different people, with some regarding it in terms of data, some in terms of services and others again as the outcome of applied artificial intelligence (Iskold 2008). The World Wide Web Consortium describes the Semantic Web as providing a common framework that allows data to be shared and reused across application, enterprise and community boundaries (W3C 2007). It must be noted that the Semantic Web is not something that is different from the World Wide Web. Rather, it is an enhancement that gives the web far greater utility (Feigenbaum et al. 2007). Whereas the original web mainly concentrated on the interchange of documents, the Semantic Web allows people or machines to range through an endless set of databases which are connected not by wires but by being about the same thing (W3C 2007), and where the semantics determine what a machine can do with the data beyond simply reading it (Vossen and Hagemann 2007).

For present purposes, the Semantic Web is perhaps best understood in the context of the 'big picture' problems facing the IT industry as a whole. These problems are technical in regard to the interoperability and scalability of global networked systems, and financial in terms of the costs to both systems vendors and their clients. Semantics can help here, in that they have to do with meaning. Essentially, in order for the services and applications on the web to work between systems and organizations, shared meanings are required. In providing a way of extracting common meanings from vast and complex data sets, semantic technologies have produced a new form of knowledge representation, and with it a way for computers to share meanings. Using semantic declarative knowledge, systems can communicate, not on the basis of natural language, which can be extremely ambiguous, but by using pure semantic codes and relationships. The goal here is that of a global web of semantically related resources that in theory could comprise all the knowledge in the world, accessible through a complex of autonomic systems that would for all intents and purposes behave like humans (Miller, P. 2007).

Although a fully functioning Semantic Web would in all likelihood represent a paradigm shift between previous systems architected and built by humans and those based on agents and intelligent technology, the transition seems likely to be gradual rather than marked by a step change. Hence, semantic techniques are proliferating across Web 2.0, and in the so-called 'deep web', which is comprised of hundreds of thousands of databases and websites and may be some 500 times as large as the surface Web (Bergman 2008). There are signs that the combination of Semantic Web mediation between a plethora of languages and concepts and the inherently structured and generally higher-quality content available on the deep web is already paying dividends (Bergman 2009).

Radical improvements in search and, in particular, improvements at the site of the information provider rather than in the search engines, were among the earliest benefits anticipated from the use of semantics (Batelle 2005). These included the use of semantic techniques for discovering and presenting associations between terms and concepts, along with personalized user profiles. However, a much more radical outcome is that posited in the view that, when genuinely semantically based knowledge computing eventuates, the need for searching will be obviated by the fact that all paths between input and output activities, including answers to questions, will already exist in the system (Miller, P. 2007). For the moment, however, Google continues to set the standard in search, and doubts continue to be cast on whether semantics alone will be sufficient to displace it by coming up with a killer search application (Iskold 2008).

However, it is clear that the Semantic Web offers much more than just improvements in searching; rather, it has implications for life cycle economies, systems integration and the elimination of data silos, along with new categories of tools and the empowerment of knowledge workers (Rohde 2008). Figure 4.3 provides an overview of the Semantic Web in operation.

In order to reach its current level of development, which enables targeted search and data browsing and the use of automated agents, breakthroughs have been necessary in the areas of data modelling and languages. Critically, these include:

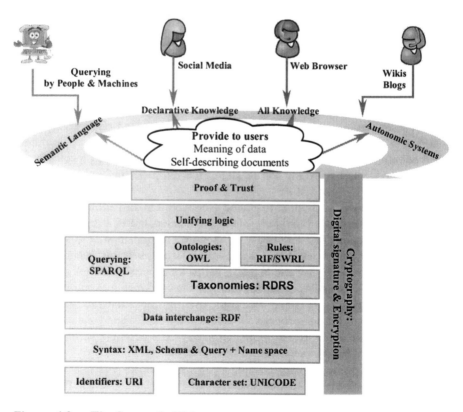

Figure 4.3   The Semantic Web

- The combination of metadata (not just to describe and annotate data, but also to enhance their meaning through semantics) and XML (to label and tag information) as the underlying foundation, along with Unicode for making everything language independent (Vossen and Hagemann 2007).
- The Resource Description Framework (RDF) as the model for data interchange. This simple XML-based model can easily be represented graphically and enables general concepts to be expressed based on a simple and uniform syntax. It allows structured and semi-structured data to be mixed, exposed and shared across different applications of the RDF model (Feigenbaum 2009).
- Ontologies to define the concepts and relationships used to describe and represent an area of knowledge. Ontologies are used to classify the terms used in a particular application, to characterize possible relationships, and define possible constraints on using those relationships (W3C 2007). The OWL Ontology Web Language employed in the Semantic Web explains and defines the theories left implicit within a metadata structure and how to derive its logical consequences, i.e. facts not literally present in the ontology but entailed by the semantics (W3C 2007).
- SPARQL as a standard query language and data access protocol for use with the RDF data model. This SQL-like language enables the querying of sets of RDF graphs and the querying and search of disparate data sources. It also helps to 'gluc' separate software applications together by transforming data from one vocabulary to another (Feigenbaum 2009).

All book publishers, some more consciously than others, are to some degree or other engaged in using semantic tools. Increasingly this applies to search based on taxonomies built on the 'wisdom of crowds' approach, where content for specific purposes and contexts drawn from previous searches is aggregated and ranked to reveal the structure as well as definitions of content discovered (Schwartz 2009). Taxonomies can be the backbone of a publishing business, enabling the sorting, inventorying and merchandising of content. By way of example, taxonomies of learning objects are in widespread use in educational publishing, and more generally, Wiley operates accounting, cooking and psychology taxonomies (Dawson 2008). The increasing popularity of digital publishing standards and the extent of activity in both digital content creation and the design of reading devices indicates that book publishers are well aware of the opportunities as well as the threats inherent in technological change. Moreover, as will be seen in the next chapter, book publishers are already quite heavily engaged in creating and exploiting digital content, using everything from blogs and wikis to feed aggregators and social networking.

Another set of semantic tools is the Calais suite, which is designed to make content more accessible, interoperable and valuable, and is available free. The OpenCalais Web Service is shown in www.opencalais.com. By using Natural Language Processing, machine learning and other methods, this automatically creates rich semantic metadata which are delivered to the user as tags which can be used for incorporation into specific applications such as blogs, catalogues or content aggregations.

While not a complete solution, Calais offers particular benefits to publishers. This is basically owing to their need to find ways of producing and adding value to content and delivering it to customers. In operation, Calais would enhance this content with rich semantic metadata, generated in industry-standard formats for integration with whatever commercial, open source or proprietary content management system was in use. The tags supplied could, for example, be applied to content archives, rendering them open to search and integration with other content assets, and employed as the basis of value-added products and services.

The role of semantics will become increasing apparent to book publishers as they take advantage of web-based internal-process integration and customer-facing services. To this end they will employ semantic-form declarative knowledge and knowledge tools to avoid the limitations of language-based approaches, and enjoy substantial savings of time and money. As in other areas, however, it is important that book publishers take early advantage of these opportunities, lest others beat them to it (Davis and Walter 2004).

The future of the Web

Despite doubts over its practicality, the Semantic Web is now well established in a range of industries from telecommunications and health care to pharmaceuticals and biotechnology.

It is present in the form of standards and in the tools used in tagging systems on social sites such as MySpace and Flickr and as Digital Object Identifiers (DOIs) in publishing (Feigenbaum et al. 2007). Search engines such as Google, Yahoo! and Ning all use semantic technologies, while domain-specific semantic search offers great potential in areas such as real estate and music. These and related developments suggest not only that semantic technologies are attaining critical mass, but also that in the process they could be ushering in Web 3.0, which has been described as a stage of cleaning up previous messes and harvesting the value created in Web 2.0 (Krill 2009). Much more exciting and, in ways, a logical evolution from Web 2.0 as the Semantic–Social Web, is the case for aligning Web 3.0 with concepts such as the 'Internet of Things' and 'Augmented Reality'.

In the meantime, the phenomenon that Li and Bernoff (2009) describe as the groundswell would appear to be pointing clearly in the direction of radical change not only in technology and its adoption, but also in the nature and operation of businesses. This spontaneous demonstration of people power is manifest in the use by consumers and potential consumers of online tools to take charge of their own experiences and obtain whatever it is they need, be this information, support, ideas, products and services and bargaining power, from each other. It is important to reiterate, moreover, that the real breakthrough here lies not in the technology but in the relationships it makes possible. Proponents of the groundswell phenomenon argue that it is already changing the way that companies do business. This includes everything from how they locate and connect to customers, for example by listening and responding rather than shouting at them through now inappropriate mass advertising channels, to empowering their staff to engage with the groundswell effectively in order to learn from customers and build long-term loyalty (Li and Bernoff 2009). The likelihood that such activity might become ubiquitous sits well with our own perception that any new version of the web should amount to more than iteration, and should embody truly radical breakthroughs. Such ubiquity would mean that the groundswell would become embedded across the spectrum of human activity, and not just in computers, but on mobile devices of all kinds.

Mobile Technology (Pervasive Computing)

Often referred to as ubiquitous or mobile computing, pervasive computing is just what its name suggests, using familiar interfaces to email services and web services using everything from mobile telephones and PDAs to laptops and Global Positioning System (GPS) navigators (Radziwill and DuPlain 2009). Also referred to as 'participative computing' it is collaborative and user-centric, consisting of participative networks creating value through user engagement and interaction on multiple levels (Radziwill and DuPlain 2009).

In many ways the future of the web will be mobile, with current trends leading away from the desktop and towards entire new families of browser-enabled mobile devices, from handhelds to smartphones. Increasingly all such devices will be equipped with the ability to render web content in the form of widgets, with GPS and track-pad fingerprint-recognition security options, and running on open source software. However, the transition from desktop to device has significant implications for the user experience, whether in terms of the viewing conditions in place and the attention levels required, the skills required of the user and the levels of information involved (Shea 2008). Furthermore, beyond issues of browser capabilities, all designers of handheld devices must address ongoing problems to do with screen resolution and with user interface and interaction.

Screen resolution

The basic problem here is that of different screen sizes, with designs perfected for small screens not scaling well to large screens, and vice versa. Furthermore, users may well prefer to have two versions of screen layout, that for their specific device and the regular, large-screen version (Shea 2008). This is significant, because although the W3C's vision of 'One Web' is important, provision of the exact same experience on all devices may well devalue the benefits of context and mobility delivered by mobile devices.

User interface and interaction

Key issues here involve those of navigation, location and pagination. In all cases the use of zoom facilities can be helpful, although for pagination, which involves much greater user involvement, the target area is more important. Most pervasive of all may be the difficulties involved in entering text on a device that has a small physical keyboard, or a touch screen or some other form of software keyboard. Typing is typically much slower, and concepts that are second nature on the desktop may not be available. The obvious answer may lie in advanced touch screen technology, which, as well as being easier to use, leaves space on the device for additional functions, hopefully including entirely new interface elements. Beyond issues of functionality per se, however, there is the question as to whether users will choose to acquire different devices for specific purposes or prefer to invest in one all-encompassing, multifunctional gadget. Currently a strong contender in the multifunctional arena is the latest generation of mobile phones, colloquially known as smartphones.

Smartphones

As people tend to like handheld devices for their portability and convenience, the need to carry several devices around at any one time is unlikely to have widespread appeal. Not surprisingly, therefore, the current generation of smartphones is seen as having a great deal of promise in this regard. More than just telephones, these devices enable users to access the internet and to download a growing range of applications, including games, social networking programs and productivity tools. However, despite their popularity with specific groups of users, there are still conflicting opinions as to the viability and purpose of these devices. On the one hand, they have been criticized for being essentially content consumption rather than content creation devices, and also as being prone to compatibility and performance problems where different operating systems and even IT policies are involved. On the other hand, there is the view that services such as Twitter and Posterous have resulted in a change in the direction of content creation, and that it has been smartphones that have made this shift a reality. Indeed, arguably the term 'smartphone' is already outdated, with all phones become smarter with the provision of internet access, email and other capabilities. The distinctions between these various devices will be based variously on their degrees of openness and applications extensibility, and on whether they are prized for their utility or their entertainment value. However, the really significant distinction is that between their use for content consumption or for content creation (Dignan 2009).

Only a decade ago there were fewer than 500 million mobile subscriptions in the world, whereas today there are around 4.6 billion (*The Economist* 2009). The market for mobile handsets is a lively one in which a growing number of companies are competing on the basis of products which differ more in degree than in substance. In many ways the real breakthrough with smartphones came with the advent of yet another cult product from Apple, in this case the iPhone. With its user-friendly interface and wide screen, along with multimedia and networking facilities, the iPhone has, since its inception, set the benchmark for smartphones.

Accordingly, despite the success of competing devices such as the Blackberry, particularly with business users, it was going to take the entry of another really significant player into the market to seriously dent the aspirations of Apple and its fervent iPhone community. In retrospect, this was only likely to happen if Google entered the market for smartphones, and so it transpired with the arrival of the G1 device. This 3G smartphone had much to commend it, from its Wi-Fi networking capability to its touch screen interface that could be customized to provide user access through widgets, profiles and consolidated views of all communication with a contact, whether this was through email, text or multimedia message, Facebook status updates or photos (Cha 2009). Perhaps even more significant was the inclusion of the Android Open Software Stack for mobile devices and the involvement of the Open Software Alliance. This is a consortium of leading technology companies, including computer and chip makers and telecommunications providers, as well as leading mobile telephone companies. Together these had the potential to provide a platform for thousands of different mobile phones operating under licence from Google and the Open Handset Alliance (Cox 2008).

However, the competition between Apple and Google became even more intense with the launch in January 2010 of its new so-called 'superphone' the Nexus One, built in partnership with the Taiwanese manufacturer HTC and again, running on the Android operating system (Cellan-Jones 2010). The manufacturers distinguish this superphone from previous smartphones on the basis of its open platform, its processing and storage capacities and the extent of choice it offers to consumers (Topolsky 2010). The initial response by the technology press has been positive, although stopping well short of regarding it as the last word in mobile development (Cellan-Jones 2010). Some indeed have described this so-called superphone as being basically an Android clone of the iPhone (Topolsky 2010).

Already the operating systems employed by these devices have significantly impacted upon the previous hegemony of the Microsoft Windows operating system, and on the ability of network providers to dictate what could be connected. The iPhone is currently well ahead of Windows mobile in popularity. Furthermore, it is a clear example of a user experience-driven business model which has disintermediated the telecommunications space. In terms of the future, however, the Nexus One could be an altogether different prospect, because it represents much more than an enhancement of handset functionality. Essentially it is a response to the challenges and opportunities presented in the growing user migration from computers to mobiles for internet access. The real game here is to safeguard Google's search-linked advertising business, from which it draws the bulk of its revenue (Johnson 2010a). So far as book publishing is concerned, with such functionality available in a single device, the question of what else could possibly be needed is moot. This is especially the case when mobile phones are capable of performing the functions of specialist gadgets such as eBook readers. It is to the subject of eBook readers that our attention now turns.

eBooks

Few topics seem more geared to stir the emotions of publishers and the reading public than that of eBooks. At its most extreme this manifests itself in polarization between those fiercely loyal to the 550-year-old codex format and those who, seeing this as obsolete, have embraced the vision of digital texts displayed on computers, PDAs, notebooks and other handhelds, including eBook readers specifically designed for the purpose. Increasingly, in the case of specialist eReaders, the trend is towards multifunctional devices which combine reading with communications and a range of social and business functions. Although there are still people who reject such developments on the grounds that eBooks are not really books, those more comfortable with electronic formats would argue that the carrier or container is irrelevant, and that the delivery of content in a more convenient and flexible form is the important thing. Shatzkin (2009c) summarizes the four stages of eBook development as those of Vision, Establishment, Transition, and the New Marketplace, pointing out that things are currently at the Establishment stage. Table 4.1, borrowed from Shatzkin, illustrates these four stages.

Doubtless there will be people who will choose to adhere to the printed book, shunning all and any electronic substitutes. This is fine as far as it goes, but the problem for such people could be that already there are indications that the supply of hard-copy products will dwindle to the point where, if they are available, the unit costs will make them extremely expensive. Clearly we are talking about the future here, but not the distant future. The practice of reading everything from newspapers to personal and business documents on some kind of a screen is already so widespread as to be a fact of life. Furthermore, so far as eBooks are concerned, there is already a thriving market both in reading devices and for downloads from the various eBook libraries. The proliferation of the latter is also important, as witness the deal struck by Simon & Schuster to sell around 5,000 eBooks on Scribd, a web service that currently attracts 60 million unique visitors a month and where people can buy, share, sell or comment on material using the latest social networking tools (Ante 2009). Almost one million dedicated eBook reading devices like the Amazon Kindle and the Sony eReader were sold over the period 2005 to 2008, leading to predictions that eBook sales would grow from around $150 million a year in 2008 to around $550 million annually by 2011 (Weinstein 2009).

This last point suggests to us that the technology as it currently stands is adequate in terms of the quality of the reading experience, which so far as clarity of image on the better screens is concerned is now hard to distinguish from reading on paper. Furthermore, the experience is more than adequate as regards the convenience factors of reading on the move, of not having to carry physical

Table 4.1   The four stages of eBook development

Stages	Period	Major features
Vision	Late 1990 to 2007 entry of Kindle into the market	Minimal market, less than 1% of trade sales Development of the ePub standard Established terms of trade Grants intermediaries approximately the same margins as in the physical print-book world Lessons of DRM have been learned
Establishment	Now	eBook revenue growth Competition among devices Minimal changes to overall power relationships in the publishing value chain
Transition	Next 1 to 3 years	Real shifts in value chains Most publishers offering direct downloads DRM expected to disappear Explosion of potential purchase points Devices only importing from a single source will lose importance Large horizontal aggregators will struggle to maintain loyal customer base as the vertical web takes hold
New Marketplace	In 10 years' time	eBooks become the norm Authors will have less need for publishers eBooks will be routinely updated and enhanced and linked to other content in ways that printed books simply cannot match Printed books will have very specific uses

objects around, and of being able to access and increasingly download additional books while in transit. There is clearly a need for cheaper devices and for more low-cost digital content, but arguably proof of concept has been resolved in the best place of all, the marketplace.

eBook reading devices

In this marketplace the clear leaders have been Amazon and Sony, with respectively, the Kindle and the Sony eReader. Their latest offerings, the Kindle DX and the Sony Daily Edition, have both much to recommend them in terms of eInk electronic paper screen displays (9.7 inch diagonal on the DX and 7 inch on the Daily Edition), 3G wireless functionality and battery life (lasting up to one week on a single charge in the case of the DX and up to two weeks for the Daily Edition). The DX enables access to over 400,000 books in its Kindle bookstore, far surpassing the 90,000 available through its Sony counterpart. However, Sony offers access to over one million public domain documents available through Google, and also the opportunity for users to borrow ePub formatted books held in public libraries (Bradley 2009).

The key distinctions between these two eBook readers are to be found less in specific features and levels of performance than in the fact that the Sony device uses the ePub open standard publishing format. This XML-based file format allows the production and distribution of a single digital publication file and offers consumers interoperability between software and hardware for unencrypted, reflowable digital books and other publications (Conboy 2009). So far as the Sony device is concerned, this means that it can also read PDF and Word formats, whereas the DX uses the proprietary Kindle (AZW) format, making its content very much device specific and excluding material in the ePub format. Although hitherto Amazon has dominated the market on the basis of its global reach and large content store, logic suggests that with publishers of the stature of HarperCollins, Houghton Mifflin, Random House and Simon & Schuster supporting the ePub standard, this is the way of the future (Paul 2009b).

As competition within the eBook market has increased, one long-anticipated arrival has been that of the QUE Plastic Logic reader. Almost a decade in design and development, it was launched at the Consumer Electronics Show at Las Vegas in January 2010. The first devices were scheduled for shipping in mid-April 2010. These are high-end devices aimed initially at business users, but are expected to be followed by a series of specialized eReaders for students, teachers, health care professionals and other niche markets (*The Sydney Morning Herald News* 2010). Its key features include a proprietary display technology, where transistors are built on plastic rather than silicon, a fast eInk 11 inch by 8.5 inch touch screen, a battery that lasts for days rather than hours and the absence of navigational buttons. In addition, the QUE proReader is linked to the BN.com online book store from which books can be searched, downloaded and purchased (Paul 2009a).

There are currently two models of the QUE proReader to choose from, the 4GB model with Wi-Fi costing US$ 649 and the 8GB model with Wi-Fi and 3G at US$ 799. Buyers can purchase devices either in-store at Barnes & Noble bookshops across the United States or online at BN.com (Plastic Logic Press Release 2010). The system can accommodate thousands of regular office documents in formats such as Word, Excel, PowerPoint and PDF without the need for conversion, and can be used to read books, newspapers and magazines.

Although clearly an impressive device, the QUE proReader emerged into a market not only already replete with established players and open to aggressive new competitors, but also where Apple has just made its long-anticipated appearance with the iPad tablet computer. Introduced to the market by Steve Jobs at the end of January 2010, the iPad comes with a whole host of exciting features, including web browsing, email, games and presentation software. For present concerns, however, what is most significant is that the major target for this touch screen device is the market for eBooks. Promoted as being a third category of device, being more intimate than a laptop and much more capable than a mobile phone, the iPad comes with an iBooks program using the ePub format and an iBooks bookstore similar to iTunes (Johnson and Arthur 2010).

The iPad is the same size as the Amazon Kindle but its 9.7 inch (24.6 cm) touch screen comes in colour rather than in than in black and white as with the Kindle. Priced from US$ 499 to US$ 829 and to be sold through Apple's online Apps Store, the iPad comes with 16, 32 or 64GB flash memory and has built in Wi-Fi and Bluetooth connectivity. The battery last for 10 hours and although it can sit for a month on standby without needing a charge, its basic life is unimpressive when compared with the competition (AOL News 2010). The iPad has also been widely criticized for its lack of a camera. Much more important, however, is the absence of a facility for multitasking and of Flash software for video and animation. The backlit screen is harder on the eye and offers less clarity than the eInk version, there is no 3G (promised in later models) nor as yet any alternative to connectivity through the AT & T network (Stone 2010). Experienced IT industry watchers were quick to point out that this absence of features had to be seen in the context of two factors. The first was that the price point of the first iPad was set sufficiently low to assist Apple in its efforts to create a market for the device. Second, only not did this represent a major shift in strategy away from the company's traditionally high margins, but also the company was aiming to recoup lost profits through the upselling of much more expensive models embodying the missing features, and through sales of content (Stokes 2010).

Although criticism on the grounds of what features might or might not be built into any new device is only to be expected, there is another way of looking at this matter. Indeed, it is argued that, in picking upon individual points of perceived weakness in the iPad, critics are missing the point of the device, which is to do with creating new market spaces and consequently enabling new user behaviours (Sutherland 2010). In some ways this is an argument for devices that are multifunctional rather than single purpose, in that it anticipates not only the development of new media capacity, from games and video to newspapers, but also the same disruption of the value-creation process in publishing that occurred previously within the music industry. As new spaces and new applications emerge, so, it is claimed, will new consumer behaviours, and with them, new business models for publishing (Sutherland 2010).

Nevertheless, and not entirely unrelated to the matter of applications, criticism of a much more different kind emerged from within the computing and open software communities within days of the launch of the iPad. Rather than a third-category device, these critics viewed the iPad as marking a fundamental shift in the workings of the computer industry and as a monopolistic development threatening innovation and the long-term future of the industry (Johnson 2010b). To these critics, the absence of multitasking capability was much more than an inconvenience. Rather, it meant that only applications approved by Apple could be loaded onto the device, in effect overturning the long-standing position whereby users were able to upload whatever software they wished to their devices. If unchallenged, this could enable Apple to control the future, at least to the extent that it could block ideas and applications that it viewed as competitors (Johnson 2010b).

Doubtless we have not heard the last of this issue, but in the meantime, and focusing on its characteristics as an eBook reader, the iPad could turn out to be a serious player in the market. Already it has been welcomed in wider media circles both for its potential as a games platform and as very good news for the TV industry through its ability to allow video to be consumed on the move and in a dynamic and personalized fashion (Guardian News 2010). At the time of its launch, Apple had already signed deals with five major publishers – HarperCollins, Penguin, Simon & Schuster, Macmillan and Hachette – but surprisingly, not with Random House, which had been engaged in earlier discussions about the iPad. However, Random House welcomed the new device and said it looked forward to finding ways to expand distribution of its own books through the iPad and the iPhone. This would both broaden the reach of its authors and connect with new readers (Weinman 2010). Although also not a signatory to the Apple deal, McGraw Hill welcomed the iPad specifically for its potential in the areas of professional and educational publishing, with its CEO pointing out that 95 per cent of its textbooks were already in eBook format (Shah 2010). Also of interest to educational publishers was an observation by a UK academic that the iPad, owing to its personalized nature and wireless connectivity, offered the ability to access a world beyond that of the networks of particular schools. Indeed, with fundamental implications for teaching and learning, this is technology to which schools would have to adjust, rather than the other way round (Guardian News 2010).

The launch of the iPad is clearly a significant development and one which should contribute, at least in the medium term, to increased competition and a reduction in the price of devices, although not necessarily in those of the eBooks to be read on these devices. Nevertheless, concerns have been expressed about the oversupply and even the commoditization of these devices (Walters 2010), with some seeing the iPad as just as likely to cannibalize the sales of other Apple devices as to generate sales in the tens of millions (Stone 2010). Nevertheless the contenders keep coming, including particularly impressive appearances by Barnes & Noble's nook and Hearst's Skiff, and with Texas Instruments reported as seeking a share of a market that has been predicted to grow from sales of 4 million in 2008 to 12 million in 2010 (Godinez 2010). Should Google decide to make the move into eBooks, then, as has been pointed out, we could be looking at a completely different eBook world within the next year (Stone and Rich 2010).

Issues in eBook and eReader development

Whatever the features of the individual device, moreover, it will increasingly be the quality of the consumer experience that will be the differentiator, and especially in terms of platform compatibility and the range and scale of content available. Although both Amazon and Sony have become market leaders, based on the attractions of their hardware and their alliances with major publishing houses, the international market is going to demand more choice and convenience rather than mere availability. In many ways, standardization remains the Holy Grail, with widespread adoption of the ePub format seen as enabling a free choice of hardware, even if this still comes with some form of digital rights management (Schnittman 2007). There would be clear advantages for book publishing as a whole, were device vendors to move from their proprietary formats to the adoption of the ePub standard. So far as DRM is concerned, just as in the music and film industries, publishers are reluctant to remove it, lest their industry be exposed to widespread piracy (Paul 2009b). These concerns about piracy are justifiable, given that in just three months in 2009, some 9 million books were pirated (Publishers Lunch Deluxe News 2010e). The answer may well be found in a response along the lines of that coming from within the music industry, with publishing moving towards something like a rights-free, platform-neutral MP3 format. However, content owners must first accept that future value lies not so much in the content itself as in its exchange, and in the fact that readers like to be able to share and exchange this content (Rothman 2006). They also want to be involved and engaged in activities including re-sampling, mashups and reinterpretation.

We are clearly still at an important development stage for eBook readers, with seemingly new devices and options emerging all the time. It can be expected that a wave of new customer-driven applications will flow from the eBook format and delivery platform, including content that can be reformatted and printed on demand (Schwartz 2009). In this fledgling market it is important not only that book publishers remain objective and look beyond the claims of competing device manufacturers to assess what they can actually do that is different from the competition, and which promises significant rather than incremental improvements to the reader experience. What the response of the market to the Apple iPad will be, it is too early to say. Steve Jobs has expressed confidence that the existing installed base of 75 million iPhones and iPod Touches means that there are already 75 million people who know how to use an iPad (Johnson and Arthur 2010). However, the device has already been criticized for lacking sufficient new features to justify claims that it is a new category of device (AOL News 2010), as well as on the basis that with its iPhone interface it is still a device optimized for media consumption rather than creation (Johnson and Arthur 2010). It is also much too early to say whether what is, in many respects, an 'iPod for books' is likely to be the answer to the eBook challenge (Guardian News 2010). In any case, for a truly significant breakthrough to occur, changes will be required as much in mindsets and expectations as in the technology. In the ongoing discourse as to the nature of books and reading, it is important not to think of the future in terms of the present, let alone the past.

Hopefully also, publishers will have learned the lessons from the failed first generation of eBooks, lessons to do with price, the selection of content available, ease of use and, by no means least, DRM. Armed with vastly improved bandwidth and memory capacities, publishers are now in a position to offer readers a truly different experience in terms of access and interactivity, from hyperlinking to annotation to mashing and publishing. Nor need this necessarily spell trouble for print books, demand for which is predicted to grow simultaneously with that for eBooks, albeit for differentiated versions (Shatzkin 2009d). Critically, this could lead to another paradigm shift for publishing, one in which the experience provided is something truly different from that enjoyed with the printed book, an experience based on the nature of eBooks as social objects that are fluid, intangible and shareable in a digital world (Gomez 2008). Until then, and arguably until the emergence of a kind of eBook ecology involving publishers, retailers and readers, the printed book seems more than likely to have a future, perhaps to some extent prolonged by the arrival of technology such as the Espresso book publishing machine, enabling the printing of titles on demand (Publishers Lunch Deluxe News 2010f).

However, as with mobile phones, the future of eBooks may well lie in complete reinvention rather than in simply transferring print from the page to a screen. In the United States, the Gutenberg and the ACLS Humanities eBook projects were both essentially attempts in this direction, conceived as multilayered documents, aimed at different audiences and linked to many sources outside the immediate framework of the book. As a more focused example, Tim O'Reilly's *Twitter Book* with its modular, dynamic and non-linear text with links to comments, and collaborative authoring is also a step towards the future, as could be a so-called 'smartbook' concept proposed by a group of Bulgarian academics. Arguing that the book reading experience can be reinvented in a web-based context that supports connectivity and creativity among digital communities, the authors envisage a new generation of smartbooks that would be evolving, highly interactive, customizable, adaptable and intelligent. They would also be equipped with a rich set of author and reader support services, including separate author and reader spaces and a shared collaborative space, the access rights to which would be set by publishers (Koychev, Nikolov and Dicheva 2009).

It is clear from this and other examples that the eBook is still very much in its infancy, and that there is still some way to go before the various initiatives and innovations reach anything like maturity. When they do, the limits of our current perceptions of the nature and purpose of eBooks could become all too clear. However, while such devices and their successors will remain critical to the dissemination of digital content, the digitization issue has broader and deeper implications for book publishing.

Digitization of Content

The impact of the digitization of content, including the ability to reproduce and distribute perfect copies of content assets, is said to have been almost as profound as has been the introduction of the internet (European Commission 2003). At the 2009 Digital Book Conference in New York, one presenter, in outlining what he called a stimulus plan for book publishing, urged publishers to digitize as fast as possible, owing both to the inevitability of electronic formats and to the cost and business benefits of doing so (Christensen 2009). A similar message emerged at the LeWeb conference in Paris a year later, when publishers were warned not to overlook the activities of technology companies that were shaping the future through their innovations in content creation, distribution and consumption. Not only were book publishers increasingly dependent upon such companies, but also they needed to be much more closely engaged with them. The alternative was to lose further ground in matters of content control and distribution to competitors armed with free and low-cost tools for building mobile applications and eBooks with little or no expertise. Among the suggested solutions were that publishers consider making arrangements with mobile application developers, in order to be able to tap into already existing communities, or with mobile operators for the creation of local storefronts with content available for loading onto mobile devices (Johnson 2009).

That many publishers have already received the message loud and clear can be ascertained through even a casual browse on the web. At the Digital Book World Conference in New York in 2008, for example, HarperCollins reported a series of experiments in the provision of both partial and completely free access to digital content, experiments which resulted in encouraging results so far as site registrations and even sales were concerned (Hulse 2008). Another, earlier and farsighted example occurred at the ill-fated AOL Time Warner conglomerate in 2003. There, the media giant's publishing arm reconstituted all its books into thousands of digital assets in a 'search inside the book' initiative including, for example, the dust jacket, the table of contents, and sample chapters, all of which were deemed likely to drive additional sales, either as stand-alone products or in combination with other media assets such as film or television content (Cone 2003).

Currently Thomson Reuters is doing well out of a strategic focus on its professional information assets in markets where content is created and distributed digitally, and where subscriptions sold to institutions are a much more attractive proposition than book sales to single readers. The revenues generated by these knowledge groups are reported as generating four out of every five dollars emerging from an integrated digital value chain (Wischenbart 2009).

The importance of digital standards to such activities was reiterated again at the 2009 Digital Book Conference, where Random House reported the adoption of Docbook as its standard version of XML, along with radical changes in workflow and processes in a drive to transform existing frontlist and large numbers of backlist titles to the ePub format. What was particularly interesting about this initiative was that not only it was realistic with regard to the potential implementation issues surrounding adoption of the XML standards, but also it acknowledged the wider cultural and business model issues that would be involved (McCloy-Kelley 2009).

Book Publishing and Technological Change

Digital technologies are already in widespread use in the book publishing industry. Although frequently criticized for its reluctance to adopt new ideas and technologies, book publishing has successfully negotiated through centuries of technological change, from the age of movable type to Web 2.0. Moreover, where there have been problems following technology adoption, these have tended to be less a technical issue than the result of incompatibilities in outlook between business and technology people, particularly as regards specific applications of the technology to book publishing (Byrd and Daffron 2009). Despite our core belief in the primacy of business solutions over technological ones, it is easy to see how current developments in technology might be regarded as somehow being qualitatively different from those that preceded them. To some informed observers, indeed, not only are technology and publishing synonymous today, but also it is technology and technology-based solutions rather than content that will determine success and survival in the industry (Cairns 2008). Such assertions are all the more plausible when reinforced by market research predicting that between 2009 and 2013 the overall share of expenditures on digital content and services within the entertainment and media industries will increase from 21 per cent to 31 per cent. Furthermore, by 2010 digital expenditure will be that sector's main engine of growth, making further inroads into all segments (PriceWaterhouseCoopers 2009).

This brief overview of technology and its potential application in the book publishing industry continues into the next chapter, which is devoted to the topic of Web 2.0 applications in book publishing.

Chapter 5

Web 2.0 Applications and Book Publishing

Introduction

In order to understand social media it is first important to understand the debt that they owe to Web 2.0. Advances contained within this second generation of web development have enormously facilitated the key processes of communication, secure information sharing, interoperability, and collaboration. In turn this has led to the evolution of web-based communities, hosted services and applications such as weblogs (or blogs), wikis, RSS, social tagging, mashups, social networking and virtual worlds. Web 2.0 is already having a disruptive impact, and is predicted to be the driver behind a range of new business applications and processes characterized by user participation, openness and network effects (Musser and O'Reilly 2006).

Web 2.0 is the pivotal driver of the social networking phenomenon. In an environment where the social and business dimensions increasingly overlap, its support for social networking sites such as MySpace, Facebook, LinkedIn, Digg, Ning and Twitter, and for virtual world environments such as Penguin Club, Active World and Second Life, is enabling businesses and their customers to interact as never before (Sankar 2009).

For publishing, as for any other business, there are tremendous opportunities here not only for building loyal customer bases by drawing people to their sites, but also for the creation of new business models. By the same token, a failure to act on the opportunities presented by social networking is likely to result in loss of business to other, more proactive competitors (Waldram 2009). This chapter begins with an overview of Web 2.0 and its applications.

Web 2.0 and Its Applications

Originally pioneered by Darcy DiNucci in 1999, the concept of Web 2.0 gradually gained acceptance following the first Web 2.0 conference hosted by O'Reilly Media and MediaLive in 2004 (O'Reilly 2005). The concept has been variously perceived as:

- the business revolution in the computer industry caused by the move to the internet as a platform, and an attempt to understand the rules for success on that new platform (Musser and O'Reilly 2006);

- an internet-based business technology revolution where massive interconnectivity and openness in the harnessing of collective intelligence leads to business advantages (O'Reilly 2009).

In talking to publishers about advanced technologies, we eventually came to an understanding of Web 2.0 in the broader context of its use and applications. Accordingly, we see Web 2.0 in terms of the use of social software to amass and create collective intelligence in a community-driven context where the value is generated by users. The key applications of Web 2.0 are presented in Table 5.1.

In addition to a consensus on these applications, general agreement has been reached on those features now considered as typical of Web 2.0 sites, features captured by McAfee (2006) in the acronym SLATES. These are:

- Search: the ease of finding information through keyword searches.
- Links: ad hoc guides to other relevant information.
- Authoring: the ability to create constantly updated content over a platform that is the creation of many interlinked authors. In wikis, the content is iterative in the sense that users can undo and redo each other's work. In blogs, the content is cumulative in that the posts and comments of individuals are accumulated over time.
- Tags: simple, one-word, user-determined descriptions to categorize content and facilitate searching by avoiding pre-set categories.
- Extensions: powerful algorithms that leverage the web as an application platform as well as a document server.
- Signals: the use of RSS technology to notify users rapidly of content changes.

Web 2.0 technologies and applications have dramatically changed people's perception of and levels of participation in the web. Web 2.0 has become accepted as variously, a communication medium, a socialization platform, a discussion forum, a business platform, a storage device for diaries and a constantly growing and expanding encyclopaedia (Vossen and Hagemann 2007). Funk (2009) summarizes the four key themes of Web 2.0 as follows:

- power is in the hands of individual users and their networks;
- Web content is distributed, sorted, combined, and displayed across the web in formats unanticipated by the content creators;
- new technology makes rich online experiences and complex software applications possible;
- integration breaks down the walls between PCs, phones and mobile devices, between marketing and ordering channels, and the user experience across different websites.

Table 5.1   Key applications of Web 2.0

Web 2.0 Applications	Purpose and functionality	Examples
Weblogs or blogs	Personal websites that enable communication between users, including the ability to publish and distribute content.	The Penguin blog: http://feeds.feedburner.com/typepad/thepenguinblog.
Wikis	Websites that promote the collaborative creation of content. Wiki pages that can be edited by anyone at anytime. The wiki users can alter the original content and perform functions such as update, restore, delete and create, while the blog user can only add information in the form of comments.	Wikipedia: the biggest non-profit people-generated encyclopaedia with over 2 million articles.
RSS (Really Simple Syndication, and alternatively, Rich Site Summary) Technologies	An XML-based content-syndication protocol that allows websites to share and aggregate information based upon the users' needs. Users can access relevant content through very fast communication channels on a subscription basis.	iTunes offers direct access to podcasts through its iTunes Music Store. To integrate the podcast in the store, iTunes has defined an extension in the www.itunes.com/dtds/podcast-1.0.dtd namespace.
Social tagging (Social bookmarking)	The collaborative activity of marking shared online content with keywords or tags as a way to organize it for future navigation, filtering, or searching. Tagging includes a number of features such as: aggregating, searching and browsing, bookmarking and sharing.	Flickr, which allows the user to upload images and 'tag' them with appropriate metadata keywords.
Mashups: integrating information	These result from the combination of different applications in order to deliver additional value that the individual elements could not provide on their own.	App Mashes Up Digital Text on Facebook Platform.
Social networking	An application that enables interactions among people. It has two basic functions: • create and maintain a profile that serves as an online identity within the environment; • create connections between people within the network.	Facebook, LinkedIn, MySpace, Ning, Orkut, Bebo.
Virtual worlds	A category of social networking where people visualize others as being present and interact with them in virtual environments. The social interaction is via a 3-D environment and is known by the unwieldy acronym MMOGs (Massively Multiplayer Online Games) or MMORPGs (Massively Multiplayer Online Role-playing Games).	Second Life, Active Worlds, Kaneva.

Safko and Brake (2009) emphasize the contribution of Web 2.0 in its support for activities such as communication, collaboration, education and entertainment. In turn, these activities engage the capacities of social media, which in combination with Web 2.0 enable communities to form and to interact with one another. Although social media can be a disruptive element in organizations (Safko and Brake 2009), they are commonplace in the current global environment. The social media tools and applications summarized by Safko and Brake (2009) and presented in Table 5.2 are by no means mutually exclusive and are relevant to more than one category.

Users are now turning to the web not only to search for content, but also to communicate with other users. Starting with the exchange of personal views between individuals and members of social communities, this practice has now extended to the business arena. Battelle and O'Reilly (2009) argue that the current version of Web 2.0 should actually be called 'Web Squared', as it has already developed far beyond the original version. In embracing Web 2.0 technologies and applications, however, businesses must learn how to harness this dynamic, and at times chaotic, environment to the pursuit of clients and new business opportunities. Prior to discussing Web 2.0 applications within business in detail, we need first to explore two vital applications, namely those of social networking and virtual worlds.

Social Networking and Virtual Worlds

Social networking services

This generation of online communities first appeared on Web 2.0 in 1995. It is characterized by virtual communities such as MySpace, Facebook, Twitter, Friendster, Ning, YouTube, LinkedIn, Flickr and Delicious (Owyang 2009). Whereas early public online communities such as Usenet were structured by topics, social networking sites are structured as personal networks, with a greater focus on the place of the individual within these communities. The introduction of social networking sites focused primarily around people has given birth to new organizational frameworks for online communities. While most social networking sites aim for broad and exponential growth, others explicitly seek narrower (or niche) audiences. Member interaction and participation in these communities can range from activities such as adding comments or tags to a blog or message-board post, to competing against others in online video games such as MMORPGs. The pace of their development has been described by Boyd and Ellison (2007) as something which started to bubble during 2004 and has erupted since then.

The most popular social networking services vary from country to country and, indeed, continent to continent. For example, in Asia, the most popular social networking sites include Friendster, Multiphy, Orkut, Wretch, Xiaonei, Cyworld and Facebook (Wikipedia 2009). Facebook may not be the most popular network

Table 5.2   Categorization of social media tools and applications

Category of tools and applications	Primary function	Tools
Social networking	Communication and sharing of information	Arkut, Bebo, Facebook, Friendster, LinkedIn, Mebo, MySpace, MOLI, Ning
Publishing	Use of any web-based application to post content to a target audience	Blogger.com, Constant Contact, Joomla, Knol, SlideShare, TypePad, Wikipedia, WordPress
Photo	Archiving and sharing photos	Flickr, Picasa, Photobucket, Radar.net, SmugMug, Twitxr, Zooomr
Audio	Downloading songs, podcasts and other programmes to a device	iTunes, Podbean, Podcast.net, Rhapsody
Video	Creating content for viewing on screens	Brightcove, Google Video, Hulu, Metacafe, Viddler, YouTube
Microblogging	Communicating important messages in less than 140 characters	Plurk, Twitter, Twitxr
LiveCasting	Streaming live broadcasts to audiences or social networks using internet radio and other applications	BlogTalkRadio, SHOUT cast, Justin.tv, Live 365, TalkShoe
Virtual worlds	Enabling participants to assume a persona and engage in a computer-generated world which enables interaction with others in virtual communities	Active Worlds, Kaneva, Second Life, ViOS
Gaming	Enabling game playing both in competition with and in collaboration with others	Entropia EverQuest, Halo3, Universe, World of Warcraft
Productivity applications	Providing facilities for the improvement of business productivity	Acteva, AOL, BitTorrent, Eventful, Google Alerts, Google Docs, Google Gmail, MSGTAG, Survey Monkey, TiddlyWiki, Yahoo!
Aggregators	Gathering, updating and storing information for easy access	Digg, FriendFeed, Google Reader, iGoogle, My Yahoo!, Reddit, Yelp
RSS (Rich Site Summary)	The automatic feeding of current content from websites most critical to the user	Atom, FeedBurner, PingShot, RSS2.0
Search	To enable the location of content, people, places and things on the web	EveryZing, Google Search, IceRocket, MetaTube, Redlasso, Technorati, Yahoo!Search
Mobile	Using cell phones for a range of interactivity similar to that with computers	airG, AOL Mobile, Brightkite, CallWave, Jott, Jumbuck, SMS.ac
Interpersonal	Facilitating people-to-people communication and collaboration	Acrobat Connect, AOL Instant Messenger, Go To Meeting, iChat, Jott, Meebo, Skype, WebEx

site in all countries, but it is ubiquitous and its global presence makes it the major global social networking site.

In the United States, Freiert (2008) and Kazeniac (2009) reported volatility in the positioning of the top 25 social networking sites. The key metrics for assessing relative positions were monthly counts of user visits to sites, linked to total audience size and intensity of use. Their data revealed that, by 2009, Facebook had taken over the number 1 ranking position from MySpace, while the relatively unknown Twitter had jumped from almost bottom at 22 in 2008 to number 3 in 2009. Although all these sites provide broad social networking amenities, there are differences between the services available, as well as in their various users and user groups. There are also differences in the revenue models employed by different social networking sites. This is significant, given that many businesses have already included social networking activities within their business models (Leitner and Grechenig 2008).

Our research indicates that the nature of user involvement with social networking has changed significantly. Today, people want not just to read and share information, but also to participate more actively, using the extensive functionality provided by Web 2.0 technologies. In their work for Forrester Research, Li and Bernoff (2009) identified five different groups of social network users and their levels of participation:

- Spectators: basically non-participatory members centred on the reading of blogs, online forums and customer ratings and reviews. Other activities include viewing videos and listening to podcasts.
- Joiners: who not only visit sites but also create and upload their own profiles to social networking sites.
- Collectors: who use RSS feeds to access the latest content and information, to provide tags/photos to web pages and to participate regularly in online polling.
- Critics: self-appointed reviewers of the viability of products or services, and commentators on other people's blogs. Other activities include active contributions to online forums and the editing of articles in wikis.
- Creators: the most active and influential players. They publish blogs, create their own web pages, upload video, audio or music, write articles and post them. Some of them also enjoy creating their own social networking sites.

Additionally, Owyang's (2009) report on Forrester Research's social networking research project proposed five eras that marked the development of social networking sites. Table 5.3 provides an overall perspective on current and future developments in social networking sites, based on Owyang's study.

Table 5.3   The five eras of social networking services

Eras	Timeframe	Brief description
Social relationships	Started 1995 Matured in 2003–2007	Participants begin to form connections with others and commence the sharing of ideas/information.
Social functionality	Started 2007 To mature in 2010–2012	Not only does this provide a forum for sociability, but it also supports wide-ranging social interactive applications.
Social colonization	Started 2009 To mature in 2011	Every experience can now be social. Technologies such as OpenID and Facebook Connect will begin to break down the barriers of social networks and allow individuals to integrate their social connections as part of their online experience.
Social context	Will start in 2010 To mature in 2012	Personalized and accurate content.
Social commerce	Will start in 2011 To mature in 2013	Social networks will be more powerful than corporate websites and CRM systems, enabling communities to define future products and services.

Virtual worlds

A virtual world is a computer-based, simulated environment in which participants interact by means of avatars, which are identities assumed for the purpose. Participation in virtual worlds demands that users invest a substantial amount of upfront preparation time prior to participating. Consequently, their rate of growth and their reach are not anticipated to match those of social networking sites. Currently the market is dominated by a limited number of very large providers, although there is considerable activity among new entrants seeking to compete on the basis of unique genres and different value propositions (Cohen 2008).

Virtual worlds are targeted at a range of demographics and social environments. Some, such as NeoPets, are designed to operate more as gaming environments, whilst others, such as CyWorld, are more social in purpose. Some virtual worlds, for example Second Life, attempt to combine a number of functions, including those relating to business (Wetsch 2008). All these virtual world sites can be classified in terms of their specific features and categories. Examples include Free Access, which clearly does not involve payment, and Best for Techies and Mac Access, which are intended primarily for particular user groups. A detailed list can be accessed via www.virtualworldsreview.com/info/categories.shtml.

In a business context, there is recognition of breakthroughs with regard to the potential for real-time interaction with employees, customers and suppliers (Safko and Brake 2009). In fact, business is already finding ways to interact with its virtual customers and to sell goods and services through the medium of virtual worlds. Cohen (2008) summarizes the key activities as follows:

- trend-spotting: especially for style- and image-oriented companies that need to be conversant with the latest developments in order to source new ideas;
- collecting improved brand insights: where marketers can use a virtual space to gather information about their brand and related customer behaviours that might not be available through traditional research methods;
- gathering consumer research data related to design concepts: tapping into a self-selecting base of geographically dispersed subjects can yield broader input at a lower cost than would be possible in the real world;
- providing educational forums: enhancing the learning experience beyond that provided by the traditional classroom approach;
- expanding live events: using virtual worlds to extend the experience provided at organizational events;
- extending brands, in particular experiential brands: where virtual worlds present a means to extend their reach in terms of another media format and time shifting;
- leveraging new advertising formats: where virtual worlds provide brands with new forms of advertising, from virtual billboards to product placements that mimic real-life experiences.

Social and virtual networking within business

It is clear that social and virtual networking and other Web 2.0 capabilities have significant business potential. However, whereas many aspects of Web 2.0 technology, from search to content delivery, have been adopted reasonably painlessly, the uptake of social and virtual networking technologies continues to present issues both of application and of implementation (Wray and Arthur 2010). Social and virtual networking essentially entail the exchange and sharing of information and knowledge in an open and collaborative environment, activities that in some ways still remain counter-intuitive in a business context. There is a precedent here in the practice of knowledge management, initially on the basis of internal social networks, and then on an inter-organizational basis. Such networks can facilitate sharing and collaboration across the spectrum from access to and the creation of knowledge, to its transfer and exploitation, whether in knowledge-intensive processes or in value-added products and services (Vossen and Hagemann 2007).

To be successful, of course, knowledge management must relate to the basic mission and strategies of the organization concerned, and should be directed to the creation of business value. The same is true for social networking. In weighing up the risks and opportunities involved, managers need to understand why they would seek to collaborate with customers and other stakeholders in such environments, and where the likely business value would accrue. Ideally, someone within the organization should have had some immersion in the technology, simply in order to appreciate the social experience involved. Whatever the case, businesses need to understand themselves and their customers before joining what could turn out to be inappropriate social networks or spreading themselves too thinly over too many sites (Funk 2009). In turn, this posits the need for businesses to at least begin to appreciate the full extent of the social networking landscape, to understand its social norms and styles, and the implications of involvement for specific organizational cultures and practices (Funk 2009).

Meanwhile, as the popularity of social networking increases, all manner of companies are engaged in pursuit of the potential business benefits on offer. As Nimetz (2007) points out, this entails the use of social networking sites for a variety of purposes including:

- to drive traffic to their sites;
- to engage with consumers, including the encouragement of consumer feedback to aid in the product and service development process;
- the creation and reinforcement of brand awareness;
- as a primary online reputation management tool;
- for the recruitment of staff;
- to learn about new technologies and competitors;
- as a tool to intercept potential prospects.

A typical example of a social network that is used professionally and for business purposes is LinkedIn, a network that connects business by industry, function, geography and areas of interest. Other examples include Ning, the Open Business Club (openBC) and Ryze Business Networking. Leitner and Grechenig (2008) identify the use of the following primary revenue models by Ning:

- allowing users to create a network for free, in exchange for the network hosting Ning's revenue-raising advertisements;
- offering users a network, Ning for Business, where they can control the content of advertisements, in return for the payment of a monthly fee;
- allowing access to other services such as extra storage and non-Ning URLs on payment of an additional monthly fee.

Such is the popularity of social networking within business that the choice of sites now extends well beyond those business-orientated examples like Ning and LinkedIn, to much more avowedly social sites such as MySpace and Facebook. Given that there are few easier or more effective ways for getting directly in touch with customers and potential customers, the attraction of these more social sites is understandable. However, with exposure inevitably goes the potential for risk, as was illustrated all too clearly in a case involving the abuse of Twitter by an employee at a major telephone company and the subsequent suspension of access to the service (Wray and Arthur 2010). Similar examples can be found in other companies and in other countries.

Virtual worlds are also being employed as more than just platforms for game playing. They are beginning to appear more frequently in a business context, with Second Life being an obvious example.

Second Life is an online three-dimensional world that enables multiple users, called 'residents', to interact with one another as avatars in a virtual society. It can be used in both a recreational and a commercial context. A large portion of the Second Life experience involves an economic dimension, where residents trade goods and services in exchange for Linden Dollars (the currency of Second Life, which can be converted to US dollars).

The commercial dimension to Second Life includes the activities of real-world businesses as well as of those businesses that were initially created to operate within the Second Life universe. The former can use Second Life to reach their customer base through promotions and demonstrations, or by providing virtual services to residents (Safko and Brake 2009). The involvement of real-world companies in Second Life ranges widely across the industrial spectrum, from research and design (Starwood Hotels and Resorts) to news and sports simulcasts (Reuters, Major League Baseball), to press briefings and staff training (Sun Microsystems), to education (Harvard University), to IT (Dell, Sony, IBM), to in-world sales of virtual products (Adidas, Toyota) and to book publishing (John Wiley & Sons, Penguin UK) (Safko and Brake 2009).

Web 2.0 and its Application within Book Publishing

As in other businesses, Web 2.0 has brought different kinds of opportunities to book publishing. It offers many advantages over the Web 1.0 environment, which was intrinsically linked to the emergence of eBusiness and was widely perceived as essentially comprising a read-only interface (Stephen 2009), despite Tim Berners-Lee's always having envisaged it in read-write terms. Web 2.0, on the other hand, is explicitly characterized by a read-write interface. Figures 5.1 and 5.2 demonstrate the basic differences between Web 1.0 and Web 2.0 as applied to the book publishing environment.

Currently, the most visible impact of Web 2.0 on the book publishing industry is to be found in the contents of the blogosphere. All aspects of publishing are dissected and analysed in blogs, ranging from the cynical to the visionary, but which are frequently stimulating and informative. Many of these blogs are critical of book publishing for its allegedly backward and reactionary nature, particularly in regard to business practices and culture. Others are much more positive and recognize the progress represented by ongoing developments in such areas as eBooks, in bandwidth for delivery mechanisms and in the uptake of social networking (Albanese et al. 2009). While positive as regards the influence of Web 2.0, we nonetheless recognize the challenges that publishers still face in profitably

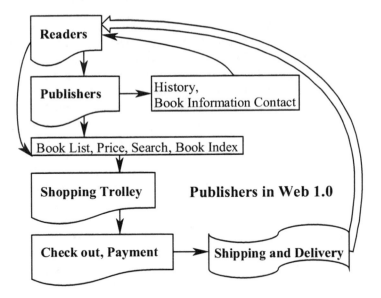

Figure 5.1   Book publishing in a Web 1.0 environment

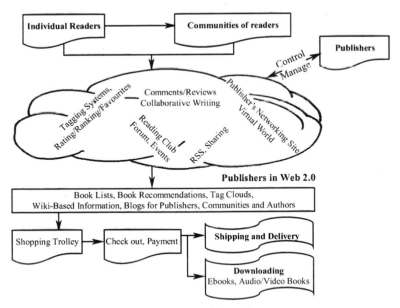

Figure 5.2   Book publishing in a Web 2.0 environment

adopting and leveraging Web 2.0 technologies and applications. These have less to do with technology itself than with changes in the nature of markets and of relationships within them, including those between publishers, authors and other stakeholders. In particular this applies to relationships with readers.

We have already encountered the phenomenon of the long tail and its hitherto adverse effects on mid-list titles, especially in the field of trade publishing. Now a combination of new technology, including self-publishing software and Web 2.0, can serve as a platform not just for the marketing and distribution of content, but also for enabling readers to communicate and interact with publishers, other trade stakeholders and each other (Cader 2008). Not only are publishers no longer able to dictate what is published or distributed, but also the traditional line between producers and consumers has become blurred, leading to a significant power shift in the marketplace. In these markets, social and virtual networking could have massive significance for book publishing. Networks will be the predominant venue for individual and group connection and expression, and for the creation and promotion of rewarding experiences, including those related to the enjoyment of reading books. Nor are we talking about the distant future. Indeed, 2010 is predicted to be the year when social networking really impacts upon book publishing, not least owing to the huge followings that certain authors have already developed in blogs and on Facebook and Twitter (Shatzkin 2009b).

In order to connect with and exploit this social and virtual networking phenomenon, however, book publishers in many cases face the need for a step change in their approach. Rather than thinking purely in terms of promoting and selling books, they must first adopt the networking mindset. This means that they have to learn to communicate with and appeal to the interests of people as networkers first, and only afterwards as consumers (Nash 2010b).

Already, from within the book trade, some are arguing that as a result of developments in the way that books are created, promoted, segmented and delivered, book publishing has changed forever (O'Reilly 2009, Shatzkin 2009b). Indeed, argues Drew (2009), with the advent of book publishing and promotion services such as BookPublishing2.com (a platform that not only claims to clarify the publishing process, but which also promises to help authors to build a long-term, sustainable platform for their work), the book publishing, industry is unrecognizable to that of 10 years ago. From the many possible examples of Web 2.0 applications currently in use by book publishers, five will be discussed here: blogs, wikis, social networking, near-time cross collaboration and widgets.

Blogs

It is virtually impossible to put accurate figures on the growth of blogs and blogging, but it is claimed that a new blog is created every second (Nelson 2006). The pace of growth aside, there can be little doubt as to their current impact in social and business circles. With their innate capability for viral marketing, and used properly, there are few more cost-effective ways to reach large numbers of potential customers. However, there is the important caveat that this is totally open and networked communication, carrying risks as well as opportunities. Once in the blogosphere, control quickly passes from the blog's creator to anybody feeling the urge to comment.

Book publishers are using blogs for marketing and promotional activities, and in order to generate interest and what the marketers call 'buzz' around books and reading. Both for would-be authors seeking to make the breakthrough into publishing and for publishers looking for new talent, blogs are increasingly the avenue of choice. They have fostered the growth not just of online conversations between authors and readers, but also of virtual communities of readers with interests in specific genres or topics, and the potential to become niche markets for the publishers concerned. Blogs are fast overtaking specialist reviewing outlets in newspapers and journals in both scale and popularity, and it seems inevitable that literary blogs and blogging book clubs will become more powerful and exert more influence on sales (Nelson 2006).

Table 5.4 presents some examples of blogs organized by individuals or groups engaged not only in sharing information about books and discussing industry-wide issues, but also in exchanging books between individuals and groups of individuals. Bernoff (2009) argues that there is already a perception within the book trade that those publishers not engaged in using blogs and related video and user-generated content risk losing crossover traffic to sites which contain such features.

The functionality of blogs has provided a point of entry for people and organizations not previously engaged with the mainstream publishing industry. In one sense this has enabled the surfacing of an alternative literary culture, members of which had previously lacked the connections that could serve as entry barriers to the traditional publishing world. As a result, writers are using blogs to build audiences to strengthen subsequent book proposals, and publishers are now offering book deals to bloggers. In October, 2005, the self-publishing company Lulu, announced the Blooker Prize for the best blog or print books based on blogs (http://lulublookerprize.typepad.com). In general terms, Nelson (2006) explains that book publishers can use blogs for the following purposes:

- To monitor trends and opinions: publishers can 'listen' to blogs for gossip, news and reactions to their books. Agents and editors can use blogs to identify topics that would attract readers or to monitor readers' responses to different types of material. Marketers can use blog data to target vital marketing or advertising campaigns. Importantly, marketers can highlight the positive comments and connect with those readers or bloggers who are commenting positively.
- To find fresh content: bloggers provide an effective communication channel and are a source both of fresh authors and of new ideas for agents and editors. Furthermore, the popularity of blogs is easily measured, enabling agents to demonstrate both traffic volumes and potential sales numbers to editors.

Table 5.4   Examples of book- and publishing-related community blogs

Name	Brief description
America's Bookshelf	One of the largest book exchange clubs in the US. www.americasbookshelf.com
Booksconnect	A book-sharing community site connecting readers, authors, publishers, librarians and booksellers. www.countrybookshop.co.uk/booksconnect
Bookcrossing	A community of users from over 130 countries who exchange books with each other at public places such as cafes, parks etc. www.bookcrossing.com
Booksquare	Constructive and at times critical analysis of the book industry. http://booksquare.com
Dr. Syntax	Scattered observations on books and publishing issues. www.doctorsyntax.net
Publishers Lunch	News, stories, interviews and forums in both electronic and face-to-face modes covering any and all issues of interest to the global book-publishing community. Viewed by over 40,000 people every day
Publishing Insider	A space for discussing topics related to books, music, movies and life in general organized by Carl Lennertz of HarperCollins Publishers. http://publishinginsider.typepad.com/publishinginsider
The Digitalist	A blog created by the digital team at Pan Macmillan which is open to anyone interested in joining the debate about books, publishing, the web, and the future. http://thedigitalist.net
E-Reads	Links authors, publishers and readers in discussing news and issues of common concern. www.ereads.com/index.html
Goodreads	A community for book readers, enabling members to review and share opinions on books they have been reading. www.goodreads.com
The Idea Logical Blog	A blog operated by The Idea Logical, a company focusing on the book industry and the future of publishing. www.idealog.com/blog
Revish	A community that enables book lovers to review and rank their favourite books, or simply to tell others what they are currently reading. www.revish.com
Harperstudio	A blog which also enables partnering with authors to publish books in a way that is effective, creative and sustainable. http://theharperstudio.com
The Brave New World	Emerging from publication of the report Brave New World (www.ewidgetsonline.com/vcil/bravenewworld.html), published by the Booksellers Association of the UK and Ireland and authored by Martyn Daniels. Contains topical items and views on the impact of digitization on publishing and the issues that make the news. http://bookseller-association.blogspot.com

- To market books: here the opportunities include word-of-mouth promotion, low-cost advertising and new ideas for publicizing authors and books. Publishers can also use blogs to make information more visible to search engines, while employing keywords in order to improve search engine rankings. Also, the more people (followers) that are attracted to a blog, and the more their comment features on other blogs, the greater is its visibility to search engines.

Whilst the blogging forum for book publishing is still at the developmental stage, there appears to be unlimited potential for expansion. Moreover, the more they participate in the blogosphere, the more book publishers are likely to be convinced of the business benefits of such engagement. A particularly notable example of a publisher's blog is that from the digital publishing team at Pan Macmillan UK, called The Digitalist (http://thedigitalist.net). This blog functions variously as:

- a sounding board, a place for listening, and participating in discussions with people;
- a news service, keeping watch on developments in the digital era and on the convergence of culture and technology;
- an interrogative, investigative domain for looking at, and challenging, new ideas;
- a place for introducing people within and outside the company to new ideas, and for discovering new ideas themselves.

Blogs are pivotal to the Web 2.0 environment, not only because of their published content, but primarily for the interaction and relationships that they enable. Funk (2009) likens blogs to spider webs in terms of the relationships they spin: relationships among blogs, between authors and their sources of inspiration, and between authors and their community of readers. Taken individually, blogs are of relatively limited value. However, when linked with other blogs to provide interaction, they assume an entirely different and much more powerful persona, that of the all-encompassing, ever-present blogosphere.

Wikis

The implications of wikis for publishing have been amply demonstrated by the success of Wikipedia. In more general terms, the availability of software for the collaborative creation and updating of content using a web browser and a simple mark-up language means, at least in theory, that anybody can become a publisher. Wikis are organic in terms of their open editing and structure, universal in allowing authors to create, organize and edit their work in one system, and convergent in their ability to synthesize knowledge from many differing perspectives (Burd and Buchanan 2004). Initially publishers were reluctant to adopt wiki technology, owing to their suspicions of a model that relied upon open, editable and reusable content that was not easy to monetize. However, the use of wikis is now widespread both in mainstream academic publishing and in Open Access publishing as a platform for online book delivery (Suber 2009).

Among the functionalities of wiki software are duplication checking, version tracking and other features to address potential quality problems (Funk 2009). Wikis offer a particular benefit in the development of participative communities, extending to links with mobile and wireless devices, including emerging advances in eReaders. More generally, wiki applications have been directed to open source software development and to business collaboration. They have also been used in data collection and publishing projects, such as WikiHow (a collection of how-to articles), and WikiQuotes (a free online compendium of sourced quotations from notable people and creative works in every language). For book publishers, the use of wikis is a comparatively new phenomenon, but one which is emerging in a variety of forms, including collaborative writing, collaborative editing and collaborative forums.

Collaborative writing   As the name suggests, this format allows multiple parties to be involved in the creation of a particular work. One example of the successful use of wikis in this context is that of the Pearson wiki project. Conducted in 2006, this involved Pearson partnering with two influential business schools to create a business book authored and edited on a wiki (Bulkeley 2006). Entitled *We Are Smarter Than Me*, this was a collection of insights from more than 4,000 members of the online community created with the express purpose of writing the book. Completed in 2007, this book made it into the list of best business books of the year compiled by Amazon (www.wearesmarter.org). An alternative instance of the successful use of wikis for collaborative publishing is demonstrated in Mini-case 5.1.

However, if Penguin's collaborative novel writing project in 2007 is any guide, there is unlikely to be any great rush by other publishers to embrace this approach. At its conclusion in 2008, one Penguin executive stated that although it was the best thing he had ever done, he would never do it again (Douglas 2008). One obvious conclusion to be drawn from the Penguin example is that the effectiveness of wikis within the context of collaborative authoring can vary from one project or genre to another. However, the lessons here have less to do with the success or failure of projects per se than with the importance of the cultural dimension and all that it can mean to the uptake and outcome of any technology.

Collaborative editing   With the use of wiki technology, anybody can contribute to the editing of a book. Furthermore, there are clear business benefits where this participation can be extended to the involvement of specialist communities of interest in publishing projects. This break from the traditional practice whereby authors write a book and publishing staff are responsible for its editing and design can, in the right circumstances, result both in better quality publications and higher long-term financial returns. This is the rationale behind O'Reilly's collaborative

---

MINI-CASE 5.1: WeBook.com

WeBook.com is a free, online publishing platform specifically designed for group authoring. It enables writers, editors, reviewers, illustrators and others to cooperate in activities ranging from writing a book to adding sentences or making grammatical corrections to or reviewing works already in progress. New works can be excluded from public view until necessary, or can be made accessible on a group-specific basis. Live feeds send updates whenever a project has a new submission or a contribution has attracted feedback. Interaction between writers, contributors and readers is facilitated by the use of live forums and research tools. WeBook retains user projects, submissions and reviews on personal WeBook profiles and homepages. The key functions can be viewed on its website, www.webook.com.

When a book is finished, opinions are sought as to its likely viability through a polling process operated by the WeBook team. This entails interested parties (community members) voting for their choice under such categories as eBooks and audio books under the WeBook imprint. The system also allows for the employment of ePublishing professionals in order to ensure adherence to certain quality standards. Distribution is handled via WeBook.com, Amazon.com and selected booksellers.

The business model is simple and effective. WeBook bears the costs of site hosting, publishing, quality control and distribution, and enjoys 50 per cent of all profits generated from book sales. Authors enjoy a highly attractive 50 per cent royalty and, just as important, win a publishing contract.

Source: WeBook.com

---

publishing initiative, the Open Feedback Publishing System (Fahlgren 2009), where public reading and feedback are integral to the system. The idea is to improve the standard of books by engaging communities of readers in collaborative dialogue with the authors in an open space. This system allows authors to publish the manuscript online as HTML, with a comment box located under every paragraph, sidebar, figure and table.

Although this system works for O'Reilly, before others seek to engage in this practice they need to consider three prerequisites to a successful outcome. These are:

- the need for sufficient capital resources, and not least the skilled personnel necessary to ensure ongoing engagement;
- an audit of existing technology, leading potentially to the outsourcing of software to a third party;
- potential levels of customer demand and of author participation.

Internal collaboration   Publishers are using wikis for a variety of purposes, including as internal learning and communications spaces for employee feedback and teamwork, and for the conduct of external conversations with readers and potential readers (Li and Bernoff 2009). The specific internal and external benefits to be derived through the use of wikis include:

- Workflow enhancements: where editors, whether internal or external, can work effectively and transparently with authors. The obvious example here would be Wikipedia, which despite recurring abuses of its open system, remains a major achievement in collaborative publishing.
- Organizational morale: where employee motivation and commitment to the company, and mutual understanding between employee and employer, can be stimulated and enhanced through the operation of an open communication channel acting as a forum where ideas and knowledge can be shared (Kirchner et al. 2009). For example, at IBM there is growing use by employees of both internal company and public blogs, with staff also active in contributing to wikis (Karena 2007). A book publishing example of the use of wikis is the selection of standing audio programmes and online browsing samples launched on a mini-site by the Penguin Group in the United States. Most of the content is created, written, shot, edited and produced by some 30 Penguin Group executives and department team members who are closest to the content (Publishers Lunch Deluxe News 2009).
- Learning improvements: already both the business and technology literatures are reporting the use of wikis in such fields as organizational learning and staff training (Edwards 2007). Our own research confirmed that the use of wikis can improve information flow and communication, helping people to learn from past experience and to share knowledge and ideas. In Sydney, a company called MOB (Mobile Online Business Pty. Ltd) has first-hand knowledge of the value of wikis in its own collaborative learning environment. Furthermore, the company is extremely active in building wikis for a range of customers in different industries. In one example MOB created a wiki-based business intelligence tool called MultiTrack. This has enabled Warner Music Australia to enjoy real-time access to sales and performance data and artist campaign information while aggregating current music industry news and information through the integration and automatic visualization of various feeds. In principle, there is no reason why book publishers could not use wikis for similar purposes, while at the same time enjoying the benefits of organizational learning and knowledge capture in a collaborative and sharing environment.

Collaborative forums   Customer service is a vital if demanding activity for all businesses, and wikis offer an exciting range of new options in this regard. As pointed out previously, it is important initially to think not in terms of book sales but rather, of locating potential readers and attracting their attention. Essentially this implies trying to engage them in conversations during which they can air their views, voice any concerns they might have and provide comment and opinions on books and book publishing. The ultimate purpose is still commercial, but it has to take account of early 21st-century lifestyles and the strategic implications of connections made on wikis or through the use of other Web 2.0 technologies. An example is shown in Mini-Case 5.2.

MINI-CASE 5.2: O'Reilly Forums

The O'Reilly Publishing forums site is an excellent example of such a strategy at work. Membership of this site enables customers to interact with O'Reilly Publishing and with each other by writing book reviews, asking questions and sharing ideas and commenting on blog posts. It also enables them to attend online or in-person events, start user groups or grab widgets for customers' websites.

The forums address many different topics, with titles such as Real World Tech, O'Reilly Books, Digital Media and Head First. Readers can click on the '+' sign at the right hand side of the homepage of their website (http://forums.oreilly.com) in order to access any particular forum, post their opinions and learn from others.

Source: http://forums.oreilly.com

Although wikis are not easy to incorporate because of the control issue, they are nevertheless proving popular among both businesses and customers. However, before embarking on their use, publishers must be sure that both they and their customers are ready for such developments and that:

- they have people who are interested in contributing;
- they have sufficient high quality and useful content to make it viable;
- they understand the need to listen to what is being said;
- they have a proper and easily understood wiki policy and set of rules.

Collaboration has been described as a derivative core competency that contributes to the tightening of business value chains. In wider terms, it is viewed as an umbrella under which supply chain planning and management, mass customization and personalization, dynamic pricing and a host of new models and processes can be assembled (Andriole 2005).

Social networking

The use of social networking by book publishers has grown with their realization of the need to develop and open up more practical channels of communication with their readerships. Furthermore, in order to keep pace with the demands of dynamic and turbulent markets, publishers must respond in a manner compatible with those radical changes in technology which precipitated these market changes in the first place. Today, waiting for technological maturity is no longer an option and hence, publishers must rapidly embrace and develop the necessary infrastructure and skills. Social networking sites such as Facebook can provide access to the kind of market intelligence that traditionally has come from expensive market research.

However, in all such cases, more than the simple use of social technology is involved. Hence, while describing the marketing benefits of a successful collaborative publishing initiative using Twitter, Hunter (2009b) emphasized the need to have an underlying strategy for the use of the social technology. Potential approaches could involve posting interesting content in the hope that followers would be intrigued by it and pass it on to friends, who in turn might share it with others, in effect operating as broadcasters and viral marketers. This kind of strategy has proved effective in the advertising industry for those companies that have been able to realign their thinking. The result has been creation of an innovative and relevant product discovery experience for people engaged in conversing and connecting on social networks (Lichtenberg 2009). Furthermore, in seeking to exploit such sites effectively, publishers must bear in mind that the profiles they contain are people-specific, and not product-specific, that users are only attracted to communities by things that interest them and that the integrity of the social networking process should take precedence over any desire to control interactivity (Reed 2009).

Some publishers have not only begun to immerse themselves in existing social networking sites, but also have started building their own sites to cater for the needs of their employees, authors and readers. An excellent example is that of Random House UK, which has launched ReadersPlace as a site for its book clubs (Mini-Case 5.3).

Through digital marketing, book publishers can more easily identify ways to engage with their readers. As discussed previously, virtual worlds such as Second Life offer publishers an opportunity to convert people's love of books into engagement and marketing reach. In 2006, Penguin UK became the first major publisher to operate within Second Life, with a project based on a book originally published in 1992. It followed this up in 2007 with a project comprising a virtual bookshelf with a sample of 10 titles. The publisher did not expect quick results from these projects, arguing that long-term engagement would be necessary before satisfactory outcomes occurred (Kurosawa 2007). Readers who are registered Second Life account holders are able to log in and locate the Penguin UK site, where they can purchase selected printed, audio and eBooks at a discount. The following link contains the details of the Penguin UK site in Second Life: www. penguin.co.uk/static/cs/uk/0/articles/secondlife/index.html.

So far as the choice of particular social networking sites is concerned, there is little evidence for the superiority in terms of strategic effectiveness of one site over another, apart from the reported preferences of individual publishers. Twitter is reported as the site of choice for publishers such as Harlequin Books, O'Reilly Media and Harper Perennial (Hendrickson 2009). An explanation for such interest

---

MINI-CASE 5.3: Random House ReadersPlace

This book club community engages with members and authors by means of features including:

- individual book club profiles
- rating and reviews of favourite titles
- access to pictures and videos of reading group discussions.

This site hosts a live chat session with a Random House author every month, with members being eligible to win a personal book talk with an author living in their area. This kind of activity has helped Random House UK to engage more effectively with its customers. The detailed structure can be viewed from ReadersPlace's website, www. readersplace.co.uk.

The company has complemented this site with AuthorsPlace (2008), which allows its authors to establish, personalize and update their own web pages and manage their online presence.

Resource: www.readersplace.co.uk

---

has been offered by Woodstra (2009), who argues that there are five compelling reasons why publishers should focus on Twitter:

- to interact with other stakeholders in the industry, including for the collation of information and ideas;
- to familiarize themselves with the activities of bloggers and reviewers;
- to update their knowledge of industry news faster than through other news outlets;
- to obtain feedback on books and services useful for both publishers and their authors;
- to obtain exposure for events, books and authors, while keeping readers informed.

However, popularity with publishers need not necessarily mean that Twitter is the most suitable site for that industry (Don 2009). Nor does it do anything to lessen the steepness of the learning curve involved in mastering how to talk to people and maintain relationships online (Ratzlaff 2009). Clearly, with an ever-increasing range of social networking sites available, publishers must take considerable care in matching site selection to intended outcomes and use. Although it seems obvious that all such attempts at alignment should occur in the context of wider social networking and community strategies, there are as yet surprisingly few indications that book publishers as a whole have moved to create such strategies (Shatzkin 2009b).

In the meantime, book publishers are learning from experience, both their own and that of others. They have already learned that they need to embrace innovation, both in the form of technology and in finding new ways of doing business. In doing so, they need to understand that the development and maximization of new digital opportunities cannot succeed in the context of one particular department, or be reliant upon a single person in each department. It has to be a natural part of everything publishers do, and it has to be constant and continuous. It is important also to emphasize that these social networking strategies will have major implications for human resource policies. For example, rather than simply paying people to tweet or to put up a Facebook page, publishers will need to engage in recruiting subject-matter experts who can plan for relevant interaction within networks and for aggregating platforms to bring together products, services and people (Spark 2009). Furthermore, the experience gained as people use and experiment with these tools can frequently result in the creation of virtuous circles based upon their connectivity.

Near-Time: Cross-organizational collaboration

One interesting development in Web 2.0 technologies is in the field of platforms for cross-organizational collaboration. A leading example is Near-Time, which claims to offer the capabilities of wikis, weblogs, forums, tagging, bookmarking, content-embedding and other key social media publishing technologies. It also claims to have user-friendly administrative and operating features which provide businesses with a platform that enables them to interact with their customers, prospective customers, partners and suppliers (www.near-time.com). An example of the use of Near-Time for cross-collaboration is Contentnation.com (www.contentnation.com).

The Content Nation website uses Near-Time to enable the rapid construction of many forms of content. Content Nation is a global community of media, other enterprises and personal publishers who share their insights and expertise on the subject of social media services. Members can participate as follows:

- post news on trends that are impacting on social media;
- write and collaborate on articles and forum topics that can provide deeper insights into social media;
- contribute directly to editing in the Content Nation environment, in the case of *Live Book*, John Wiley & Sons' first effort at a crowd-sourced book, which was later released in edited print form in 2009;
- post files for downloads of white papers, research and demo links;
- post information on upcoming events relating to social media;
- add their own ideas;
- Near-Time has also been adopted by a number of book publishers for its rich collaborative features. According to the Vice President and Executive Publisher, Professional/Trade Division of John Wiley & Sons, the Near-

Time platform offers a catalyst for true community building. Wiley chose Near-Time for a number of reasons, including its enablement of a richer experience for their readers, with content that was more relevant and valuable. Also important was the ability to inject new life into backlist titles and to expand market reach. This wiki forum was also chosen for its inbuilt controls, enabling publishers to maintain the integrity of their content while building a community of interest around the book (Wire 2007). It should be pointed out, however, that most wikis offer something of this nature and that, for example, Wikimedia's wiki platform Mediawiki has a full audit trail with revision control.

Widgets

The marketing function has been at the forefront of book publishing's response to the challenges of technological change. One prominent feature of this response has been the implementation of widgets. Essentially, widgets are an informal internet application easily embedded into a web page. There are plenty of definitions available, but as good a one as any is that of Babalina (2009), who describes widgets as portable chunks of code that people can include on their web pages and which enable others to display pictures, music, videos and text.

Random House and HarperCollins both launched sophisticated widget initiatives in 2007, called respectively Insight and Browse Inside. Both embody search capabilities that allow readers unprecedented access to book titles, chapters and sample pages. Feedback to date from the book publishing community suggests that the facility offered by Random House is superior to those of its competitors, as it offers easier navigation and faster loading. They are also leading the race for the number of titles available through their site, reported as amounting to 5,000 for Random House, compared with 3,700 for HarperCollins in 2009 (Babalina 2009).

Random House's Insight, takes more than one form. The smaller version of Insight (195 × 335 pixels) is compatible with any website and can support the operation of forums for interactive book previews by permitting customers to browse pages back and forward or to identify keywords in the text without ever leaving the web page. The act of clicking to its main screen results in this version converting to the larger version via its own full-size, pop-up window (600 × 700 pixels). This produces high-quality, readable preview pages, the facility for text searching and a thumbnail page navigator. The larger version also has the capacity to embed itself into a web page, should the publishers wish to prioritize the promotion of a title. The Insight widget is now available in audio book format. The audio version is a completely embeddable player that links the user to the recorded sample of the audio book made available online (www.randomhouse. biz/webservices/insight/widget).

The Random House widget offers functionality similar to Amazon's Search Inside the Book widget, but unlike the Amazon example, which is restricted to its own website, the Insight widget is designed for use on almost any website, including social networking sites such as YouTube and MySpace. This is extremely advantageous to the publishers, as it allows the possibility of electronic access to readers. Iskold (2007) summarizes the key business benefits of the Insight widget as:

- they showcase Random House books everywhere online;
- they help to promote the Random House brand;
- they enable users to preview books;
- they enable users to buy books;
- they spread the widget virally.

At Amazon, the Search Inside widget is particularly useful in that it enables readers to search for a book title by using keywords. In initiating its prototype in 2003, Amazon created a site where readers had keyword access to over 120,000 titles, all of which included a number of sample pages and other relevant information. So far as book publishing is concerned, the enabling of consumers to add information to widgets, resulting in the cross-pollination of information between publishers and consumers, has dramatically altered the dynamics of marketing (Babalina 2009).

The HarperCollins widget is compatible with both MySpace and Facebook, whereas the Random House widget is not (Babalina 2009). The main purpose of HarperCollins's Browse Inside widget is to enable readers and authors to embed sample pages of their favourite books directly into social networking sites and blogs, making this the first time that a significant direct link had been created between the book and the reader. In fact, HarperCollins has confirmed that the Browse Inside widget was designed with the intention of marketing titles to the MySpace generation online, and to extend the company's reach beyond its own site to social communities, blogs and author sites where many potential new readers were to be found (Crum 2007).

In all these cases, the use of widgets was expected to create a greater revenue stream from online communities. There were, however, cost-efficiency issues to be considered, such as whether to create future titles as eBooks and to convert all existing titles to eBook format, and whether the technology aspects involved were to be handled in-house or outsourced. These are still valid concerns today, and accordingly, a number of publishers, including Penguin Group and Simon & Schuster, have gone for the outsourcing option. Whatever the business decisions eventuating, however, the relentless development of social networking seems to guarantee a rosy future for the technology itself (Babalina 2009).

In the space available, we have of necessity had to select sparingly from the many Web 2.0 applications available to book publishers. Although there is already ample evidence that publishers are taking advantage of these opportunities, the exploitation of Web 2.0 and its impact upon book sales is still very much a work in progress. Abbott (2009) provides a feel for social media developments in reporting some points emerging from his research in relation to the positive outcomes from using social technologies:

- Many participants testified that they had purchased up to 10 books on the strength of recommendations via social networking sites.
- Random House sales representatives reported that more than 30 per cent of their readers involved in the forum Books on the Nightstand had bought up to five books, based on recommendations from the site, and that 14 per cent had bought six or more.
- A survey of lit blog readers showed that 56 per cent of those surveyed bought books primarily based on blog influences (Dawson 2009).
- A book entitled *Ignore Everybody* written by Hugh MacLeod reached Amazon's Top 25, a performance attributed by the publishers to MacLeod's network prominence, with his blog attracting more than a million visitors a month, and his 17,474 followers on Twitter.

Although these examples are encouraging, it is still too early to pronounce with complete confidence on the most significant implications of social media for the activities of book publishers. What can be said with certainty is that social media are established as a form of interactive, participative experience founded on an atomized culture where speed and diversity of communication are pivotal.

Innovation and Web 2.0 strategies

While frequently potent in it effects, innovation does not necessarily happen in one transformative step. Rather, it is likely to be iterative in nature. This is as true for innovation in book publishing as for that elsewhere, and would apply, for example, to such current innovations as the increased emphasis on dealing with readers and on managing their expectations. Dealing with readers properly means thinking like readers, anticipating their wishes and trying to satisfy them. Essentially, this comes down to the development of genuine and lasting relationships with readers on a company-wide basis. This calls for listening as well as communication skills on the part of publishers, with all the indications being that what many people want is contact and involvement with authors, publishers and other readers (Funk 2009). Although Web 2.0 and its applications provide a multitude of opportunities for business, it is important to match the tools chosen to the specific business application. Baker (2009) argues that all the excitement surrounding the uptake of social networks, wikis and blogs for business dealings ignores the potential risks involved, including that of time wasting. This might at first sight seem to be a somewhat negative approach. Nevertheless, it is important that the use of social networking can be shown to contribute directly to the creation of business value (Hansen 2009). This said, continuing innovation based upon new technology is inevitable. Accordingly, book publishers need to recognize the opportunities and the associated risks presented by Web 2.0, while seeking to devise the necessary strategic responses.

Responding strategically involves much more than the mere adoption of such technologies. Within the abounding complexity of competing sites, features, tools and applications, there is an incredible amount of 'noise' (Lawlor 2008). Consequently, there is a risk of businesses not fully understanding the tools they are using, or of spreading themselves too thinly across a number of different networks, making it nearly impossible to decide what to share and with whom. For every new application that relies on a network, another crops up that helps users to manage it. While success in such ventures was once measured in terms of visits or 'eyeballs', it is now clear that a strategy of aiming for smaller, well-targeted niches can lead to much better returns than one of marketing to a large, undifferentiated mass of users (Lichtenberg 2009). Whatever the target, publishers should aim to make their websites the most comprehensive source of information possible about their authors and books, their general and specific activities and their reader groups. The technology to do this is available and is no longer an issue. The challenge lies in leveraging already existing knowledge for conversion into engagement and marketing reach. This could result in the widest possible dissemination to existing and potential readers and reading communities. Furthermore, rather than confining their editorial and marketing expertise to some kind of back-office status, publishers must release their hidden value by using the power of social networking (Cader 2008).

Nor are publishers operating entirely at a disadvantage in such relationships. While it is true that it needs to be better informed about readers and reading communities, this readership base still shows signs that it values the role and contribution of publishers. For those with a desire to publish their own books, association with a mainstream publishing house may still be as much about social recognition as about the mechanics of appearing in print. Readers also value the networks of contacts, activities and experiences that are more likely to occur with established imprints than with low-cost, universally accessible facilities located in cyberspace. The key to success here resides not so much in what book publishers have to sell, but in what they know and in how they can use this knowledge both to solve the problems of readers and to avail themselves of the associated business opportunities. Moreover, by using social media to keep their audiences engaged, publishers would be more likely to ensure an increased supply of an even scarcer commodity, namely, attention. Put differently, by responding to the need for networking in order to engage with and retain the interest of consumers, publishers would be behaving like knowledge-intensive businesses.

Book publishing is a combination of many businesses working in harmony. Advanced web technology and its applications will not only provide avenues of opportunity, but will also present associated pitfalls that need to be avoided. In face of a virtual maelstrom of technological development, publishers must enhance and refine their organizational and management skills, and reassess their capabilities and their relationships with other industry stakeholders, not the least with readers.

The diversity and sophistication of web tools and applications requires a sensitive yet practical approach, at a time when management guidelines and governance principles for such technologies are still in development and, in all probability, still likely to lag behind the pace of change. In essence, this is a strategic matter, with implications for such fundamentals as value propositions and positioning within the industry.

PART III
Business

Chapter 6
Knowledge-intensive Organizations

Introduction

This chapter looks at how changes in organizational structure can lead to the emergence of new forms of organization. Organizations come in all shapes and forms, from large and complex bureaucracies to operations run by a single person. In one way or another they comprise particular sets of relationships assembled for the creation of value. This value can be directed either towards the generation of profit or for the provision of goods and services on a not-for-profit basis. Changes in organizational form have been a constant of business life through the ages, with market forces mandating new ways of arranging assets and resources to respond to customer needs and expectations (Miles et al. 1997).

Today as organizations respond to the challenges of globalization, technological change, turbulent markets and changing customer demands, answers continue to be sought in changes to organizational forms. Some observers interpret such changes in terms of the emergence of Enterprise 2.0, with organizations restructuring around Web 2.0 technologies in order to leverage the value of their knowledge workers (McAfee 2006). This is understandable given that the principal driver and vehicle for change today is the need to create and exploit value from knowledge based on capabilities and competencies embedded in the social and physical structure of organizations. Seen from this perspective, knowledge is a form of organizational architecture, and knowledge-intensive organizations are those dependent upon activities such as collaboration and social networking for the creation of long term business value (Stephens 2009). Before exploring the concept of knowledge-intensive organizations, let us briefly revisit the core construct of knowledge.

Knowledge Revisited

In an economy increasingly dominated by intangible resources relevant, reliable and timely knowledge, whether as raw material or end product, is vital to the survival of many organizations. The business literature documents an extensive range of knowledge types, from explicit, implicit and tacit knowledge, to knowledge *what* and knowledge *how*. There is also the knowledge resident in expert groups as compared with that individual knowledge accumulated through life experience gained in particular situations (Greenwood 2008).

Different kinds of knowledge will be found at different levels in the organization, ranging from cognitive knowledge and systems understanding, to advanced skills in technology, collaboration and governance, to intuition and self-motivated creativity (Brooks 2002). Through effective knowledge management these various forms of knowledge can be converted into corporate assets, not least in the form of that knowledge embedded in business processes that facilitate maximum value through deployment. This also reflects a trend away from standard transactional business processes towards those that are more complex, which involve more stages and players, and that being based largely on human knowledge, experience and creativity cannot be easily replicated by competitors (Marjanovic and Seethamraju 2008).

Important across the industrial spectrum, these knowledge-intensive business processes are already widespread in book publishing from activities such as content acquisition and packaging, to distribution and warehousing, to marketing and rights management. The effective embedding of knowledge in value creating processes and practices requires the appropriate technological and human infrastructures. These are necessary in order to support both the creation and exploitation of knowledge, and to leverage the social capital inherent in knowledge-intensive operations (Ladegaard and Syversten 2005). It is the combination of empirical and latent knowledge, the former comprised of physical and social artefacts and interactions, the latter of beliefs, identities, goals and values (Hargadon and Fanelli 2002) that has propelled the development and enabled the survival of different kinds of knowledge-intensive organization. So apart from this fundamental knowledge dimension, how are these knowledge-intensive organizations to be distinguished from other forms of organization?

Knowledge-intensive organizations

Discussion around the concept of knowledge-intensive organizations probably peaked during the closing decades of the 20th century. This does not mean that the concept is no longer relevant, but rather that it has become embedded in a wider organizational landscape where some degree of knowledge-intensity tends to be the norm. Indeed, with most if not all businesses to some extent engaged in a process of knowing and reflection, it has become more difficult to draw clear distinctions between knowledge-intensive organizations and other kinds of organization (Greenwood 2008). Nevertheless, given the continued currency of the concept, it is important to understand why it remains relevant and what it actually means in everyday operational contexts. For one thing, the use of the term 'knowledge-intensive' does not necessarily mean that this format is universally superior to or more progressive than others. It simply reflects the realities of operation in markets where knowledge is the key driver and resource. For another, however, what it does indicate is the emergence of a new kind of organizational paradigm, a knowledge paradigm with fundamental implications for the role of management, for functions, and for social and other responsibilities (Zumbansen

2008). Organizations located within this paradigm can be described in terms of certain core characteristics.

Characteristics of knowledge-intensive organizations

In responding to the demands of markets, customers and other stakeholders, knowledge-intensive organizations are generally regarded as being less bureaucratic and more responsive to change than traditional industrial-age organizations. Typically they also tend to have highly qualified staff and innovative structural and operational arrangements. They are also similar to learning organizations in their ability to modify and align their behaviour and organizational structures creatively with the environment. A full range of the characteristics of these businesses is included in Figure 6.1, but prominent among these are:

- they sell knowledge both as a product and as a service;
- people are the key source of value creation;
- intellectual capital is the most important asset;
- they are open and are aligned effectively with the external environment;
- organizational structures are frequently based upon projects, and can be changed flexibly to meet business objectives;
- the creation of value requires ongoing adaption to changing conditions through collaborative learning processes;
- senior management directs and coordinates rather than commands, with a wider range of management decisions diffused broadly across the organization.

Members develop a widely shared vision and the kind of solidarity and trust that enhances organizational flexibility and adaptiveness.

To aid in understanding of this construct, each of the characteristics included in Figure 6.1 is explained in Table 6.1.

These features will not be found universally in such organizations, nor will they be distributed evenly among them. This diversity of characteristics is testament to the range and complexity of knowledge-intensive organizations and to the ways in which they are perceived. For example, doubts have been cast upon the role of knowledge as a determinant of knowledge-intensive status, with the possession of knowledge being seen as less important than the particular set of institutional arrangements in place (Greenwood 2008). Conversely, the significance of structural or other organizational properties to knowledge-intensive status, has been questioned on the grounds that this is often a matter of contingent interpretation as of anything else (Grey and Sturdy 2009). Consequently, it is important to bear in mind that knowledge-intensive organizations are neither unique in form nor precise in definition (Karreman and Alvesson 2004). Furthermore, they will engage with knowledge in different ways and at different levels of intensity.

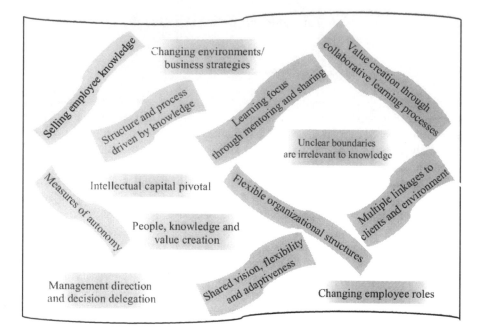

Figure 6.1   The characteristics of knowledge-intensive organizations

But all may not be as it seems   Just as the mere possession of knowledge is not sufficient in itself to justify the appellation 'knowledge-intensive', so the use to which this knowledge is put is also significant. In the case of those companies that employ a range of knowledge to provide, and in some cases, to co-create business solutions for clients, knowledge-intensive status is not an issue (Scott-Kemmis 2006). However, this is by no means the case for all companies engaged in solving client problems. For example, despite their evident knowledge credentials in this regard, the knowledge-intensive status of professional services firms in law and accounting have been questioned on other grounds such as for example, their adherence to much more traditional forms of recruitment and organizational structures (Newell et al. 2002). Perhaps even more surprising would be similar criticism leveled at universities on the basis that for all their educated staff and the knowledge they possess, knowledge-intensive operation is hindered by centralized decision-making processes and the basic disconnect between much of the knowledge that universities generate and large sections of the external environment (Greenwood 2008). On the other hand, in companies for example, the oil and mining industries, despite their old industry connotations, employ significant knowledge-intensive operations and structures, which amount to at least a sub-set of knowledge-intensive operation. As such they are not untypical of a wide range of hybrid organizations that are engaged in both knowledge and non-knowledge intensive activities.

Table 6.1 The characteristics of knowledge-intensive organizations

Characteristics	Brief description
Selling employee knowledge	They are engaged in selling the knowledge of their employees rather than in manufacturing a product or delivering a service.
Intellectual capital is pivotal	Intellectual capital is the most important organizational asset.
People, knowledge and value creation	People are seen as the ultimate repositories of knowledge (both tacit and explicit) and the key source of value creation.
Changing environments/business strategies	Their business environments can change very quickly, mandating consequent changes in business strategies.
Structure and process driven by knowledge	Their structures and processes are determined by the role of knowledge as the fundamental driver of value creation within an integrated value chain.
Changing employee roles	The roles of employees have changed from those involving simple, controlled work to more complicated knowledge work.
Flexible organizational structures	Organizational structures are frequently based upon projects and can be changed flexibly to meet business objectives.
Value creation through collaborative learning processes	Recognition that the creation of value requires ongoing adaption to changing conditions through collaborative learning processes.
Learning focus through mentoring and sharing	A focus on the creation of ongoing learning opportunities through mentoring, sharing information, brainstorming and communities of practice.
Organizational boundaries are blurred and have little impact upon knowledge	Boundaries with the environment are unclear and typically irrelevant to the knowledge production process.
Multiple linkages to clients and environment	Linkages to clients and the external environment are multiple and occur at many levels in the organization.
Widespread autonomy	Individuals and teams enjoy a measure of autonomy both to determine their own courses of action and to assess and adjust to conditions in the external environment.
Management direction and decision delegation	Senior management directs and coordinates rather than commands, with a wider range of management decisions diffused broadly across the organization.
Shared vision, flexibility and adaptiveness	Members develop a widely shared vision and the kind of solidarity and trust that enhances organizational flexibility and adaptiveness in an organization that is open and aligned with the external environment.

Sources: Greenwood (2008) and Lönnqvist (2001)

The importance of organizational structures

Among the major advantages associated with knowledge-intensive organizations are the perceived synergies between the business requirements of the organization, the skills and motivation of its employees and the needs of its clients. As the trend towards knowledge-intensive operation gained momentum, considerable emphasis was placed on the need to find alternative organizational forms that would offer greater flexibility and responsiveness to the demands of customers and the market. Essentially, this entailed a search for alternatives to traditional hierarchical and bureaucratic organizational structures, with proposed solutions ranging from the flat and the flexible to so-called 'Adhocracies', within which self-forming project teams operated on the basis of decentralized decision making, and with very little in the way of formal rules and procedures (Newell et al. 2002). Both flatness, in terms of reduced layers of management and flexibility in terms of response to markets and organizational boundaries (Bahrami 1998) are features of adaptive and agile organizations. Both these organizational forms have in common such characteristics as those of engaging in real-time communication and networking, and in collaboration, learning and innovation. They differ mainly in their fundamental categorizations, with adaptive organizations described as taking a 'sense and respond' approach and their agile counterparts characterized in terms of 'anticipate and lead' (Calabrese 2006).

Finally a more recent addition to the organizational literature is Enterprise 2.0, which is defined by Corso, Martini, and Balocco (2008) as a set of organizational and technological approaches steered to enable new organizational models. Among the models or paths they identified were:

- Social enterprises: emphasizing collaborative schemes to overcome temporal and geographic limitations and organizational barriers to communication and knowledge transfer, and the attainment of new organizational and strategic effectiveness and flexibility.
- Open Enterprises: broadening and opening up the virtual workspace in order to respond to the mobility and dispersion of people, to reconnect them to their networks and ensure flexibility, speed and robustness in operational and decision-making processes.
- Adaptive Enterprises: focusing on flexibility and re-configurability of processes to enable alignment with the changing needs of the company and its employees.

Amid the growing roll call of new organizational forms there are key commonalities as regards their capacity for responsiveness and agility and for learning and innovation. Increasingly moreover, these are organizations that are 'virtual' both owing to their involvement in cyberspace, and to the fact that typically they are not quite what they seem to be (Hedberg 2000). Here we shall call them 'networked' organizations. Networks are a hybrid organizational form combining the arms-length relations of the market with the hierarchical relations of a formal organization, and where the division and coordination of labour is different owing to the fact that knowledge is the main driver of value creation (Ladegaard and Syversten 2005).

In networked organizations, the barriers of time, distance and organizational boundaries are removed or in the latter case lowered, and the locus of knowledge is diffused across the network. Put differently, these are innovative organizations seeking to achieve or apply breakthrough technologies and practices in markets where the interests of various participants overlap and where customers can be co-creators of value (Jansen, Steenbakkers and Jagers 2007). These new networked organizations operate as cells or nodes of knowledge and expertise that combine and are formed and reformed in order to respond to opportunities on a business unit, company-wide or intra-company level (Brooks 2002). The commonalities between these innovative and networked knowledge-intensive organizations are evident in explanations of why innovations tend to take place in networks:

- The integrated solutions required by the market often demand core competencies beyond those likely to be found within a single company.
- In order to obtain the innovative products and services they require, customers increasingly must contribute knowledge to the development process.
- The pace of market change is often such that the reaction times required are well beyond the capacity of single organizations.
- The costs of innovation and the risks involved are too high to be borne by individual organizations (Jansen, Steenbakkers and Jagers 2007).

In addressing the issue of structural change it is important to remember not only that all organizations are in some way unique in their structural configuration, but also that they are social constructs, sets of nodes, relationships and interactions that have evolved and been shaped for particular social and economic purposes (Allee 2003). Whatever the structures and resources available, however, in the final analysis the success or otherwise of any business will inevitably come down to the quality and effectiveness of its management.

Managing knowledge-intensive organizations

The management of knowledge-intensive organizations is a subject that merits a book in itself. Here all that is possible is to provide a brief overview of the most important areas for management action. In doing so it is important to remind the reader of the need to balance the rhetoric of management theory with the reality of organizational change. Not every organization will be found to be creative and innovative, or with the management and organizational structures likely to motivate and empower its employees. This is a fact of organizational life and perhaps even more so in turbulent and uncertain markets. Nevertheless, if management is to cope with these and other challenges, it is clear that it must respond in ways that fall within the broad parameters of knowledge-intensive operation. This will entail the need to deal with issues concerning innovation, technology, processes, intellectual capital and people.

Innovation   Innovation is a fact of life for knowledge-intensive organizations and the markets in which they operate. Innovation involves making new concepts and ideas relevant to individuals and communities. However, the ideas it produces must connect to particular contexts in order to add value to systems, people, processes and other ideas (Radziwill and DuPlain 2009). Ranging from the breakthrough or structural form of innovation, to that which is more incremental and gradual in nature, innovation can involve multiple actors and organizations engaged in various permutations of product and service, market and business partner combinations (Hauschildt 1997). In addition to occurring at operational and management levels, innovation can apply with regard to the business model, with new approaches and technologies combining to create breakthroughs in supply and value chains (Hamel 2007). Almost inevitably, the management of innovation entails management of the uncertainty associated with available resources, including uncertainty over the capacities of the personnel involved, and the nature of the relationships between them. Commonly this results in the creation of spin-out organizations free from the constrictions of the parent bureaucracy, but this is not always the answer. Less radical and perhaps more in tune with the networking principle, is the creation of hubs as focal points and competence centres around which the innovation may be exploited (Jansen, Steenbakkers and Jagers 2007).

Technology   Technology is essential both as an enabling infrastructure and as a change agent within the organizational landscape. In knowledge-intensive organizations, where the key focus is on creating and leveraging value from intangibles, technology has a role to play at strategic, tactical and operational levels:

- strategic: rethinking strategic purpose and identifying new sources of knowledge and value creation in value networks;
- tactical: deciding how best to create, use and apply knowledge in knowledge networks;
- operational: codifying and sharing knowledge in technology networks (Allee 2003).

Ideally the management of technology begins before a single system or application is purchased. All too many businesses continue to fall into the trap of specifying and implementing technology which is later found to be inappropriate and inimical to the business functionality and performance outcomes desired. Technology is an indispensable enabler in modern businesses, but its implementation must align with business processes and practices. The deployment of technology in itself cannot deliver business performance. Technology must be willingly adopted by users, integrated within their respective work contexts and effectively utilized, while being driven by the performance outcomes of the enterprise. This is most likely to result in the choice of technologies across the continuum from strategic to operational and capable of performing the following functions:

- automating the capture, creation, organization, dissemination and sharing of knowledge assets;
- connecting people with relevant interests and/or skills within an environment conducive to knowledge exchange;
- shaping the organization by automating routine work and circumventing barriers;
- facilitating intelligent problem solving.

These kinds of technologies have featured in previous chapters and are in widespread use today, including in the book publishing industry. Apart from issues of technical functionality, interoperability and security, their management involves evaluation and planning for upgrades or replacements. For management this means continuing to put out the message that what really matters is not 'technology push' but 'strategy pull', which means not buying the latest version or artefact just because it is available, but ensuring that organizational need rather than technological change drives technology acquisitions. It also means consulting widely with systems users, internal and external, and seeking to educate customers, while ensuring that all staff understand the need for and are trained in the use of the specific applications and systems concerned. Although this is all pretty obvious, none of it is as simple as it sounds. Quite apart from the potential internal cultural and behavioural issues around technology adoption and use, the pace of change in such areas as Web 2.0 stands as a continual challenge to the 'strategy pull' philosophy, not least because increasingly it is customers who are calling for the ever more rapid take-up of new technology. This is where the input of management, business and technical, strategic, tactical and operational becomes so important.

Processes As mentioned above, business processes in knowledge-intensive organizations tend to be more complex than in previous standard operational environments. The knowledge-intensity of such processes and the range of stakeholders likely to be involved in their design and subsequent improvement can vary. For example, those operational business processes that are highly repetitive in nature, such as electronic procurement processes, tend to be tightly structured in terms of the task involved and the order in which they are to be completed, and are comprised mainly of explicit knowledge. Beyond the operational level however, say, in processes related to the design of new products or structures, both tacit and explicit knowledge are involved through input from and collaboration between a wide range of decision makers (Marjanovic and Seethamraju 2008).

The creation and improvement of such processes and their integration into the business requires a highly consultative and persuasive approach from management, possibly including the use of some form of incentives. This will be aimed at motivating different individuals and work groups and persuading them to collaborate and share knowledge for the greater good, even where this might imply some surrender of power or status.

Intellectual capital   Knowledge-intensive enterprises were once evocatively described as being 'brain rich' and 'asset poor' (Quinn 1992), meaning that their real wealth lay not in plant and equipment but in their intellectual capital, namely the combined knowledge, innovative skills and experience of their people (Edvinsson 1997). The management of intellectual capital has proven to be challenging, and has still a fair way to go before it can be claimed to be totally effective. This is because of its ambiguous nature, the difficulties inherent in the capture and codification of its intangible elements, and the lack of a clear consensus on how it might be measured and reported.

As the visible representations of organizations, their structures, procedures, products and services increasingly become temporary materializations of the underlying intellectual capital, the management of that capital becomes even more important. This includes all the usual planning and control activities, the strategies for the acquisition and, exploitation of intellectual capital, and the human and structural systems involved. Nevertheless, much of this continues to take a back seat to the issues around measurement and performance management. Used properly and in context, however, these systems can be as effective in planning as in measurement, with metrics designed to capture strategic knowledge-intensive activities such as learning, change, innovation and organizational renewal (Lönnqvist 2001).

People   Just as people sit at the centre of value creation and realization in knowledge-intensive organizations, their relationship with management is easily the most critical issue. These words have been chosen deliberately to draw attention to the by now conventional wisdom that in knowledge-intensive organizations, people tend to be treated differently by management. This is because in such organizations, the relationship between employees and the means of production has changed significantly. Much of the knowledge upon which so much else depends resides, not in management or in systems, but in the minds of individual employees, who as a result have a wide range of options as to what to do with it. The realization that knowledge critical to the organization can leave the premises on a daily basis, and perhaps forever should its real owners choose to leave, sparked major interest in the practice of knowledge management. Initially, this amounted to efforts aimed at capturing and codifying knowledge, including the tacit knowledge of employees, in systems.

However, when faced with the limitations of such exercises, management has come to realize that the key challenge resides in being able to manage people who, by being valued for what they know, have in many cases acquired the status of knowledge workers. Nor has acknowledgement of this status simply involved the adoption of a semantic variation on the theme of white collar work. Rather it entails a clear recognition of the growing centrality of a different kind of work based upon know-how and problem-solving activities in both individual and collaborative settings. The people capable of performing such work are not so easily replaced or as interchangeable as are assembly-line or clerical staff. This inevitably gives them a certain amount of negotiating power within the organization, an influence manifest in the exercise of a considerable degree of autonomy in what they do and where and when they do it (Liebowicz 1999). If anything, this room for organizational manoeuvre on the part of knowledge workers has been extended by the phenomenon of social networking. Today, an increasing proportion of employees are daily users of such technologies at work as well as in their private lives (Li and Bernoff 2009) and hence possessed of skills and a level of networking awareness that carries considerable potential to make them more valuable to the organization. This said, such employees are unlikely to attain their full potential in the absence of management that appreciates the need to nurture and support them.

In seeking to respond to the changing status of employees, management itself has frequently had to undergo a change, not only in operating styles but also in mindsets. As bureaucratic and hierarchical structures gave way to flexibility and networks, much of the old industrial age command and control mentality was swept away. The primary challenge for organizations seeking to manage their knowledge workers is twofold. It entails first being able to motivate these people and second, being able to capitalize on their attributes in ways that contribute to the overall performance of the enterprise (Amidon 1997).

For management this has necessitated the acquisition of both new roles and new skill sets. For senior management in particular, this has resulted in an acknowledgement of the importance of leadership over the mere imposition of decisions based on position within the organization. At a general level, this means leadership in fostering access to knowledge and to ensuring its use in support of organizational objectives. In more detail, it involves providing support for group and intergroup learning, for the management of anxiety and uncertainty amidst shifting patterns of power and politics, and ensuring that appropriate structures, resources and reward mechanisms are in place within the organization. New skills have been much in demand with the growing complexity of organizational activity networks, and with this has emerged a need to find a new balance between centralized direction and local inventiveness. For this to happen, a high degree of effectiveness in communication, consultation, listening and persuasion is essential.

When it comes to the actual organization of workforces, teams including virtual teams have proved their effectiveness as regards the motivation and involvement of employees, and in particular in persuading them to buy-in to corporate vision and goals. Teams are highly effective in most aspects of knowledge-intensive operation and also for fostering innovation. They enable a process of independent decision-making around agreed priorities and the effective allocation of people and resources as required. They allow different areas of expertise to combine, thus facilitating optimal levels of knowledge sharing and creation, and the integration of responsibility for a range of activities from concept development to application.

In the final analysis, all organizations have to be designed to align with their fundamental objectives, be these related to making a profit or in a non-profit context, providing a service. Knowledge-intensive organizations operate within structures and systems that balance operational control on the one hand with employee motivation and autonomy on the other. However, not only will the success of such efforts vary from place to place and from business to business, but also there may be much more to such openness that at first meets the eye.

By way of example is a recent anecdote from industry, where questions about the true relationship between knowledge worker autonomy and operational control were raised in a company that by any obvious criterion would have been recognized as being knowledge-intensive. More specifically and indeed, in terms of knowledge-intensive status, importantly, the corporate culture at the company was accepted as being sufficiently inclusive that the empowered and autonomous knowledge workers were happy in the belief that they operated largely independent of managerial controls and monitoring mechanisms. Imagine their surprise however, when as the result of subsequent research, considerable doubt was cast upon the conventional view of employee-management relations at the company. Most significantly, the researchers raised the possibility that what had hitherto been perceived as open and consultative management practices at the company were in fact anything but that. Indeed, in successfully instilling a culture and belief system that was favourable to the organization and warmly welcomed by its employees, management had apparently succeeded in establishing a kind of 'command-and-control by stealth' regime. In the process it appeared, the empowered and highly motivated workforce had become nothing more or less than tools of management (Edenius and Styhre 2009).

This cautionary tale is recounted here not to cast doubt on the broader reality of knowledge-intensive structures, or to suggest that in this case it marked a return to command and control approaches. Rather it is to emphasize the degree of ambiguity that continues to surround the management of such organizations, ambiguity it must be said that applies as much to the circumstances of book publishing as to those of any other industry.

Book Publishers as Knowledge-intensive Organizations

In one sense to enquire as to the knowledge-intensive status of book publishing is to pose the most rhetorical and redundant of questions. Surely the entire edifice of book publishing is built upon and dedicated to the creation, packaging and dissemination of knowledge of all kinds? As with the case of universities, the knowledge-intensive role and status of book publishing must surely be indisputable. And yet, as has been pointed out earlier, not even universities can be universally or unquestionably assumed to be knowledge-intensive, largely on the grounds of inappropriate cultures, organizational structures and management practices. Much like universities, the fundamental knowledge-intensive status of book publishing as based on its core purpose, processes and outcomes remains unassailable. Nor is it necessary for a company to exhibit the complete range of characteristics to qualify as a knowledge-intensive organization. However, like its sister institution, book publishing is by no means entirely convincing as a knowledge-intensive activity when it comes to aspects of its commercial practices and organizational structures.

In attempting to assess the status of book publishing against the seven key characteristics identified above, due allowance has to be made for differences, not only in performance levels but also in size, strategy and market segment. It is also the case that assessment against some criteria is easier than against others. All publishers meet at least the first three of the fourteen criteria outlined in Table 6.1, in that they sell knowledge both as a product and service, and that people and intellectual capital are their most important assets. This is because book publishing is a business that relies on knowledge content and on the ability of people on the one hand to create, package and distribute this knowledge and on the other hand, to pay for access to it. Comparison against most of the other characteristics is much more difficult however. Whereas information about structures and processes is quite easy to obtain, that pertaining to issues of organizational climate and culture and of management style and practice is often a different matter altogether. Much of the corporate information available for public consumption is routine and standardized in format. This means that perceptions of reality, of what the company really does and how it does this, can vary widely when seen from both inside and outside the firm. Some firms which might appear quite enlightened to senior management, may be viewed as controlling and restrictive from lower down the organizational structure, or indeed when seen from an external perspective.

It is clear that perspectives on the present condition of and future prospects for book publishing are heavily polarized and in cases diametrically opposed. To the strongest critics, the wholesale entry of media moguls and accountants into book publishing has put at risk the entire fabric of the industry by abandoning its core business principles. This issue is seen as being particularly acute in trade publishing where management has come in for criticism on at least two grounds. First, there is the perceived quest for unrealistic profit margins through the pursuit of bestselling authors and titles. Second, there is the alleged sacrifice of valuable intellectual capital by replacing experienced and knowledgeable publishers with finance and marketing specialists. Somewhat less strident are those voices that while calling for wholesale change across the industry and not just within trade publishing, base their arguments on a much more positive perception of the current status of and future prospects for book publishing. Here the call is for increased digitization and the uptake of specific technologies such as social networking in pursuit of new markets, products and services. Even more significant are the calls for a new vision within the industry, along with wholesale changes to industry and firm cultures. There are clearly arguments on both sides in these matters, but on the face of things a failure to respond to either perceived weaknesses or opportunities that go to the fundamentals of the industry would not bode well for the credibility of book publishing as a knowledge-intensive business.

Not surprisingly the critics are divided as to their proposed remedies. In the specific case of trade publishing, it is interesting that not even the most severe of critics is proposing a complete return to any perceived golden age where publishing was a business comprised largely of gentlemen entrepreneurs possessed of a developed social conscience. However, there are persistent calls for a revival of familiar tried and tested business practices based upon editorial judgement and a knowledge of readers and markets, something deemed more likely to succeed in the absence of the aforementioned media moguls and accountants. In rather more constructive mode, there is that range of viewpoints that would embrace the need for organizational and technological change. These changes are necessary owing to the emergence of new generations of readers, and indeed, of non-readers in markets where audience participation has taken on an entirely different dimension, and where publishers no longer enjoy unchallenged supremacy.

As an example of the latter more pragmatic response to the needs of book publishing, we would cite the case of a small Australian company that combines a conferencing business with online publishing. With two principals and a core staff of under a dozen, this company was a pioneer both in its early understanding of the wider potential of digitization and in its use of imaginative resource management techniques.

Case study 6.1: Knowledge-intensive Organization – Common Ground Publishing[1]

Common Ground is an Australian publisher engaged almost entirely in the production of digital output, serving a niche market grounded in the academic conference sector. This involves reliance upon a very expensive and sophisticated technology infrastructure. The basic value proposition entails the provision of a digital publishing service which combines the traditional virtues of quality and provenance with those of digital production and distribution. The major area of activity for the company is that of refereed journal papers sourced from their conferences. However, they have traditionally operated a hard copy book publishing operation, comprising about 20 standard texts with an educational and learning focus. When launched, the company spent significantly on technology, and on editorial and technical staff. Central to the delivery of its value proposition

---

1   *Sources*: Interviews and emails; www.commongroundpublishing.com; http://newlearningonline.com.

was the need to develop and promote its own proprietary mark-up language for describing digital texts. Based on an aggregation of common terms and concepts, this language is capable of mapping to some 17 different standards. It would have been extremely difficult to fund this development and to pay for the editorial and technical staff, without massive subsidies from the conference business.

Common Ground has evolved into a producer and manager of content for print and the internet. They have minimal trade in hard copy books (4 per cent of output), but offer a full ePublishing service to an ever-growing client list. They are an innovative academic and general publishing company, but in order to attain their business objectives, they still need to be both dynamic and flexible. They focus their attention on four main areas of business: Conferences, Publishing, Research and Software Development as demonstrated in Figure 6.2.

The company has recently passed the publishing milestone of 10,000 peer reviewed journal articles and it is currently publishing approximately one book per week.

The Common Ground value chain is derived directly from conference papers (where authors lodge papers for refereeing). If the papers are accepted, a content management system channels them via a workflow process which incorporates formatting, quality control and insertion into websites and databases. The final process is that of Distribution, which entails providing the product to consumers via various options including direct to customers via community and author portals, linking to the retail trade through a B2B eCommerce channel, and in smaller quantities through traditional distribution processes. The primary business model is the *conference processing* model. Although the company can be described as

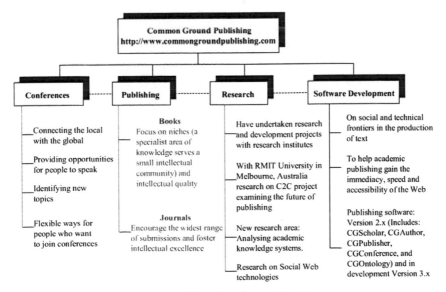

Figure 6.2   Common Ground's key business structure

an academic publisher, its major income stream comes predominantly from cash flows from conferences.

In linking its publication activity to its conferencing business, Common Ground is working to an underlying vision. This vision involves the alignment of conferencing with publishing within an overall knowledge acquisition, creation and transfer process, one element of which entails selling the knowledge. Their business focus is centred on building and strengthening knowledge communities, often linked to or nurtured by conferences. Common Ground believes that ideas nurtured in the conference arena generally dissipate quickly, and a key purpose of these conferences is to seek to capture these ideas. The adoption of these ideas and their conversion into knowledge is achieved through a formal knowledge-creation process that runs from the submission of a proposal (for a paper or book), to its formal presentation to an internal audience to obtain feedback, to its submission and peer refereeing within a formal journal process. This process is illustrated in Figure 6.3.

Regarding the publishing process, Common Ground has its own unique publishing programme which is illustrated in Figure 6.4. This enables members of the company's publishing communities to publish through three media outlets.

- First, by participating in Book Conferences, community members are able to access a world of publication that, resulting from the responsive, non-hierarchical and constructive nature of the peer review process, is very different from the traditional academic publishing forum. For example, The International Journal of the Book (http://booksandpublishing.com/journal)

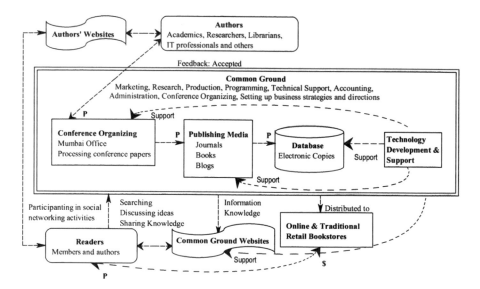

Figure 6.3   Common Ground's knowledge processing model

provides a process for double-blind peer reviews which offer authors an alternative avenue to publishing in well-respected academic journals.

- The second publication medium is through the book imprint, Books and Publishing (http://booksandpublishing.com/books). This forum encourages the submission of book proposals and manuscripts and enables the publication of innovative titles in both print and electronic formats.
- The third major publishing medium is the news blog Books and Publishing Community (http://booksandpublishing.com), which is constantly publishing news updates and snippets. It also covers major developments in the fields of publishing, libraries, information systems, literacy and education.

Common Ground's publishing process embodies three distinct elements: innovation, collaboration and the use of technology. The innovative features of Common Ground Publishing include:

- niche markets: catering to a narrow, culturally based market;
- timely publication: which generally involves a turnaround time of two to three months per publication;
- academic acknowledgment: all titles receive accreditation for acceptance by the Australian Department of Education, Science and Training for

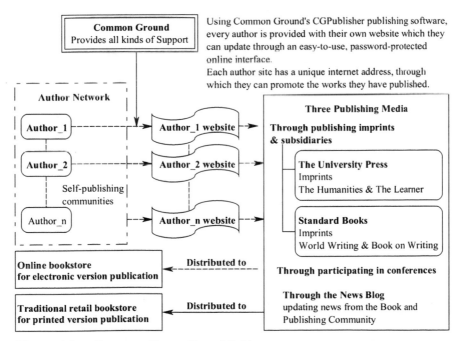

Figure 6.4   Common Ground's publishing programme

purposes of regular audits of institutional research performance;
- CGPublisher: publishing software developed in house, the details of which are included in Table 6.2;
- mixed-media publishing: involving publication in print or electronically via the internet;
- collaboration: aiming to achieve a cooperative effort between publishers, writers and their various communities, enabling Common Ground to access their joint experience and skills to publish content in the most accessible format;
- anti-style guide: a flexible arrangement allowing publications to contain a consistent pattern and follow normal protocols that acknowledge other people's works and ideas.

Table 6.2   Key software developments in Version 3.0 of CGML

Software	Key features
CGScholar	A social networking space that provides an avenue for academics and other knowledge experts to: • highlight and promote their professional profiles • interact with peers • be informed and find out about its focus: events and news relevant to their respective areas of expertise. Such as, Facebook and MySpace, but where individuals and communities are categorized by disciplines and subject matter.
CGAuthor	Represents an online authoring and word processing tool which has as key functions of: • knowledge research (including citation management) • peer-to-peer cooperation • variable outputs for web, print and word processing environments. This is similar to Google Docs, but contains specific properties (for example, citation management and typesetting) which Google Docs does not contain, but which are considered essential in academic publishing.
CGPublishing	A publishing workflow engine, which enables publishers to have control over aspects of designing and managing the publishing processes, including peer review.
CGConference	A conference management system for collating proposals, registrations and programmes, in addition to capturing and publishing conference presentation content, a great deal of which would hitherto have been largely lost to the organizers.
CGOntology	A tool for developing, comparing and publishing formal knowledge systems as Semantic Web ontologies, and the foundation of Common Ground software integration.

Collaboration is a key feature of Common Ground's publishing business. The company employs unique practices when communicating with its stakeholders along the supply chain, sharing knowledge during the processes. The key features include:

- Outsourcing: Common Ground has engaged an outsourcing company in Mumbai, India which has several areas of expertise. This includes expertise in data harvesting or trawling the internet. This includes a search for email addresses which attendees at Common Ground conferences might find useful for sourcing clients and marketing to them. The Mumbai operation also handles all typesetting and PDF generation. Common Ground regards this outsourcing partner essentially as a stakeholder that provides quality control, and not simply as a source of cheap skills and labour. The Mumbai operation also engages in the checking of manuscripts, ensuring that they comply with templates and process documentation, and are thus compatible with the standard technology and review compliance checklist.
- Using research projects to link researchers, universities, academics, research institutions, and government with Common Ground publishing. For example, in the year 2000, they instigated a digital publishing project (Creator to Consumer: C-2-C), in collaboration with the printing industry and RMIT University in Melbourne, Australia. This was a significant research programme with a focus on examining the future of publishing. A significant number of academics and researchers were subsequently involved in the process of creating a series of seven books relating to the transition to a digital-age book production format. Since then the company has been engaged in similar projects aimed at the development and application of new technology and involving a range of academics from various backgrounds.
- Building collaborative communities: Common Ground provides the platforms and social technology (such as its own social networking facility) to enable user-friendly communication for a variety of interested parties, including creators, consumers and retailers, with links between these stakeholders and its own publishing activities. These links provide a common pathway, allowing everyone to work together in a cooperative and efficient environment for content creation, printing and distribution. For example, it is not uncommon for creators, contributors and publishers to work together on drafts. Authors can create their own web page and link to other authors or creators via an author community. They can share their ideas, discuss issues and create content.
- Collaboration with third parties, involving publishing, distribution, marketing and sales. An example of this is where Common Ground provides an online connection to a printing company, providing the option of printing and dispatching directly to customers using POD. Common Ground also

       collaborates with Google to list its book titles and with Amazon to sell its books.

- Collaboration with other publishers: Common Ground cooperates with several imprints and journals, as circumstances dictate.

* * *

When it comes to the use of technology, Common Ground is similar in approach to O'Reilly Media in that it focuses on internal software development to provide support to its entire knowledge process and publishing activities. They are keen to exploit the significant opportunities provided by the internet to revolutionize the means of production and distribution of knowledge. However, the full potential of these opportunities has yet to be realized. In the meantime, Common Ground is pursuing what is fundamentally a research and development agenda, with the aim of developing cutting edge social web technologies and investigating new relationships in the processes of knowledge creation and knowledge validation. From 2000, they have actively engaged in researching and developing publishing software, version 2X of which built upon the Common Ground Markup Language (CGML) and is still being utilized in business processes. They are currently working on an updated Version 3.0, the details of which are shown in Table 6.2.

    The company continues to work on the expansion of social and technical frontiers relating to the production of text, in order to enable academic publishing to benefit from the immediacy, speed and accessibility of the web. They have adopted these software tools in their publishing programme in order to support emerging knowledge communities. The communities interact via innovative face-to-face conferences in addition to 24/7 virtual relationships through a blog, peer reviewed journal and book imprint, all contributing to exploration of the affordability of the new digital media. Members of these knowledge communities are generally academic-based. Internally, the company seeks to hire people who have specialist skills in areas such as technology, innovation, and thinking outside the box, or who have a background in research. They encourage and seek to motivate employees to involve themselves in various research projects and learning processes in order to continue their self-development. Their focus is on the attraction of the kind of person likely to fit best with their business aims and objectives.

Dr Bill Cope is employed in a dual capacity with Common Ground. He is both a director and an active researcher. He is the co-creator of the website (Learning Theory and Practice), along with Dr Mary Kalantzis who is a core author and editor for many titles published in cooperation with Bill Cope. The website comprises a portal linked to areas of educational research and development. Its purpose is to encourage others to share knowledge and ideas, and also to provide some background information on trends in the work, ideas and initiatives of the Common Ground team. The website has five key dimensions:

- New Learning: to question the theory of learning in an environment of continuing social upheaval.
- Learning by Design: a collaborative project with teachers engaged in the process of documenting their curriculum. This is achieved through the medium of a tool called Learning Elements, the purpose of which is to detail the array of task types or 'Knowledge Processes' with which the learners are involved.
- Multiliteracies: a method of approaching literacy by drawing attention to the variations in language pursuant to various social and cultural situations. This also relates to the inherent multimodality of communications, which is particularly relevant in the context of the current, evolving new media.
- The Assess-As-You-Go: this project is a work in progress and involves the construction of a web-based working environment specifically for learners. It incorporates both a formative form of assessment (diagnosis and feedback) and a summative assessment (a time-based comparison of student progress when compared with others of similar status).
- The Knowledge Systems: the platform which introduces their research, investigating the changing nature of scholarly publishing as an essential aspect of their evolving academic knowledge systems.

However, the Common Ground case may be employed to reinforce the virtues of intelligent, knowledge-intensive change it is nonetheless important to recognize that more than one point of view exists in these matters. No matter how sincere and passionate the critics of alleged crass commercialism in publishing might be, there is always another point of view. Nor, in less controversial terms, is it necessarily the case that only the smaller publishers can be innovative and flexible in their response to changing markets and technologies. Much of the furore over the issue of bestsellers attaches to the activities of trade publishers, and especially to those publishers who operate as elements of global conglomerates within the mass media and entertainment industry. Ultimately the pessimists may be right as to the poor business judgement involved in such activities, and there is already evidence for a change of heart and a return to more familiar pastures in the flight from publishing of the likes of CBS, ABC, RCA, and MCA Universal (Epstein 2002). Nevertheless, global conglomerates led by the likes of News Corporation and Bertelsmann continue to feature among the top revenue earners in book publishing.

Furthermore, logic let alone mandates introducing a semblance of balance into the debate, and suggests that we at least consider the possibility that some of the owners and senior managers of these conglomerates actually know what they are doing. Indeed, rather than engaging in asset stripping and the abuse of intellectual capital, these big conglomerates could be acting intelligently as regards both their intellectual capital and the demands of their core markets. If for example, a group that has prospered in selling content to the mass ranks of cinema and television audiences decides to engage in book publishing, it would make sense for it to aim primarily at similar markets in that domain. Logically this could entail the mass market for bestsellers written by big name authors. In the circumstances these organizations can hardly be blamed if they bring to the task the same organizational and management approaches that have stood them previously in such good stead. This of course is just another point of view, but presumably time will tell and in the market, this should not take very long.

The picture is also complicated by the fact that some of the very companies that would be most heavily criticized for selling the soul of publishing in pursuit of bestsellers are in fact, also engaged in a range of distinctly different practices. Indeed, these are practices which by any measure are those of the intelligent, knowledge-intensive businesses that organizational theorists and some publishing reformers argue are the way of the future. It would be hard for example, to think of one major mainstream publisher that was not engaged in knowledge-intensive activity over and above the three core characteristics of the sale of knowledge both as a product and service, the recognition of people as the main source of value, and of intellectual capital are the most important asset. By way of example we present two short cases describing digitization initiatives at respectively HarperCollins and Random House.

Case study 6.2: Knowledge-intensive Activities at HarperCollins

HarperCollins, one of the largest English-language publishers in the world, is a subsidiary of News Corporation. Consistently at the forefront of innovation and technological advancement, it has taken the lead in the provision of both partial and completely free access to digital content, an activity commonly associated with knowledge-intensive operation. The company made the headlines in 2005 with the announcement that a year later it planned to launch a digital library for all its books and audio content, focusing initially on it backlist and then on all new titles (HarperCollins News 2005). At that time, the popular attention in the media focused on its Browse Inside feature, which like Amazon.com's Search Inside and Google's Book Search program, allowed readers to replicate in cyberspace the experience of going to a bookstore and flipping through a few pages before buying a book, with additional features that included interviews, tour schedules, reading group guides, photographs and links to author blogs (Rich 2006).

However, there was much more to this initiative than access to information and purchasing facilities. It marked the first digitization exercise by a major book publisher and represented a direct challenge to the hitherto dominant activities of Amazon and Google. It was also intended to counter potential copyright violations by major search engines and others by gaining control of digital files and valuable intellectual capital, while enabling creative responses to market demands for alternative digital formats. At that time, HarperCollins also announced its intention to negotiate deals with online social networking sites like MySpace and Friendster to allow users who were fans of particular authors to link to the Browse Inside function (Rich 2006).

This multimillion dollar investment, with future predicted annual expenditures of seven figures, was intended to catch up on earlier *sampling* initiatives in the music and film businesses, as well as targeting younger generations who were spending so much time on Google, MySpace, Facebook, author websites, Yahoo and MSN. The main aim was not to sell books directly to customers online, but rather to use the Browse Inside feature to attract readers to its web pages. Readers who want to buy the books are directed to links to a number of online retailers, including Amazon and Barnes & Noble, as well as to the websites of smaller independent booksellers like the Tattered Cover in Denver and Copperfield's in Sebastopol, California. However, HarperCollins left little doubt that it aimed to become what one executive called the number one marketer on the web (Bangemann 2005).

Also in 2005, HarperCollins announced a forthcoming partnership with NewsStand, Inc. a leading provider of digital content and delivery solutions to the book, newspaper and journal publishing industries. Working exclusively with LibreDigital, a Division of NewsStand Inc., the goal was to develop a global digital warehouse hosting all HarperCollins' digital content in multiple formats. The warehouse development was part of an ongoing effort to build the digital infrastructure necessary to market and eventually monetize content to emerging digital markets, while allowing HarperCollins to maintain control of its digital files and intellectual property and protect the rights of its authors (HarperCollins News 2005).

By 2007, the structure and potential value of this alliance had become apparent. The combination of HarperCollins' content and marketing expertise with LibreDigital's secure digital warehouse and comprehensive fulfilment and delivery model, resulted in the provision of end-to-end solutions from editorial to consumer service. This included the supply of digital services in discrete, modular segments including digital typesetting, production, digital warehousing, internet distribution, and online marketing. This modular approach enables publishers to start with the right set of services for their particular purposes and adjust the mix as business needs change (PR Newswire News Release 2007).

In addition to its potential benefits in terms of marketing and profitability, this alliance reduced HarperCollins' previous dependence on external digitization facilities and enabled the company to regain control of its customers from these third parties. They took the view that such a capability would become essential to all publishers wishing to remain competitive and to reach digital consumers, whether on an in-house basis or through out-sourcing (PR Newswire News Release 2007). Within a year, HarperCollins had moved significantly along the spectrum of knowledge-intensive operation with its decision to enable free access to complete books on its website, the only conditions being that the user was unable to save or print the material. However, there is a direct link to book purchase (Wischenbart 2008).

Finally, in March 2009, HarperCollins launched a beta version of its digital sales catalogue. Along with the customary information about books and authors this includes promotional videos, audio samples, and provides the ability to read some galleys and ARCs. The information is updated many times a day. Titles can be sorted and booksellers can create lists and write, store and share notes. This is largely a tool for publishers, booksellers and librarians (Biba 2009).

* * *

A further example of a trade publisher engaged in the pursuit both of bestselling titles and of intelligent knowledge-intensive practices is Random House.

Case study 6.3: Knowledge-intensive Activities at Random House

Back in 2006 Random House initiated a 'search inside the book' facility that allowed readers to view and buy content online, ranging from a few pages to an entire book. The initiative enabled the indexing, searching and display of text, with separate agreements to be reached with online booksellers, search engines and entertainment portals. This allowed readers to read pages of Random House books for around 4 cents a time (Allen 2005). The intention was to share the money on a 50/50 basis with the authors of fiction and narrative non-fiction titles, with different pricing models to be developed for other types of book such as cookery books.

In 2006 Random House also launched a programme called Amazon Upgrade where for a small extra payment, customers who bought print books from Amazon could access the content electronically (Mills 2005). The company also announced their intention to launch a movie division, in partnership with a production company called Focus Features, in order to parlay its books into films. This was in fact just one part of an attempt by the company to establish itself within a new milieu, where visual presentation was more popular than traditional text and including the transmission of educational content using cell phones (Business Week Media 2005)

More recently, in the United States, the company has started a drive to transform both frontlist and backlist titles to the ePub format, and significantly, it is also addressing the wider cultural and business model issues involved (McCloy-Kelley 2009). This included a drive to increase the contents of its eBook catalogue from 8,000 in 2008 to 15,000 within a matter of months (Dear Author News 2008). Meanwhile in the United Kingdom, Random House has been an innovator in launching its own social networking site for its book clubs called. Readersplace. co.uk following the creation of Authorspace.co.uk a year earlier (Smith 2009).

In 2009, Random House reminded the market that it had not lost sight of its core commercial imperatives when a letter was sent to literary agents by the CEO of the parent company Bertelsman, claiming the digital rights to all books it had published before the advent of a market for eBooks. Like many publishers Random House saw this as a potentially lucrative future revenue stream. Rights holders and the Society of Authors strongly objected to this move and at least in theory, authors could retaliate by taking their content elsewhere. Interestingly a similar impasse occurred when Rosetta Books sought to publish digital editions of in-copyright works owned by Random House. The eventual outcome was that the expected court case never went to trial and that Random House granted a licence to Rosetta to release eBook versions of 51 titles (Rich 2009).

* * *

These cases have been presented owing to their representative nature and because they involve two major trade publishers. To these examples of knowledge-sharing alliances and the valorization of intellectual capital in book publishing others can be added, including the appointment in February 2008 of a Chief Digital Officer at Simon & Schuster. The role entails responsibility for the full range of the company's digital activities including strategy and new business development, consumer-focused digital marketing, the website, electronic publishing and digital infrastructure (Wischenbart 2008). At the time of writing, moreover, HarperCollins has announced the creation of two new digital groups within the company. HarperCollins Digital, led by a Chief Digital Officer, will be comprised of three teams focusing respectively on author services, consumer products and business development. The Digital Technology Services group is tasked with providing technology services across the company, and with developing new technologies that align with the company's global digital strategy (Publishers Lunch Deluxe News 2010c). Similar initiatives in knowledge-intensive activity could be made across the spectrum of publishing categories. With the qualifications just made, and with due allowance for company and market circumstances, we would argue that book publishing should not only be seen to be knowledge-intensive, but also that it must strive to become even more so in the future.

Chapter 7

Supply Chains and Value Chains in Knowledge-intensive Organizations

Introduction

Throughout history the connections between business development, profitability and the creation of value from the provision of goods and services have been clear and reasonably straightforward. Traditionally, businesses competed for market share on the basis of cost or differentiation, and links between them were limited to exchanges of raw materials, components or business services. Although these strategies are still relevant today, they operate within industries and economies where connectivity and interactivity are the watchwords.

At its most basic, this transformation can be seen in the fact that competition is no longer simply a firm-to-firm issue, but also something that happens between complex chains of supply and value. Indeed, as we shall argue later in the chapter, the extent of connectivity and interactivity between businesses, their partners, suppliers and customers is best seen in terms of networks rather than chains of relationships. First, however, it is necessary to illustrate the emergence of the process of firm and industry connectivity in the form of supply chains and value chains.

Overview of Supply Chains and Value Chains

Supply chains

At their most basic, supply chains are comprised of flows of raw materials or parts from suppliers to manufacturers to customers. The primary focus is on costs and efficiencies of supply, on utilization and inventory turnover rates, and the flow of materials from their various sources to their final destinations (Feller, Shunk and Callarman 2006), along with an emphasis upon distribution rather than product enhancement (Rainbird 2004). The complexity of the supply chain will vary with the size of the firm and the intricacy and number of items manufactured.

Although originating in a manufacturing context, supply chains are equally important to service industries. Traditionally their management has embodied five basic components (Wailgum and Worthen 2007):

- Plan: developing a strategy to manage all the resources required for meeting customer demand, including metrics for monitoring the efficiency and cost effectiveness of the supply chain.
- Source: choosing suppliers and developing pricing, delivery and payment processes, along with metrics to monitor and improve relationships.
- Make: producing, testing and packaging for delivery of the product, with metrics for quality, productivity and worker output.
- Deliver: the logistics of coordinating orders, networks of warehouses and the selection of carriers to deliver the goods and setting up of invoicing systems for payment.
- Return: creating a flexible and responsive system for receiving defective and excess products from customers and supporting customers who have problems with delivered products.

Before the advent of the internet, supply chains were viewed largely on a firm-by-firm basis and, as has been seen, with a focus on manufacturing industry. However, the development of internet connectivity and communication standards has enabled the integration of company supply chains with those of their suppliers and customers, resulting in exchanges of data between trading partners and greater visibility along the supply chain (Wailgum and Worthen 2007). This has also led to increasing sophistication in supply chain management and to its extension beyond the manufacturing environment. Furthermore, the transition from patchworks of manual interactions and exchanges with partners, suppliers, distribution centres and carriers towards globally integrated supply chains has been as rapid as it has been dramatic. This has been driven both by unremitting pressures to reduce costs and by the availability of new bundles of technology and business processes which have provided unprecedented views into supply chains (Wilcox 2009).

So far as the technology is concerned, the critical breakthroughs have come in the areas of supply chain software and in visibility or tracking systems. For example, supply chain management has benefited greatly from the adoption of enterprise resource planning software that combines all the information about enterprise functions into a single source. For the tracking function, the use of bar coding has proved to be highly successful, although major improvements are anticipated from the use of radio frequency identification technology. Not for the first time, however, it is important to emphasize that supply chain effectiveness depends on much more than the application of technology. The fundamental point is that all participants must not only appreciate the value of being part of mutually beneficial end-to-end relationships, but also embrace the essential principles of visibility and collaboration, even at the risk of exposing their data to others (Wilcox 2009). This message is reinforced in the further perception of supply chains as core capabilities embodying the right combinations of talent and technology, internal and external collaboration and change management (Jusko 2009). These core capabilities are ultimately directed to the goal of customer satisfaction, as are those embodied in value chains.

Value chains

Whereas supply chains delineate the processes from creation to delivery of a product or service, value chains comprise a series of activities that create and build value, whether in regard to specific products or services, individual departments or the entire organization. They embody the key activities necessary for the transformation of raw materials into products, including activities such as design, production, marketing, distribution and support (Jansen, Steenbakkers and Jagers 2007). The creator of the concept, Michael Porter (1985), describes a value chain as a sequence of activities through which a firm develops a competitive advantage and creates shareholder value. Porter defines value as the amount that buyers are willing to pay for what a firm provides, and he conceives the value chain as a combination of nine generic value-added activities within a firm that combine to provide value to customers (Feller, Shunk and Callarman 2006). This includes the primary activities of inbound logistics, operations, outbound logistics, marketing and sales, and service, and the support activities of firm infrastructure, human resource management, technology development and procurement. All these activities add value to the firm's services and products and are essential to its pursuit of competitive advantage. The original value chain concept is illustrated in Figure 7.1.

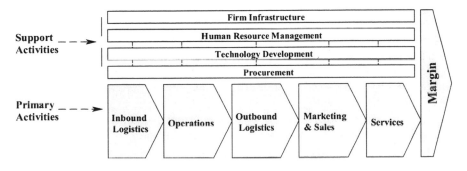

Figure 7.1   Porter's original value chain model

The difference between supply chains and value chains

Supply chains and value chains can be seen as providing complementary views of an extended enterprise, with integrated business processes enabling the flows of products and services in one direction, and of value as represented by demand and cash flows in the other. Furthermore, both chains are related to the same network of companies and both are made up of companies that interact to provide goods and services. However, there are differences between the two concepts. The primary focus in supply chains is on the costs and efficiencies of supply and on the flow of materials from their various sources to their final destinations. Efficient supply chains reduce costs. The primary focus in value chains is on the benefits that accrue to customers, on the interdependent processes that generate value and on the resulting demand and funds flows that are created. Effective value chains generate profits (Feller, Shunk and Callarman 2006).

There is also a key difference in the directional flows within the respective chains. Supply chains focus upstream by integrating supplier and producer processes, improving efficiency and reducing waste, while value chains focus downstream, on creating value in the eyes of the customer (Feller, Shunk and Callarman 2006). There is a fundamental difference in focus between the upstream flow of goods and supplies from the source to the customer, and the downstream flow of value from the customer, in the form of demand, to the supply base. As we have already argued, these flows of supply and value are increasingly more likely to occur across multi-directional networks than along linear chains.

Supply Chains and Value Chains in Book Publishing

Traditional supply chains

The publishing supply chain is comprised of independent but interconnected organizations, situated at various points along the chain, which perform certain tasks or functions for which they are remunerated in some way. This includes such tasks as the creation and development of content, design, quality control, marketing, printing and sales (Thompson 2005). The book industry supply chain is particularly complex, embodying a large number and wide variety of products, many different players, common processes and related information flows (for buying, distribution, selling, customer service and returns). In general terms, the supply chain can be categorized into the three stages of publishing, printing and retailing (Euromonitor International 2003). Figure 7.2 shows a traditional supply chain model for book publishing.

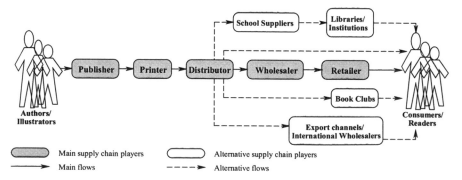

Figure 7.2   A traditional supply chain for book publishing

Supply chains in digital publishing

The digitization of book publishing carries major implications for production, for supply chains and for distribution channels. This implies not only new possibilities for value creation and for eBusiness (Akkermans 2001) and the integration of customers into the value creation process (Piller 2002), but also the potential for disintermediation, or the removal of processes or players from the chain. However, this focus on disintermediation basically emphasizes product and cost issues, and pays less attention to the other value-adding roles of intermediaries, such as those of brand and customer management. In the event, the outcome has frequently been the opposite of what was expected, that is to say, it has resulted in reintermediation rather than disintermediation. In this case, new markets and opportunities have led to the emergence of additional intermediaries, including so-called cybermediaries operating on the web and others working to extend existing physical channels (Gallaugher 2002). These new players contribute value by aggregating buyers and suppliers into new markets, and by exploiting existing connections to obtain cross-channel synergies, for instance by using corporate websites as order sources, for product and service information and for online problem solving. Figure 7.3 illustrates both a traditional physical supply chain and the changes anticipated by the uptake of digital technologies.

Digital publishing ultimately has to do with the provision of market-ready digital content to customers. It offers choices and flexibility in the selection of the most suitable supply chain and delivery options in responding to changing market circumstances. For example, sales and marketing can operate through traditional or via new, online distribution channels, and in some instances, direct to the end-user. These digital processes can still embody physical attributes, or the content

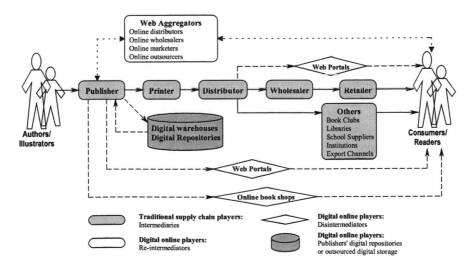

Figure 7.3 A digital publishing supply chain

may be printed on demand or distributed via downloading, on CD-ROM/DVD or online (Daniels 2006).

It is clear from Figure 7.3 that traditional supply chain concepts have undergone a major transformation with the advent of digital technology. Despite these improvements, the book industry supply chain is still coming under fire for its industry-centric nature and a lack of responsiveness to the needs of both writers and readers. This includes claims that the current supply chain is a reflection of the use of new technology by book publishers not to restructure the writer–reader relationship, but to limit reader choice and to move product rather than engage with consumers (Nash 2010b). This suggests that further changes to the industry supply chain are needed, which in turn will have implications for new value-adding activities, and hence, for different perspectives on value chains.

Book publishing value chains

In the early days of publishing, the value chain basically comprised the author, the printer and the publisher. As book publishing gradually evolved, the value chain became more complex (Thompson 2005). This complexity increased with the movement of physical books into digital format.

The components of Porter's original value chain can easily be adapted to the needs of the book publishing market. Instead of the customary value chain activities of inbound logistics, operations, outbound logistics, marketing and sales, and service (Porter 1985), others more relevant to value creation in publishing can be substituted. Among such alternatives, Daniels (2006) suggests that the elements pivotal to digital content are aggregation, search and discovery, authority and relevance. These would be supported by the customary infrastructure elements of Porter's model. Figure 7.4 shows a value chain model for book publishing based on the work of Porter (1985) and Daniels (2006).

The dotted lines in Figure 7.4 reflect the fact that human resource management, technology development and customer/supplier/partner relationships can be associated with specific publishing activities as well as supporting the entire chain. These infrastructure components and activities are the building blocks by which a corporation creates a product or provides a valuable service to its customers. The respective support and process activities operate as follows.

Support activities   As indicated in Figure 7.4, the infrastructure of support for book publishing includes four elements: top management, human resource management, technology development and relationships. These are now each considered briefly in turn.

Top management: Top management has ultimate responsibility for the strategies underpinning business decisions and for providing the resources and leadership necessary to implement them within departments and across departmental and organizational boundaries. Not only does this involve responsibility for coordinating the various infrastructure components which support processing activities, but it

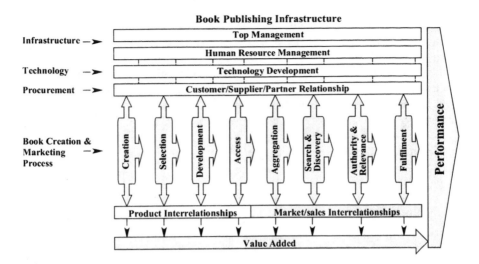

Figure 7.4   A value chain for book publishing

also includes the task of transforming intellectual property into a business asset (Lee and Yang 2000). This latter represents something of a change in perception as regards the role of management. Recent structural and organizational changes have also seen changes in responsibilities, with the emergence of a new set of positions at senior and middle-management levels, with titles such as Digital Director, Digital Strategist and Digital Editor.

Human resource management: As with other value-adding assets, human resources need to be managed effectively if the organization is to attain its objectives. This is neither as obvious nor as easy as it might seem. In the first place, there are concerns about the concept itself, which in the eyes of many observers is a hangover from the industrial age and the Taylorist practices of the factory system. In the second place, the role and status of employees in organizations and industries heavily dependent upon personal and corporate knowledge have changed beyond recognition from what they were in the industrial age. So whereas activities such as recruitment, training and staff development continue to be relevant, the organizational environment has changed to such an extent that they must accommodate the changing status of staff, in particular of knowledge workers, and build in structures for employee-directed professional development. As potentially valuable knowledge assets that can take their expertise and skills with them should they decide to leave, staff need to be nurtured and empowered in order to commit to the corporate vision and the sharing and collaborative behaviours required in knowledge-intensive organizations.

Technology development: Developments in ICTs have opened up new possibilities for value creation, notably in the co-engineering of information goods and services, in new information-based value-added services and in information-rich physical goods. ICT enables customers to become an important part of the value creation process, for instance by personally configuring their value package (Briggs 2009, Maskell 2001). This carries clear implications for eBusiness which Akkermans (2001) described as the epicentre of amalgamation between value creation and information technology, the place where technology push and market pull interact. Technology development is important at both infrastructure and process levels, with changes to technology routinely requiring reconfiguration of the value chain (Porter 1985). At the infrastructure level, technology features in the networks and the computerized systems that enable the conduct of functions from finance to production to marketing, and in the communication and exchange of ideas between partners, suppliers and, increasingly, customers.

Relationships: Relationships have always been important to book publishers, whether these be relationships with authors, printers, distributors or booksellers. Good relationships have been important for the acquisition and retention of authors, and for the maintenance of stability and loyalty along the supply chain. As supply chains and value chains have grown in complexity in the digital age, the need for relationship building has, if anything, become even more urgent. At a time when value is increasingly disembodied and delivered in virtual contexts, such relationships are regarded as intangible assets. Furthermore, they are assets exposed to the volatility of markets reeling from the combined impact of relentless technological and organizational change and from an implosion in the relationship-building environment. What was once a linear chain of relationships within book publishing has fragmented into a multimodal network of traditional and new players whose roles and status have changed dramatically.

Processing activities   As noted in Figure 7.4, book publishing extends over a range of activities, including creation, selection, development, access, aggregation, search and discovery, authority and relevance, and fulfilment (Daniels 2006).

- creation: the writing and submission of the original manuscript by authors
- selection: with publishers filtering through the mass of submitted material in order to acquire suitable content from authors;
- development: managing the production cycle, pre-press, printing and binding to produce the finished product;
- access: ensuring that the work is available for purchase on the market;
- aggregation: consolidating the total range of content available through traditional warehouses or wholesalers or, increasingly, by means of digital stores or repositories;
- search and discovery: facilitating the visibility of the content both within the book trade and to the reading public;
- authority and relevance: communicating the integrity of the brand, the status of the author and the appropriateness of the content for its stated purpose;
- fulfilment: completing the sales transaction, including after sales and, if necessary, a returns service.

Each element of these value chain activities can create value, which flows to the endpoint to achieve an optimum publishing performance. This value arises in both tangible and intangible form, evaluation of which is not always straightforward. Tangible outcomes such as revenue or profit can be assessed using standard performance management indicators. Intangible value is much more difficult to measure, however, and although there is a growing range of systems for this purpose, firms commonly settle for the use of proxies such as lead times and customer satisfaction. So far as the creation and exploitation of value are concerned, however, there is merit in shifting the focus away from value chains per se and towards what happens in value networks.

Value Networks

Value chains are now regarded in many circles as inadequate both for explaining the complexities of value creation in the knowledge-based economy and for dealing with the role of intangibles in networked enterprises. Furthermore, in global markets where the co-creation of values with others sits at the core of strategic planning (Normann and Ramirez 1993) and where more than the value chain of one organization is involved, it is better to think in terms of value networks or value webs rather than of value chains (Jansen, Steenbakkers and Jagers 2007). The purpose of these value networks is to generate economic value and other benefits through complex dynamic tangible and intangible exchanges between two or more individuals, groups or organizations (Allee 2002). Participants in these networks convert their expertise and knowledge into tangible and intangible deliverables that have value for other members of the network. These complex exchanges of value sustain the success both of participating companies and of the network as a whole, and without these mutually beneficial outcomes, participants would withdraw or be expelled and the network might collapse or be reconfigured (Allee 2002). Along with traditional value chains and supply chains, value networks have a significant relationship with the development and operation of business models.

Value networks in the digital age

With regard to the issue of potential disintermediation discussed above, Porter (2001) has pointed out that even the internet need not necessarily have a disruptive effect, often being complementary to existing technologies. He has also argued for the superiority of value networks over value chains in non-linear markets for content. Within such markets, new intermediaries are emerging to create new value and enable more sophisticated and effective exploitation of content by combining assets (particularly knowledge assets) from a variety of organizations.

The value network creates value by linking clients who are, or wish to be, interdependent. The firm itself is not the network, but is part of or a contributor to a networking service. Value is created through interactivity between network members acting as mediators in flows of services and management of the network (Afuah and Tucci 2001). Osterwalder (2004) and Briggs (2009) indicate that in value networks the value-creation logic is one of linking customers, while the main interactivity relationship logic is that of mediation. Osterwalder (2004) further argues that the three primary activities of a value network (shown in Figure 7.5) are:

- network promotion and contract management: identifying and selecting potential network customers, and managing the various contracts governing service provisioning and charging;
- service provisioning: establishing, maintaining and where necessary terminating links between customers, and charging for value received, based on the use of network capacity;
- network infrastructure operation: maintaining the physical and information infrastructure of the network.

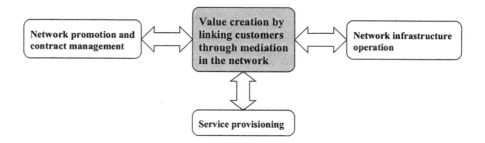

Figure 7.5   Three primary activities of a value network

Value networks in book publishing

Any attempt to illustrate the workings of value networks inevitably requires a degree of simplification and abstraction. However, in depicting the main flows of content, and the transition of value from creator to end-user, value networks represent a set of functions common to the content industries, notably those of content creation, content packaging and aggregation and content distribution (European Commission 2003).

- Content creation: the main component of value creation, where the creators may derive income in the form of licensing fees and usage payments derived from the use of digital rights management technologies.
- Content packaging: the internet and related technologies enable the creative and sophisticated packaging and reuse of content by either content owners or aggregators. Service packages are marketed to end-users, along with

content management functions controlling access to content and channels provided within the package.

• Content distribution: the sale of transmission and distribution rights into secondary markets, the reformatting or reproduction of content in packaged media formats (for example, DVD and audio CD), and the use of electronic distribution technologies such as syndication services and internet content distribution networks to optimize the value of web-based distribution.

Just taking account of these three functions alone presents a challenge. Apart from the complexity involved, there are problems to do with showing where the value is created (or being lost) and with the difficulties that stem from the fact that much of this value is intangible in nature. Figure 7.6 presents another generic picture, this time of a potential value network for book publishing. In such networks publishers would work in close collaboration with their authors, customers, suppliers and partners, creating value through the entire process from initial creation and development to distribution, marketing and sales. This network of engagements results in the creation of both tangible and intangible value. Within the network, the book publishing infrastructure, featured in the triangle at the bottom left of the diagram, plays an identical role to that within value chains, one of supporting the entire value network.

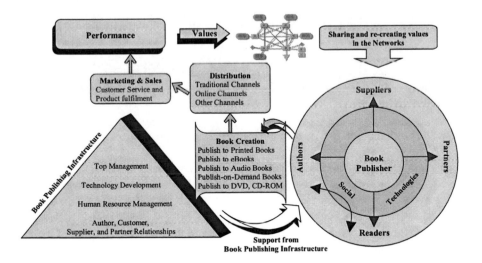

Figure 7.6   A generic value network model for book publishing

This model also can be presented in rich picture format thereby, capturing more of the detail of what goes on in the network. Figure 7.7 is an example emerging from our research into book publishing in Australia.

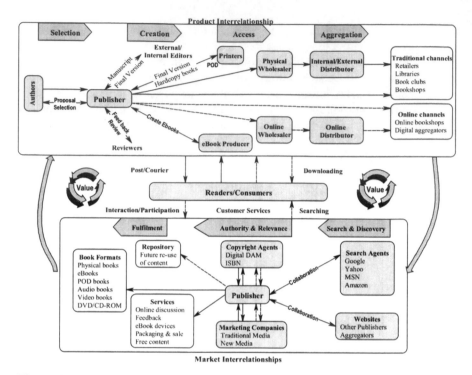

Figure 7.7   A rich picture of a real value network in book publishing

In a time of changing technologies, organizational structures, supply chains and business models, the quest for new sources of added value has become increasingly urgent.

Tangible and intangible values in book publishing value networks

Jansen, Steenbakkers and Jagers (2007) distinguish between the values in business models that are offered to the organization and the customer respectively. They then make a further distinction:

- value is the result offered to the customer of the activities performed by the organization or network;
- reciprocal value is the result of the process the customer offers to engage in as compensation for what is received from the organization.

Increasingly, the search for new value comes in the form of extra services to customers. ICT has played a major role in this regard by making it possible to harvest and process the information and knowledge provided by customers. Today, in selecting business models it is first and foremost important to reflect on what values and reciprocal values the various players wish to offer and receive. Subsequently, thought must be given to the ways in which these values might arise in the electronic world, in the physical world or in both.

Clearly, reciprocal values include both tangibles and intangibles. Allee (2002) defines tangible values as those which are created during the spectrum of business transactions. Intangible values encompass tacit and explicit knowledge that complements the transaction and, as such, is considered to be a valuable asset. In book publishing, as in other value networks, all participants create and receive value from a wide range of flows and transactions. Figure 7.8 shows the transfer of tangible and intangible values between two key players in book publishing value networks, namely publishers and consumers. The dotted arrows represent intangible values and the solid arrows represent tangible values.

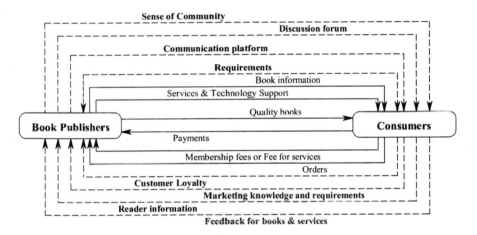

Figure 7.8   Tangible and intangible value flows between publishers and consumers

To explain Figure 7.8 more clearly, Tables 7.1 and 7.2 show how publishers and readers receive value (both tangible and intangible), from whom they receive it and from which activities.

Table 7.1   Key values to publishers

Tangible value

What publishers receive	Comes from	Activities	Tangible impact	Intangible impact
Payment	Consumers	Marketing and sales Enhancing customer loyalty	Operating capital All relevant expense	Increases business knowledge Enhances knowledge of sales and services
Orders	Wholesalers, retailers, consumers	Order entry	Requires handling costs Improves balance sheet Increase profits Reduces inventory level	Market validation of books Increases business knowledge
Requirements	Stakeholders	Informal emails, phone calls and faxes	Requires handling costs	Increases knowledge of stakeholders
Intangible value				
Loyalty	Consumers	Efficient communication Customer management Provision of high-quality service	Requires handling costs Investment in IT infrastructure	Enhances relationships with customers Enhances knowledge of customer behaviours Enhances knowledge of new technologies
Books information	Consumers and other stakeholders	Efficient communication Interaction with consumers Sales and market analysis	Requires handling costs Requires marketing costs Requires increasing payment to employees	Expands publishers' knowledge of book sales Expands knowledge of customers' needs and market requirements
Loyalty	Authors	Efficient communication Paying reasonable royalties Supporting book promotion High level editorial support Provision of high-level copyright and licensing services	Requires handling costs Increasing royalty payments Requires editorial costs	Enhances the relationship with authors Enhances the knowledge of copyright and licence issues Enhances knowledge of author behaviours
Various knowledge	Consumers, authors, others	All the above activities	Requires handling costs and other expenses	All the above
Relationships	All stakeholders	Efficient communication Efficient interaction High-level services and support	Requires handling costs Marketing expenses Enhances knowledge of new technologies	Enhances knowledge of behaviour Enhances knowledge of new technologies
Reputation	Markets	Good relationships Advanced services High-quality books	Investment in books, services, marketing and sales, relationships, IT infrastructure	Enhances knowledge of production, services, behaviours, IT, marketing and sales

Table 7.2   Key values to readers

Tangible value				
What readers receive	**Comes from**	**Activities**	**Tangible impact**	**Intangible impact**
Books	Publishers Retailers Wholesalers	Searching online Visiting physical bookshops Social networking	Cost of the books	Knowledge of books
Services	Publishers Authors			Enhanced relationships with publishers and authors
Requirements	Publishers	Informal emails Surveys		Time
Intangible value				
Book information	Publishers Retailers Authors Social networking sites Others	Efficient searching Interaction with others	May require membership fee Investment in internet connection	Expands knowledge of books
Loyalty	Publishers, Authors Retailers	Efficient communication Book purchase records Provision of valuable suggestions	Cost on books Discount	Enhances the relationship Increases the frequency of book purchases Enhance personal knowledge Increases personal satisfaction

The tables show that all players in the network are both providers and receivers of value. In principle, the more value one provides, the more one receives. In such circumstances it is important for book publishers to ask themselves how they can increase their value outputs by extending value to others through service enhancements. For example, in the area of communication channels, the value enhancements or value added may include:

- email
- provision of a personal representative

- web-enabled transactions
- online discussion forums
- more transparency in transactions
- multiple communication channels
- extended R&D activities
- enhanced ICT infrastructure
- conversion of traditional one-way channel into two-way or multiple channels for product feedback
- social networking services management
- establishment of communication strategies.

Book publishing is undergoing a transformation from the employment of traditional processes to digitization. This undertaking will necessitate significant change in supply and value chains, and in value networks. In a digital environment, intangible value will carry more weight than tangible value. These changes will, of necessity, impact upon business models. The next chapter deals with the topic of business models in a digital environment.

Chapter 8

Business Models in
Knowledge-intensive Organizations

Introduction

Although originating in the 1950s, it was not until the 1990s that the term 'business model' became widely accepted and that business modelling was employed as an essential business practice (Lawrence et al. 2003). The business model concept gained momentum at that time partly through the growth of eBusiness, together with the effects of globalization and related strategic challenges (Cassidy 2002). It has taken time for anything like a clear perspective on the nature and implications of business models to emerge, with progress being impeded by continuing ambiguity. One area of confusion lay in the perceived relationship between business models and business process modelling. It is important at the outset to draw a clear distinction between the two concepts, the detailed activity of business process modelling serving a very different purpose from that of the higher-level representation of business logic, found in business models (Gordijn and Akkermans 2000). Not so much a matter of confusion, but another point that needs to be made at the outset, is that the activity of business modelling is exactly that. It involves making models that are conceptual representations of the real world as seen through the theoretical eyes of the model builder. While extremely useful for illuminating relationships between players and processes in business contexts, these models are rarely so clearly demarcated or so straightforward in operation in the real world as they are on paper.

The very idea of business models has received short shrift from Porter (2001), who has described the concept as being murky at best, and if anything, an invitation to faulty thinking and self-delusion. In more constructive terms, Porter criticized business models for their lack of connection both to industry structure and to the creation of value. In very different vein, Osterwalder and Pigneur (2009), while recognizing the lack of consensus on the subject of business models, nevertheless view them as important vehicles for communication and understanding between players in the market. They describe business models as the conceptual implementation (blueprint) of a business strategy that allows the alignment of strategy, business organization and information systems, and represents the foundation for the implementation of business processes and information systems (Osterwalder and Pigneur 2009). From a different perspective, business models can also be seen as patterns for organizing exchanges and allocating various costs and revenue streams so that the production and exchange of goods and services becomes viable on the basis of the income it generates (Brousseau and Penard 2007).

The transition from traditional to digitally based processes inevitably carries significant implications for business models. Originally, the business model concept was both broad and comprehensive in scope, capturing the complete range of value-creating activities of a firm. While this approach is still in use, it has also become common practice to represent such activities as collections of atomic sub-models, each with its strategic objectives, value propositions, sources of revenue, critical success factors and core competencies that can be broken down into further detail as required (Weill and Vitale 2001). These activity systems are thus sets of interdependent organizational activities which are centred on a focal firm, and which also include activities conducted by the partners, vendors and customers of that firm (Zott and Amit 2009).

This chapter seeks to explain the fundamentals of business models, including how the concept has been defined, the classification of business models, their component elements, the impact of ICT on business models and business model strategies and modelling procedures.

Defining Business Models

Definitions

Given the extensive literature that surrounds the concept, there are hundreds of definitions of business models to choose from. Here we start with two which not only capture the essence of the concept but also connect effectively to the explanation of digital business models that follows this section. The first is that of Osterwalder, Pigneur and Tucci (2005), who defined a business model as:

> A conceptual tool that contains a set of elements and their relationships, that allows the expression of the business logic of a specific firm. It is a description of the value a company offers to one or several segments of customers, and of the architecture of the firm and its network of partners for creating, marketing, and delivering this value and relationship capital, to generate profitable and sustainable revenue streams.

This definition was later refined by Jansen, Steenbakkers and Jagers (2007), who described a business model as:

> A unique configuration of elements consisting of the strategies, processes, technologies, and governance of an organization, a configuration formed to create value for the customers and thus to compete successfully in a particular market.

Informed by these perspectives, our research led us to compile our own definition of business models, which was influenced heavily by the potential for divergence between activities within web-based value networks and mainstream publishing. Accordingly, we define business models as:

> Representations of the value and revenue-creating activities and relationships within networks of producers, intermediaries and customers that capture both tangible and intangible value and reflect the competitive stance of the various players.

The essential focus of any business model or eBusiness model is on the interaction of the firm with its marketplace (Jansen, Steenbakkers and Jagers 2007). Whether bricks-and-mortar, electronic or some combination of the two, all definitions contain common characteristics and posit that a business model incorporates the fundamentals of a company's competitive strategy and how its processes are formulated and delivered in order to generate value and achieve profitable results (Rappa 2006).

Currently, most business models are influenced by technology, in both its familiar and emergent forms. This would include, for example, technologies for managing supply chains and customer relationships and those embodied in Web 2.0 (Briggs 2009). However, careful consideration of the nature and role of this technology remains essential. Despite pronouncements to the effect that it is almost a question of one being *in* eBusiness or *out* of business (Cassidy 2002), the experience of the dot.com crash in the late 1990s drove home all too clearly the fundamental significance of viable business models (Hagel 2002).

Digital business models

Given the onset of new functionalities and, indeed, of new businesses to provide these functionalities, digital business models might well be expected to differ quite radically from those designed for operation in the industrial age. Among the most anticipated of changes to business models were those expected to result from disintermediation, which, as has been seen in a previous chapter, did not occur to anything like the expected extent. Intermediation and, indeed, the services of new intermediaries, was still necessary in order to ensure the effective interaction of buyers and sellers, and of the information and processes required to perform value-adding transactions. The difference between traditional and digital business models is frequently, in fact, one to do with a process of reintermediation, with additional players being attracted to the marketplace. This is reflected in the business models of companies such as eBay, Amazon and Google, whose platforms enable the bundling and delivery of goods and services, corresponding to the increasingly complex interests and specific needs of consumers (Brousseau and Penard 2007).

Digital business models also differ with regard to the specific characteristics of the goods and services they provide. Digital business models represent relationships between three categories of agent, namely producers, assemblers and consumers. They reflect the production of functionalities or modules linked to the provision of either tangible goods or information services or both, and which are assembled to generate value for users. The goods and services themselves are modular and composite in nature, embodying specific combinations of digital content and information processes. Critically, the role of the consumer is different in these models, having changed from that of recipient of value to potential participant in its creation through the contribution of feedback and insights (Brousseau and Penard 2007). In everyday practice, the output of producers, tangible and intangible, is processed by assemblers (potentially everybody from so-called 'infomediaries' marketing information packages such as TV channels or internet portals, to industrial aggregators such as computer manufacturers) for delivery to consumers.

As discussed in Chapter 5, Web 2.0 enables myriad groups of demographically and geographically diverse people to engage in the co-creation of value. Critically, this has led to changes in business models, with the key locus of value creation residing not so much in the products or services themselves as in emerging sets of relationships. This includes not only relationships between products, services and consumers, but also relationships between consumers (Briggs 2009). Furthermore, easy-to-use facilities such as blogs and wikis are providing organizations with the opportunity not only to access an almost infinite range of knowledge and ideas, but also to publish their own information within global networks. In such networks, moreover, the uptake of Web 2.0 technologies and applications is contributing both to a reduction in the costs of R&D (Cardoso, Carvalho and Ramos 2009) and to an increase in business innovation (Radziwill and DuPlain 2009). These emerging digital business models are collaborative as well as competitive in nature, and are built around value-creating networks of suppliers, customers and even competitors.

Categories of business model

As the digitization process has gained momentum, researchers have sought to categorize eBusiness models according to, for example, the nature of their value proposition or their mode of revenue generation. Clearly, these generic classifications will not necessarily be relevant to every firm and, as a result, companies will choose from what is available, either singly or in combination. A book publisher, for example, might combine the diverse activities of infomediary, affiliate and community, acting respectively as information provider, as an affiliate to the business models of third parties such as Amazon or Google and as the host or member of an online community. This issue of business model classification in book publishing is taken up again in the next chapter.

Table 8.1 summarizes two of the most popular generic categorizations of eBusiness models. In an everyday context, the choice of business models and their composition will vary even within firms in the same industry. In some cases,

Table 8.1   Categories and examples of digital business models

Source	Category	Examples
Rappa 2001	Brokerage	Marketplace exchange; buy/sell fulfilment; demand collection; auction broker; transaction broker; distributor; search agent; virtual marketplace
	Advertising	Portal; classifieds; user registration; query-based paid placement; contextual advertising/behavioural marketing; content-targeted advertising; intromercials; ultramercials
	Infomediary	Advertising networks; audience measurement services; incentive marketing; metamediaries
	Merchant	Virtual merchant; catalogue merchant; clicks and mortar; bit vendor
	Manufacturer	Purchase; lease; licence; brand integrated content
	Affiliate	Banner exchange; pay-per-click; revenue sharing
	Community	Open source; open content; public broadcasting; social networking services
	Subscription	Content services; person-to-person networking services; trust services; internet service providers
	Utility	Metered usage; metered subscription
Applegate, Austin and McFarlan 2003	Focused distributor models	Retailer; marketplace; aggregator; infomediary; exchange
	Portal models	Horizontal portals; vertical portals; affinity portals
	Producer models	Manufacturer; service provider; educator; information and news service; custom supplier
	Infrastructure provider models	Infrastructure portals

businesses confine themselves to the use of a single type, and in others they will operate more than one form of business model.

While most of these categories are a clear reflection of financial transactions between buyers and sellers, the list contains a range of models based on the provision of free services to consumers by companies that are, nonetheless, able to make a profit (de la Iglesia and Gayo 2009). This would include models such as the following:

- advertising: building audiences and communities to gain the attention and participation of consumers by giving away high-quality services in the form of tools, content and applications, all of which are paid for by a third party, the advertiser;
- freemium: where most of the users obtain a basic level of service for nothing, and where a small percentage of them pay subscriptions to receive a premium service;

- work exchange: where, in using the free service, consumers provide value to the company that provides it, either by participating in online polls or by contributing knowledge or opinions;
- mass collaboration: where users participating in communities contribute by giving away their work free, on the understanding that it will remain free to everybody.

Different versions of all these categories of business model, frequently with variations in nomenclature, are to be found in different industries. In our own research into book publishing the following categories (in practice variants or combinations of one or other of the models in Table 8.1) emerged as particularly relevant:

- Bricks and mortar: the traditional book publishing model based largely upon physical entities, including distribution and sales through warehouses and bookshops. This is still widespread in trade publishing and in the education sector.
- Clicks and mortar: which reflects the combined effects of digital technology and electronic commerce, and can feature both disintermediation and reintermediation.
  - Disintermediated: reflects the disruption of book publishing as evidenced by the emergence of new products and services such as eBooks and digital warehousing.
  - Reintermediated: reflects further disruption through the emergence of models built around new players in the book-publishing industry, such as online bookshops.
- Collaborative: book publishers are engaged in a wide variety of collaborative activities involving business partners, outsourcers, other publishers and consumers. Within this category the emergence of community models is a significant development.
- Freemium: where publishers provide free access to certain types of content while providing a higher level of service to those willing to pay for it. Examples here would include material available through sites such as O'Reilly.com and PublishersLunch.com.

Key components of business models

From the extensive list of potential components for inclusion in business models, most authors would include the following four: value proposition, cost structure, revenue model and market segment. A more comprehensive list is provided in Table 8.2.

Our own research identified the following components as being particularly relevant in a book-publishing context:

Table 8.2   Business model components

Source	Components
Chesbrough and Rosenbloom 2000	Value proposition Market segment Structure of the value chain within the firm Cost structure and profit potential Position of the firm within the value network Competitive strategy
Petrovic and Kittle 2001	Value model Resource model Production model Customer relations model Revenue model Capital model Market model
Osterwalder and Pigneur 2009	Value proposition Client segment(s) Communication and distribution channels Relationships Key resources needed Key activities necessary Partner networks Revenue streams Cost structure

- value proposition: the value created across the spectrum of the book publishing process, including value to creators, intermediaries and consumers;
- products and services: the range of products and services involved, including those exchanged between business partners as well as provided to end customers;
- participants: all the players represented in the model, from authors to publishers and their business partners to readers;
- intangible resources: in particular, corporate and individual knowledge, competencies and capabilities and relationships;
- cost structure: all the costs, fixed and variable, associated with the business of book publishing;
- revenue model: how the revenue from the business is generated;
- strategy: a description of the company's response to the environment in which it operates.

In the final analysis, any understanding of business models will be founded on a secure grasp of the relationships between people, products and services, and values (both tangible and intangible), as represented in the generic business model depicted in Figure 8.1.

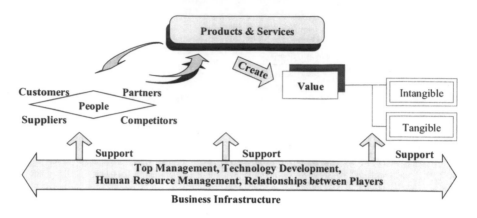

Figure 8.1   A generic business model

Business Model Strategy

Difference between business models and business strategies

For all its importance, the relationship between business models and strategy is complex and at times ambiguous. Furthermore, while often used interchangeably, there are differences between the two concepts. Hence, argues Magretta (2002), whereas business models describe how the pieces of a business fit together, they do not factor in the presence of competition, which is where strategy comes into the picture. Put differently, business models have an internal focus on economic value creation, whereas strategy is more outward looking and focused more on competitive positioning (Seddon et al. 2004). These differences between business models and strategy were further explained by Seddon et al. (2004) in terms of two perspectives. In the first of these perspectives, business models were viewed as being derived from strategy, and as an abstract representation of some aspect of firm strategy. In the second perspective, both business models and strategy were viewed as being conceived at different levels of abstraction, and focused to a greater or lesser degree on competitive positioning. Any attempt to compare the two concepts must bear these differences in mind (Seddon et al. 2004). In recognizing the subtleties involved, along with the need for as much compatibility as possible between the two concepts, Figure 8.2 (based on an original created by Osterwalder 2004) depicts their relationship in terms of different business layers and their processes.

In creating the relationships depicted in Figure 8.2, Osterwalder perceived a business model as being essentially the translation of a company's vision and strategy into value propositions, customer relationships and value networks (Osterwalder 2004).

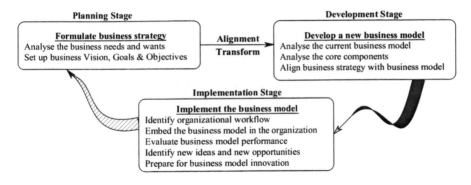

Figure 8.2 Business layers and processes

Importance of business model strategy

Lawrence et al. (2003) noted that successful businesses were those that either had devised their own models or had employed a combination of models to achieve their goals. A good business model is essential to every successful organization, whether it is a new venture or an established player. It can serve as a kind of organizational glue and, being subject to continuous external forces, must be capable of redesign and adaption (Osterwalder 2004). Business models also provide a potentially valuable unit of analysis, since by depicting basic company functionality they enable a deeper understanding of firm performance (Wu 2005). Indeed, beyond such considerations it is likely that several large corporations in the United States owe their survival and profitability during a period of economic difficulty in the early 1990s at least in part to their effective business models. These included Southwest Airlines, Microsoft, Wal-Mart and eBay (Afuah 2004).

Distinctions between different kinds of business model are a clear reflection of their different approaches to the generation and capture of value. Jansen, Steenbakkers and Jagers (2007) make a further distinction between value per se and what they term reciprocal value in business models. Value is the result offered to the customer of the activities performed by the organization or network. Reciprocal value is the result of the process the customer offers to engage in as compensation for what is received from the organization or network. This distinction is important to the design and selection of business models, whether for operation in the electronic or physical worlds or in both. Another important distinction between digital strategies involves that between, respectively, the assembly strategy and the valorization strategy. The assembly strategy refers to the scope of targeted assembling and the depth of targeted integration between functionalities in the network. The valorization strategy refers to the way that value is to be extracted from users of the service, either in the form of revenues from sales or advertising or in reciprocal form (Brousseau and Penard 2007).

As a result of the implementation of such strategies, digital business models can range in form and scope from the pure to the integrated. This includes intermediation services in pure forms, focusing on a single functionality and in the form of bundled, standardized packages, and those integrated assemblers that can cross-subsidize between services and market players to provide a better service (Brousseau and Penard 2007).

Managing change and redesigning business models

With constantly changing economic and environmental conditions, organizations must guard against the possibility of obsolescence in business models by monitoring both the internal and the external environment (Kotelnikov 2002). This can frequently require the redesign of business models to render them appropriate for the networked economy (Rappa 2006).

Pressure for the design of new business models can be technological in origin, with technology facilitating improved coordination within markets (Brousseau and Penard 2007) and the creation of new pricing mechanisms, as well as making it easier to compare the prices of competing products and services (Klein and Loebbecke 2000). Increasingly, the search for new value comes in the form of additional services to customers, with ICT enabling the harvesting and processing of information and knowledge provided by customers (Jansen, Steenbakkers and Jagers 2007).

Businesses, however, need to use foresight when formulating models, in order to anticipate any disruption that may occur in the future, causing the need for reconfiguration of the proposed model. This approach provides firms with flexibility in adopting new technologies and changing their business models (Pateli and Giaglis 2004). In amending or recreating business models, however, it is essential that allowance be made for the incorporation of softer values such as a sense of community, knowledge sharing and idealism into the reconfigured model (Jansen, Steenbakkers and Jagers 2007).

Jansen, Steenbakkers and Jagers (2007) provide a methodology for business model comparison and assessment which could be useful in the consideration of changes to business models. This involves addressing the five key areas of value model, design and strategy, revenue model, governance and IT. However, Briggs (2009) suggests that before seeking to change their business models, firms should first ensure that they understand their current ones. For this he recommends the application of a three-stage test, which he terms the 'locus-creator-scarcity model', which works as follows:

- Locus: where is the value located? In the product or service or elsewhere?
- Creator: who are the creators of value in the model? Is it the original designers or does this include business partners and customers?
- Scarcity: what resources in the business are infinite (and can be given away free) and what are scarce (and can be charged for)?

Lastly on this point, there is clear support in the literature (Prahalad and Krishnan 2008, Pateli and Giaglis 2004, Auer and Follack 2002, and Petrovic and Kittle 2001) for the application of three stages to the transition from a current business model to that embracing a digital scenario, namely:

- understand: assess the current business model in the context of the current business environment;
- identify the capabilities: including their potential influence on the model itself, as well as for new roles and, indeed, the emergence of new businesses;
- adopt: design, describe and implement new business models presenting alternative scenarios and outlining the changes anticipated.

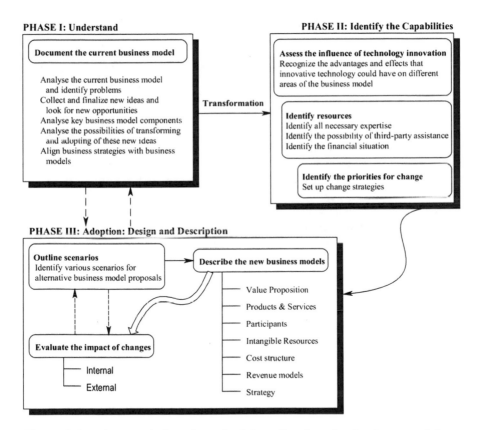

Figure 8.3   A scenario-based methodology for changing business models

Developments in Business Models for Book Publishing

Inevitably, given the nature and scale of the changes covered in previous chapters, there remains considerable scope for changes in business models for book publishing. Although to some extent this is necessary owing to changes in markets and technology, in many cases it is related to failures in existing business practices. Hence, it has been claimed that those publishers unable to survive in current markets without recourse to price-fixing activities and the punitive application of DRM should be left to suffer the consequences of poor business practices, with those remaining advised to figure out new business models (Nash 2010b). Clearly, there will be differences not only between individual firms, but also between those operating in traditional and digital markets, differences which will be reflected in their business models. Variation is also to be expected within market segments, with, for example, Thompson (2005) identifying four categories of business model within the field of scholarly publishing alone:

- Virtual Library Model: based on the creation and storage of electronic books and content which can be accessed free of charge by end-users, with the revenue being generated by selling licences to host institutions such as libraries and universities.
- Digital Warehouse Model: similar to a traditional warehouse, except that the content is maintained by the owners, usually academic publishers, in digital rather than paper form. As with virtual libraries, ownership of the content is retained by the publisher. However, there are no licensing arrangements.
- Scholarly Corpus Model: publishers, acting either alone or in collaboration with other publishers, create a corpus or repository of scholarly book content (essentially an online database) where access can be sold on a subscription basis to academic institutions.
- Scholarly Community Model: where an interactive community of scholars can gain access to a range of services, including scholarly content.

These models serve both as examples of developments in digital publishing and as pointers to the digital publishing models that form the subject of the next chapter. This chapter has summarized understanding of the term 'business model' in traditional, eBusiness and digital environments. It has provided an overview of the concept and context of business models, from definitions to design and modelling. It is clear that, when faced with the challenge of adopting a new model, businesses may initially need to identify potential new value elements that will enhance the benefits expected. This will require consideration of several areas, including strategy, organizational structures, business processes, value chains/ networks, revenue streams, competitive advantages and core competencies. In the next chapter we will present an analysis of traditional and current business models for book publishing which is based on our own research.

Chapter 9

Business Models for Book Publishing in Australia: An Extended Case Study

Introduction

The previous chapter provided an overview of the nature and composition of business models, ranging from the traditional to the digital and the hybrid in nature. This chapter is different in that it narrows the focus and looks in some detail at a range of business models in use in the Australian book publishing sector. It is based upon 14 separate case studies conducted during our earlier government-funded research into digitization within the industry, carried out from 2006 to 2008. Although to an extent limited by a requirement for anonymity on the part of the 14 case companies concerned (three trade book publishers, four educational book publishers, one professional publisher, three specialist book publishers and 3 university presses), this is in effect a case study of the progress of digitization in Australian book publishing at that time. Apart from the fact that much of what is reported from that period is still current, this earlier research exercise enabled us to test and iterate the methodology later employed in building the models amassed during the later phase of our research, in 2009. Furthermore, with the exception of the specialist and university publishers, all the remaining case study companies feature in Table 9.1, which depicts the leading book publishers in Australia on the basis of their market shares. We begin by providing a brief overview of book publishing in Australia.

The Australian Book Publishing Sector

In Australia, book publishing accounts for around 49 per cent of publishing activity, with the remainder accruing to the publishing of telephone directories (49 per cent), maps (1 per cent) and other (1 per cent). For the period 2008–9, book industry revenues in Australia amounted to AUD 4,181.6 million (IBISWorld 2010), with an earlier report anticipating an average annualized real growth rate for industry value added at around 2.8 per cent in the five years to 2011–12 (IBISWorld 2008). These figures mask the fact, that out of an estimated 4,000 publishers in Australia, most of the revenue comes from a small number of global firms that have emerged from the merger and acquisition process to capture the lion's share of the market (IBISWorld 2010).

In Australia, as elsewhere, there is a major international presence. Most of the activity in book publishing is attributable to a handful of large-scale, foreign-owned multinationals, exploiting the benefits of global economies of scale and distribution. Locally owned companies account only for around 10 per cent of the book publishing segment's revenue (IBISWorld 2010). Furthermore, instability in the market resulted in frequent changes in market share prior to 2007. After 2007, as illustrated in Table 9.1, the key players consolidated their market positions. It is important to point out, however, that although these conglomerates dominate the publishing arena, many small firms have survived, owing to their pro-activeness in focusing on niche markets. It is also important to mention the increased market share attributed to the category described as 'Other', which represents the influx of new entrants into the industry and, particularly, the emergence of online players such as Amazon.com (IBISWorld 2010).

In many ways, Australian book publishing can be seen as a microcosm of the industry worldwide. Hence, any analysis of business models for Australian book publishers is likely to have relevance for those in similar countries elsewhere. As elsewhere, the Australian book publishing industry is complex in terms both of industry and of organizational structure. As explained in Chapter 2, we used a familiar, fivefold categorization of the industry publishing into:

Table 9.1   Market shares in publishing in Australia 2003–2009

Major players	Market share (%)					
	2003–04	2005	2006	2007	2008	2009
Allen & Unwin Pty Ltd		3.69	3.52	2.66	2.50	2.40
Australian Consolidated Press Pty Ltd				1.40	1.40	1.40
Hachette Livres Australia Pty Ltd				2.00	2.00	2.30
John Wiley & Sons Australia Pty Ltd				1.40	1.40	1.40
McGraw-Hill Australia Pty Ltd		6.00	5.00	2.50	2.40	2.50
News Australia Holdings Pty Ltd	8.00	8.00	8.00	2.17	2.20	2.20
Pearson Australia Holdings Pty Ltd	7.00	10.00	11.00	6.24	5.70	6.00
Publishing and Broadcasting Pty Ltd	2.81	1.00	3.00			
Random House Australia Pty Ltd				2.28	2.20	2.20
Reader's Digest Australia Pty Ltd	2.00					
Reed Elsevier Australia Pty Ltd	12.00	12.68	13.35	2.71	2.70	2.70
Sensis Pty Ltd	45.00	30.00	31.00	42.57	42.60	39.30
Scholastic Australia Pty Ltd	6.00	5.00	5.18	2.82	2.80	2.80
Cengage Learning (Thomson Corporation Australia Pty Ltd)	13.00	12.00	5.21	1.00	1.00	1.00
Wolters Kluwer Australia Pty Ltd	3.00	6.00	6.27	1.90	1.90	
Other	1.15	5.63	8.47	28.35	31.10	33.80

Sources: IBISWorld 2005, 2006, 2007, 2008, 2009, and 2010

- trade publishing
- educational publishing
- professional publishing
- specialist publishing
- university presses.

All the case companies were prominent within their respective publishing categories. They included independent Australian and multinational trade, educational, professional and specialist publishers, along with university presses noted for their pioneering and innovative approaches.

Components of Business Models for the Five Categories of Book Publisher

Within the foregoing categories, the major focus of the case studies was on the comparison of company business models across a range of key constructs drawn from the literature. These were:

- products and services
- value proposition
- stakeholders
- intangible resources
- cost structures
- revenue models
- strategy.

Products and services

Although all the case companies were engaged in producing books, in at least three instances – those of a specialist feminist publisher, an online publisher and a university press – this was not in hard-copy format. As an indication of changes both in markets and in boundaries between publishing categories, all those publishers producing hard-copy products were also engaged in providing a range of format options from CDs and DVDs to multi-media packages, to digital formats, including eBooks. Educational publishers have been particularly innovative in producing packages which combine physical books, their electronic version and CDs or DVDs. Despite the similarities in the goals and strategies devised by individual publishers, however, there were, inevitably, differences in the value propositions that they offered their customers.

Value proposition

Value propositions are at the heart of business models and are generated by a set of internal capabilities which represent the ability of a firm to perform functions that create value for a range of stakeholders (Bagchi and Tulskie 2000). As in other industries, book publishers work closely with their partners, customers and suppliers to create a range of value propositions. Publishers must tailor their value propositions to meet the needs of targeted external parties, as well as to align with their existing internal capabilities. Despite differences between firms operating in different publishing categories, and in the aims and objectives of those in the same category, a strong element of similarity emerged in the value propositions of the 14 case study companies. This enabled the identification of a broad generic value proposition for book publishing which would embody some or all of the following characteristics and components:

- full service provision
- publishing and marketing knowledge
- culture of knowledge sharing
- strong brands
- multimedia content distribution and marketing
- use of advanced technology
- extensive digitization of processes and practices
- efficient and flexible management team
- efficient partnership networks and communication systems
- advanced strategy for customer engagement
- rich pool of authors
- sophisticated websites
- strong focus on copyrights
- adoption of international standards
- provision of high-quality content in a variety of formats.

All publishers in all categories place particular emphasis on the importance of three potential elements of their value proposition. These are the provision of high-quality content (in either print or digital format), the organization of content, including editorial competencies, and the ability to negotiate licensing and royalty arrangements. However, the capabilities that go into generating additional elements of value propositions vary from category to category. This is illustrated by comparisons between business practices in the trade and educational categories, on the one hand, and in the professional, specialist and university categories, on the other hand.

Key value propositions in trade and educational publishing include:

- Operation of full service strategies: in addition to its core publishing operations, one trade publisher has undertaken the deployment and development of international distribution subsidiaries in its major publishing centres (UK, USA and Australia). These subsidiaries not only cater for their parent publishing arms, but also reap the benefits of additional revenue streams by providing a range of services to third parties. This includes a rights distribution facility and a Publishing Services Unit that is focused upon sales and marketing. The intention is to expand the level of provision of these services in order to enable the provision of additional added value.

- Variety of products and of product formats: although alternative formats continue to emerge, for many publishers the major focus remains the hard-copy book. In educational publishing in particular, textbooks continue to dominate, and indeed show few signs of flagging, so far as the foreseeable future is concerned. They provided the mainstream revenue source for all the educational publishers investigated in our research. This was complemented by a modest trade in eBooks, PDF formats and the delivery of classroom content via digital or mobile whiteboards.

- Provision of sophisticated websites: this is especially noticeable in the case of trade publishers. Their websites are all extensively customized and provide detailed and specific information for their stakeholders. Furthermore, although they all have website ordering and purchasing facilities, the major emphasis is on improving and strengthening the quality of their communications and relationships with all other parties. To achieve this goal, trade publishers are engaged in the use Web 2.0 applications such as widgets, and other publishers are developing multiple websites to serve different groups of customers. The educational publishers are more focused on the provision of multifunctional websites. Typically, these offer stakeholder access to question and answer facilities, and in some cases, to a service that enables academics to select chapters from different sources in order to create customized textbooks.

- Multi-channel marketing and delivery facilities: the ability to exploit a range of channels, including multimedia, is increasingly necessary as publishers strive both to service existing customers and to increase sales and client diversity by reaching out to new ones. Educational publishers are noted for the provision of strong technical support and services for classroom teaching and learning activities when their textbooks are purchased by schools. In one case this includes an optional facility based on the use MP3 players in the classroom.

- Collaboration and the availability of partnership facilities: all the case study publishers are committed to the principles of collaboration and partnership. In practical terms this means that they are all engaged to different degrees in sharing knowledge, costs and time with a range of partners. This includes other publishers, as well as technology, production, design, distribution and marketing companies.

- Meeting international standards for book title metadata: most publishers have adopted the ONIX international standard for book title data. This system provides a number of benefits, including those of access to complete book title details for inclusion on websites and the efficient production of catalogues and leaflets.

Value propositions in professional, specialist and university publishing place particular emphasis upon the following:

- Operating in niche markets: all the specialist publishers investigated exemplified success in this field. One, which was the subject of a case study in Chapter 6, operates in a market linked to academic conferences and offers a full electronic publishing service for books and journals, including the provision of software, metadata, file conversion, content management and quality. It also offers the provision of an additional marketing, sales and promotion channel to its customers. Another publisher maintains a highly effective presence in the global market for travel books. The third company operates very effectively in international niches, with a particular emphasis on feminist literature and, increasingly, on eBooks.
- Provision of sophisticated information services: among the case companies, the professional publisher is an excellent example of this practice, with its provision of updated information on a regular basis through newsletters, free and premium web news, daily email alerts, and online TV programmes.
- Provision of self-publishing services: in this case a prominent university press is offering a POD-based self-publishing platform on its website. This is largely intended as a facility whereby academics can reuse and package materials to create their own textbooks and teaching packs.
- Use of leading edge technologies: all the professional, specialist and university publishers were confident that they had more than adequate technologies at their disposal. In the case of the professional publisher, the possession of such technology was seen as giving it a competitive edge over its rivals. This perception extended both to infrastructure and systems, and included the provision of search tools and a workflow solution system with an online data room, claimed to provide significant benefits for customers. By using the workflow solutions system, this company has partnered with leading service providers to offer end-to-end solutions to clients, including not only a full range of document production services, but also the facility to complete activities such as mergers and acquisitions online.

Stakeholders

As with other industries, it is necessary to think about book publishing in terms of a range of stakeholders beyond the publishers themselves, and notably, their suppliers, partners and customers:

- Suppliers: include authors, printers and distributors and a growing range of services provided through outsourcing.
- Partners: help to enhance demand for goods and services and share in the benefits. The potential list includes eBook designers, online search agents, web browsers, eRetailers, web portals, other publishers and technology

companies. In the case of the professional publisher, this list of partners extends to include government agencies and freelance authors not employed by the publisher.

- Customers: purchase both intermediate and final products and services. Different categories of publishing attract different customers. For example, the customers for trade publishers may include individual readers, libraries, book clubs, bookshops and online bookshops, and for educational publishers this will, in the main, be schools, universities and various levels of government.

As digitization takes hold, the interests and activities of all these stakeholders are subject to change. These different stakeholders are now considered in more detail.

Suppliers   For all publishers, authors remain the key supplier, the creator and provider of content. Across the industry and within its different categories, however, relationships with suppliers increasingly involve the outsourcing of everything from printing and typesetting to, in some cases, design and editorial. This occurs largely in relation to offshore locations where the quality is high and the costs are much lower than in Australia. In a variant of this approach, a leading trade publisher outsources its printing onshore in Australia, while employing its own editing and design team. This has the effect of combining a fast turnaround with strict time and quality control over content. Other variants among our case study companies include the outsourcing of activities such as printing and typesetting to India, while retaining a team of trouble-shooting experts in that country in case of emergencies. Alternatively, the entire printing process can be outsourced and use be made of freelance editors, typesetters and proof readers. As with outsourcing practices in general, however, Australian-based book publishers recognize the importance of protecting their most strategic assets. This can involve the retention of in-house staff for critical operations such as design, and the use of their own project managers to oversee and control work processes.

Partners   As has been seen in a foregoing section, partnership arrangements are widespread within Australian book publishing. This includes partnership activities among specialist publishers, who routinely operate within networks of business partners and services, including those for production, distribution, marketing and selling. In the case of one specialist publisher engaged in the digitization of content and the production of eBooks, this has led to a 50–50 partnership with an overseas technology company. The outcomes are access to specialist knowledge and cost reductions in service provision for the publisher.

Publishers in all categories have also forged partnerships through the TitlePage price and availability service which is operated by the Australian Publishers Association. Providing free access to bibliographic information for booksellers via a website, this facility offers considerable savings in time and money for publishers. Likewise, publishers are working in cooperation with each other and with the Copyright Agency (CAL) to provide their content for sale either in its entirety or on a chapter-by-chapter basis using the CAL platform and search facilities.

Other forms of partnership include those with distributors, eBook retailers and library suppliers, with digital aggregators, and with technical service companies who provide support in areas such as eBook design, website design and maintenance. Arrangements are also in place with a variety of eOperators, ranging from libraries in Australia and overseas to Google. All these partnerships add value in different ways to the products and services of the Australian-based publishers.

Customers   There are differences in the customer bases of the various categories, with trade publishing having the most diverse markets of all the categories of publishing. This mandates the need for a range of approaches that can include the targeting of individuals (via both online and traditional channels) and of schools, businesses, various levels of government, libraries, bookshops (both online and traditional), web browsers (other websites, Yahoo! and Google) and other publishers (both local and overseas). In the educational and university press categories, the customer base is more clearly delineated and extends across academics and students, libraries and other institutions. The customer base for professional and specialist publishers is similar in that it is more likely to involve various niches, demarcated in professional, educational, community of interest or subject terms, and accessed by a variety of print and electronic channels. In all categories, bookshops, both traditional and online, and libraries are a core element of the customer base.

Intangible resources

Intangibles are now a major if not *the* major economic resource. For book publishers, the key intangibles are: relationships, networks and loyalty, brand names, employee knowledge and experience, and publishing knowledge (such as of creation, production, marketing and sales).

Relationships, networks and loyalty   We have already given some indication of the scale of relationship activity within book publishing in the section on stakeholders above. In general, networking through relationships can be the path to new business opportunities. It can help companies to maintain a competitive edge and enable the generation of cost- and knowledge-sharing advantages. Networking and collaboration both inside and outside the industry is increasingly important in the search for content, up to and including collaboration with competitors. This also includes the need for collaboration with customers, which is an area in which our research found Australian-based publishers to be in somewhat of a catch-up mode. Until very recently, for example, there was limited involvement of publishers in social networking. This is changing, with a growing number of publishers now encouraging their authors to pursue this route, while themselves experimenting with blogs, wikis and widgets. Whatever the technology involved, however, it is essential that in seeking to collaborate and build networks with authors, partners and customers, publishers recognize that the 'glue' to such arrangements is loyalty, which in turn is founded on trust. However, both of these constructs are two-way affairs, and hence, loyalty and trust have to be earned.

Brand names   In publishing, the attraction of the brand lies in both the imprint and the identity of the author. Within the five categories of publisher investigated we found that:

- In trade publishing, the material is generally sourced by author name, with that of the publishing company being of secondary importance.
- In educational, professional, specialist and university press publishing, material is generally sourced by imprint, although on occasion people will look for the names of well-known authors.

As with any business, brands are absolutely critical resources in publishing. The value of imprints is frequently reflected in mergers and acquisitions, while that of author names is regularly emphasized in the level of advances paid to best-selling writers.

Experience and knowledge   The experience and knowledge of employees can be a vital factor in the success of any publishing house. Employees are potentially the greatest source of added value, and they epitomize the concept of intangibles, their contribution being based on both tacit and explicit knowledge and on accumulated wisdom and experience. The identification and recognition of the skills and experience base necessary in an age of digitization has emerged as a critical issue for contemporary book publishers. Publishers are now actively seeking people who have specialist skills in areas such as web design, digitization and social networking. This is likely to lead not only to increasing personnel costs, but potentially also to uncomfortable trade-offs between these new skills and traditional expertise and experience.

Cost structures

Allowing for the operation of different strategies, such as those focused on cost savings and those emphasizing the creation of value, all book publishers have to cover both fixed and variable costs. For traditional book publishing, the major costs include:

- Content creation: this includes the costs incurred in writing, editorial and design, and in paper, printing and binding. Most of these can be categorized as variable costs.

- Marketing: including the costs of advertising, promotion, the provision of free copies, overhead (standard 30 per cent of net sales revenues) and direct marketing ($1 × the total number of printed copies). Most of these are fixed costs.
- Other: including the costs of wages and salaries, royalties to authors (normally 10 per cent of suggested retail price), inventory write-offs (returns × unit printing, paper and binding charge), royalty write-offs (the difference between the advance and the earned royalty), printing and distribution costs, an average discount of 47 per cent (the industry range is between 42 per cent and 48 per cent), the landed cost of imported books, and copyrights or other rights (IBISWorld 2010, Greco 2005).

The cost structure and how it is modelled can vary between publishers and, indeed, between individual books from the same publisher. Frequently, for example, a traditional long-run cost model is applied to frontlist (first run) books, with the more costly short-run model or the more economical POD model both employed for backlist (re-run) titles, according to circumstances. However, all these established practices are subject to the winds of change. For one thing, printing costs are declining. This can be attributed both to significant price competition among printers (with a rise in the proportion of printing undertaken overseas) and to increases in the practice of digital downloading (IBISWorld 2010).

In the context of digital publishing, or more realistically of publishers transacting business in both traditional and digital formats, it is important when discussing cost structures to allow for potential differences in costs between the alternative channels for creation, production, distribution and marketing. Furthermore, different channels will have independent cost structures. For example, for a physically printed book there will obviously be production costs. If this activity occurs in online mode, however, the production cost will be zero or as near to it as makes no difference. With book publishing now well into the transitional stage from traditional to digital publishing there are obvious implications for the nature and scale of costs. Compared with traditional publishing, digital cost structures are more diverse between publishing houses and between their products, services and distribution channels. In general, the major range of costs in digital publishing includes:

- primary costs related to design, web development and maintenance, formatting and copyrights;
- costs of platform development (for example the website) and web facilities for, among other things, eCommerce and communication;
- ongoing investment in the redesign of websites, in infrastructure and software and, not least, in the enhancement of the product to make it attractive when compared to print books;

- costs of recruiting staff with specialist skills in web design, digitization and social networking.

Compared with traditional books, the eBook can offer cost savings under such heads as printing, stock on hand, shipping and distribution. On the negative side, however, eBooks can necessitate increased investment in the redesign of websites, infrastructure and software.

There is a range of viewpoints on cost structures for eBook production and these will be covered in more detail in the next chapter. Currently, however, there is still no substantive evidence that in Australia book publishers have succeeded in working out a price structure for eBooks which enables their production at reasonable prices while offering a satisfactory return on investment.

During our research publishers expressed different opinions on eBooks, ranging from those who considered eBooks to be something of an optional extra, to those who viewed their production as being a matter of priority. Even in the latter case, however, there was a broad consensus that business models for eBooks were still a long way from maturity. As for the future and the likely nature of the relationship between eBooks and hard-copy versions, there is still considerable diversity of opinion. Hence, some book trade players in Australia have predicted a 10 per cent rise in sales levels for eBooks between 2009 and 2010. Others, however, while admitting that sales of eBooks could soon comprise 5–6 per cent of the market, and this at the expenses of printed books, maintain that the latter will continue to have a future (Sorenson 2009). Irrespective of which of these opinions is the more realistic, however, serious cost issues remain in need of resolution, along with those to do with formatting, and compatibility between reading devices.

Revenue models

Although the details can change slightly between publishing categories, the revenue model for publishers is basically that of a traditional sales model. This said, there are notable differences between the models employed by various categories of book publisher. Hence, in trade publishing, the wholesale revenue model is widely favoured, with sales being affected through wholesalers to retailers, to customers in mass markets. In educational publishing, on the other hand, the sales commission model is common, while a combination of wholesale and commission models can be found in the domains of professional, specialist and university press publishing.

However, the emergence of digital technology has meant that there is no one single revenue model for all publishers. They all operate multiple revenue models for the provision of products and services through various distribution channels to different customer segments. Table 9.2 depicts a range of revenue models, traditional and digital, identified during our research in Australia.

Table 9.2   Book publishing revenue models currently in use

Type	Current revenue models
Traditional	Aggregation Conference Content creation Content licensing Discount sales Information collection Mass market Outsourcing Representative Sales commission Wholesale
Digital	Advertising based Aggregation Community based Content packaging Differential pricing Direct to customer eBook creation and sales Full service Multi-channel distribution Niche market Online promotion Pay per view POD Publishing service Self-publishing Shared revenue Site licensing or data licensing Subscription based Syndication

Strategy

Our initial research confirmed literature-based expectations that book publishers would understand the importance of having proper strategies for the issues surrounding digitization. This was particularly the case in relation to strategies for content creation and management, website development and staff training, POD and eBooks. Subsequent research indicated the need for a key strategic focus on promotion and communication, all heavily influenced by developments in social networking. Across the five categories, publishers are engaged to a greater or lesser degree in creating MySpace sites for the promotion of high-profile books, including the provision of different sites for different demographics by age and gender. This said, while publishers in all categories accept the inevitability of digitization, there remain concerns within the educational, professional, specialist and university press segments that, by going too far too fast, publishers might risk getting ahead of the market, a market where demand is likely to continue for both hard copy and eBooks.

One of the trade publishers interviewed routinely digitizes each new book and channels it to a digital archive. The intention here is not just to create a digital archive, but also to minimize the risk of problems over copyright. Other trade publishers have created digital departments or divisions to pursue a strategy aimed at making all their books available in various digital formats using XML-based production processes, and to deal with potential electronic rights and contractual issues. Similar strategies are being pursued in the educational, specialist and university press sectors. Publishers in the latter two categories are particularly concerned with issues to do with the copyright implications of adopting new technologies, a matter that is seen as the key to success in a digital environment.

Educational publishing is an interesting case here, in that, despite access to and ownership of a wide range of content, much of it linked to technologies such as electronic whiteboards, our case companies were quite conservative in their pronouncements on digitization. For example, they were quick to point out that the creation of digital strategies was, to a large extent, dependent upon customer requirements and on the level of technology infrastructure available within their target markets. Nonetheless, educational publishers were all too aware of the need to be vigilant in respect of changes in options and expectations, and of the growing volume and sophistication of products and services, not least those available through mobile and handheld devices.

Finally, there is a very strong belief within the specialist and university press segment that the integration of digitization with their pre-press operations will provide excellent opportunities to exploit backlists, POD and eBooks, along with the commercialization of their content into different formats.

It is clear from such examples that book publishers in all categories are well aware of the need to have strategies in place to deal with both the threats and the opportunities provided by digitization. As has been seen in previous chapters, however, good intentions alone are unlikely to solve the various problems involved. This issue will be taken up in the next chapter.

Traditional and Current Business Models for the Five Categories of Book Publisher

Our research indicates that the majority of the 14 case companies are operating traditional value and supply chains, but each with an element of hybridization. Furthermore, the focus on customers has grown in strength and the influence of digitization is reflected in the presence of new players and/or new roles for existing players. In general, educational publishers continue to exhibit greater adherence to traditional value chains, with specialist and professional publishers being further along the continuum towards digitization.

Based on interviews and discussions with publishers, we have constructed a range of business models both for individual firms and of a more generic, industry-wide nature. In this chapter, however, apart from a simplified generic model of book publishing, we have presented our findings in the form of sub- or atomic business models, which, as will be seen below, can operate either in stand-alone fashion or in combination with others. In general, these prototypes do not represent any wholesale jettisoning of tried and tested business models. Rather, they reflect a process of experimentation and combination, linked to ongoing changes in value and supply chains. Notwithstanding the evident similarities in these business models, clear differences have emerged in their scope, design and structure, and in sources and recipients of value. We now assess these models against the four key business model categories identified in Chapter 7, namely:

- bricks and mortar
- clicks and mortar
- collaborative
- freemium.

There is a wide range of categorizations and taxonomies of business models, many of which are relevant to digital markets and to book publishing. Frequently however, these taxonomies are largely descriptive in nature and have little to say about the design, description and implementation of the models concerned. In seeking to identify and construct business models for book publishing in Australia, not the least of our problems was to find a means to represent the flows and components involved. We finally came up with a notation (shown in Figure 9.1.) based upon that employed by Weill and Vitale (2001), which enabled the depiction of business model components and relationships as follows:

- Participants: represented as:
  - double-bordered rectangles (firms of interest)
  - single rectangles (subsidiaries or functional areas of firms of interest)
  - left- and -right-facing cones with rectangle (customers and suppliers)
  - rectangles with dotted lines on both sides (partners – organizations whose products or services help enhance demand for those of the firms of interest)
  - rectangles with dotted lines on all four sides (Database or websites of firms of interest).
- Relationships: where solid lines between participants indicate a relationship that can be either online or offline, and dotted lines indicate an electronic relationship between the parties. A solid line with opposite-facing arrows indicates the presence of a collaborative relationship.

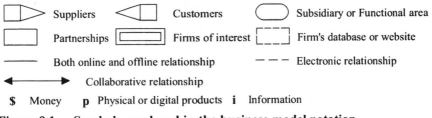

Figure 9.1   **Symbols employed in the business model notation**

- Flows: arrows represent major flows between participants, and can comprise flows of money ($), products or services, digital or physical (P) or information (I).

Bricks and mortar models

Most of our case companies are still using this traditional model, although more so in some categories than in others. In this regard, educational publishers conducting 95 per cent of their businesses using the bricks and mortar approach are the outstanding example. Bricks and mortar business models, being largely mass market in nature, do not distinguish between customer segments. Their value propositions, distribution channels, relationships and revenue streams all cater to one large, mass customer segment with broadly similar characteristics. So whereas the exact form of this traditional model varies to some extent between different categories of book publishers, and can incorporate alternative methods of operation, the fundamental structures are similar. The stages represented in this model are as follows:

Stage 1: Content acquisition: Acquiring a manuscript from an author.

Stage 2: Content development and book design: Developing and enhancing the manuscript via the editorial process, creating an appropriate book cover and page formats.

Stage 3: Prepress, printing, and binding: Preparing the finished product.

Stage 4: Marketing and sales: Managing the warehousing and the distribution of books, crafting a campaign to market and promote the book, selling the book through distribution channels, and supervision of all book returns.

Stage 5: Fulfilment: Handling all enquiries and orders from customers for new and backlist titles before, during, and in the after-sales period. Supervision of all sub-rights, foreign rights, foreign sales licensing activities and special sales.

All these stages can be encapsulated in the model depicted in Figure 9.2.

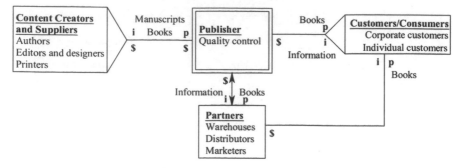

Figure 9.2   A generic business model for traditional book publishing

Case study 9.1   Traditional Business Model for an Educational Publisher

The following example, depicting the stages involved in the publication of hard-copy textbooks, reinforces the perception that educational publishers are more closely tied to bricks and mortar models than are other publishers. The entire process entails the operation of four atomic or sub-business models for, respectively, content creation, cooperative outsourcing of editing, cooperative outsourcing of printing, and selling through representatives.

Stage 1: Buy or license content from authors

This particular company has implemented two business models, one for its established authors and another for those engaged on the basis of casual contracts, for example as contributors to a book rather than as sole authors. The content creation model is shown in Figure 9.3.

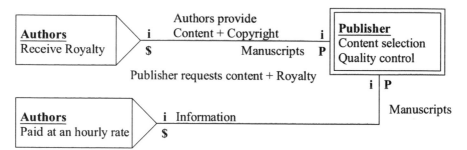

Figure 9.3   Content creation model for an educational publisher

Stage 2: Authors submit copy for editing

This stage has undergone a number of significant changes, including the online submission of author material and the outsourcing of various functions. The outsourcing model employed at this stage (Figure 9.4) was also used by the other educational publishers investigated.

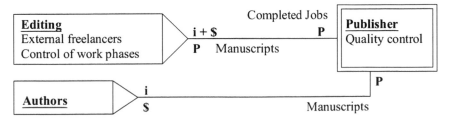

Figure 9.4   Editorial outsourcing model for an educational publisher

Stage 3: Printing

Printers (all outsourced, and mostly based overseas) produce the physical copy or, alternatively, a digital copy which is stored in databases for future use. The model is shown in Figure 9.5.

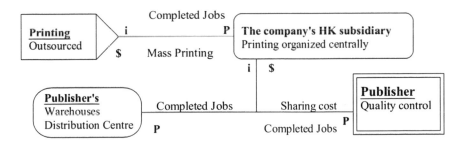

Figure 9.5   Printing outsourcing model for an educational publisher

Stage 4: Market through various channels, including sales representatives, print media and the firm's website

The company has many models linked with this stage, the most common being that of selling through company representatives. This model is shown in Figure 9.6.

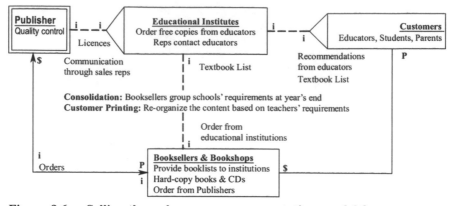

Figure 9.6   Selling through company representatives model for an educational publisher

Generally, textbooks have a three-year life cycle and their average annual sell-through rate runs at 90 per cent for the first year, 45 per cent for the second year and 10 per cent for the third year, a pattern reflected directly in profit levels. This type of model is ideal for publishers of textbooks, trade books and books such as Bibles which involve potentially large-scale distribution. Increased profits depend on the sale of units from the long-run model, which provides benefits for printers, paper manufacturers, publishers and, most importantly, the consumer, who pays a lower price for the book than if it were subject to a short run.

* * *

For different categories of book publishing, the details of each stage are different. For example, our professional publisher employs an information collection model, shown in Figure 9.7. It refers to the first stage in this model as that of harvesting information. This is achieved through the networks which it uses both to collect information and to find suitable authors (internal or external).

Clicks and mortar models

The clicks and mortar model, as its name implies, is much more digital in nature than its bricks and mortar counterpart. Our research confirmed that all the publishers interviewed were currently involved in some form of digital publishing activities, with some being more adventurous than others. None of the 14 case companies concerned described itself as being a digital book publisher. However, the specialist publishers and university presses believed themselves to be more advanced in this regard than the others.

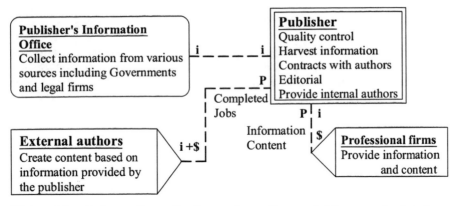

Figure 9.7   **Information collection and creation model for a professional publisher**

Case study 9.2: eBook Publishing Model for a Specialist Publisher

The example that follows is that of a four-stage business model for a specialist publisher.

Stage 1: Acquire content from authors or other owners (via licensing or payment)

These other content owners can be other publishers, both local and overseas. The content purchasing and licensing model is used in this stage, as shown in Figure 9.8.

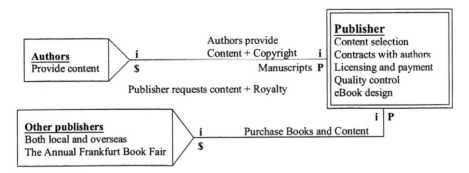

Figure 9.8   **Content purchasing and licensing model for a specialist publisher**

Stage 2: Design eBooks and upload them to the website

The major focuses here are on the design and conversion of digital files into four formats (Adobe, DX Reader, Microsoft Reader and Mobipocket), the creation of metadata and databases and, lastly, editing and quality assurance. During this stage all the technology issues are handled by a third party, whilst the publisher concentrates on managing the content. The general business models in this stage are the eBook creation model, as shown in Figure 9.9.

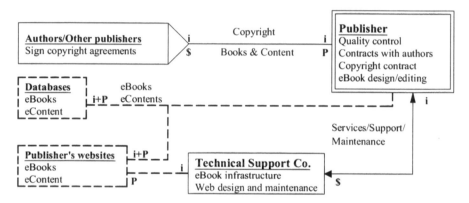

Figure 9.9   eBook creation model for a specialist publisher

Stage 3: Printing

This entails the operation of small eBook print runs of from 300 to 1,000 copies. As shown in Figure 9.10, the models employed is the POD model, which offers

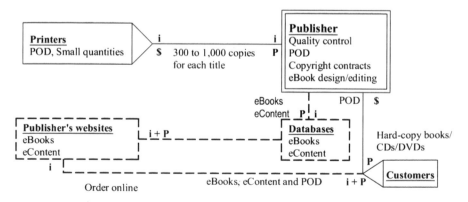

Figure 9.10   Combined POD printing and multi-channel delivery model for a specialist publisher

options with regard both to the size of the print run (single or multiple copies) and the delivery format (eBook, CD, hard copy).

Stage 4: Sales and marketing

The bulk of sales are conducted via the publisher's website. The promotion of both hard-copy books and eBooks also occurs through this medium, as well as through the websites of other eAggregators and through traditional media such as radio or TV. The business models employed are the direct-to-customer model, the aggregation model, the multi-online-distribution model and the site licensing model. A combined multi-online-distribution and aggregation model is shown in Figure 9.11.

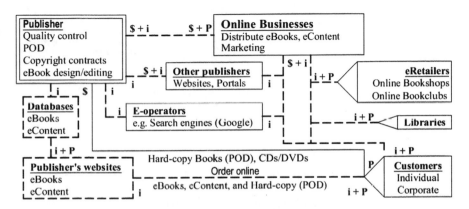

Figure 9.11   Combined multi-online-distribution and aggregation model for a specialist publisher

* * *

Used alongside traditional publishing business models, these clicks and mortar models focus on niche markets and serve various customer segments, with different distribution channels employed for different book formats. The existence of separate distribution channels, including traditional channels, can be a challenge when it comes to the setting of book prices. Costs can be reduced by using POD for small runs, but case company representatives expressed concern over the absence of a really functioning POD service in Australia, with attendant implications for any exploitation of long tail sales.

Case study 9.3: POD Model for a University Publisher

One very successful example of the use of print-on-demand is that of a university press that was visited during the course of our research. This publisher provides a POD service based largely on digitized internal content, including course notes, supplemented by the use of digital object identifiers (DOIs) for content from external sources. All material is copyrighted, with the use of DOIs ensuring that any royalties owing to other publishers are assured. The key distinguishing features of this operation are captured in three business models for, respectively, content packaging, licensing and sales. The repackaging of content obtained by purchase or licence from a range of sources is illustrated in Figure 9.12.

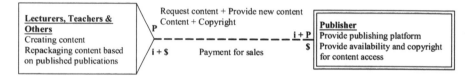

Figure 9.12   POD model for content packaging for a university publisher

The POD operation also entails obtaining and converting digital files, involving PDF and XML formats, and the creation of metadata and databases, editing, quality assurance and copyright confirmation (through the Copyright Agency DOI system). The related content licensing model is shown in Figure 9.13.

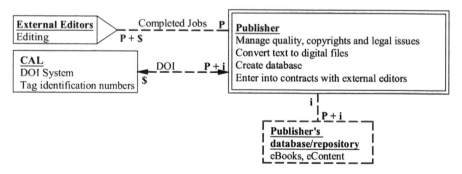

Figure 9.13   POD model for content licensing for a university publisher

Under this POD model sales are achieved either through the university bookshop or online to students and staff. This direct-to-customer model is shown in Figure 9.14.

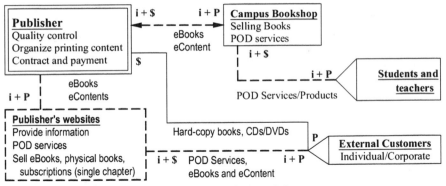

Figure 9.14   POD direct-to-customer sales model

* * *

Our research confirms that the uptake of clicks and mortar models varies from publisher to publisher. Similarly, routes to profit and the calculation of profit and loss are more complicated than in traditional publishing.

Collaborative models

As mentioned in the section on stakeholders above, collaboration is a growing and important option for book publishers. Our research revealed that trade publishers and professional publishers were actively engaged in this activity.

Case study 9.4: Collaborative Publishing Model for a Trade Publisher

The following example describes some of the current collaborative business models employed by one of the trade publishers interviewed during the course of our research.

Stage 1: Buy or licence content from authors

The company's content licensing model is shown in Figure 9.15.

Stage 2: Authors submit their copy for editing

At this stage some publishers engage in outsourcing. However, in order to exercise control over content, most publishers prefer to be independent in this area. This stage includes the obtaining and conversion of digital files, involving PDF and XML formats, the creation of metadata and databases, and editing and quality assurance. Business models commonly used in this stage include the aggregated model, the full service model and the shared revenue model.

Figure 9.15   Content licensing model for a trade publisher

The full service model for the company includes everything from the conversion of author files into digital formats and the creation of metadata and databases, to editing and quality assurance and sales and marketing. The company has distribution subsidiaries in each of its major publishing centres (UK, USA and Australia). These cater not only for their parent publishing arms, but also to the needs of third parties. This includes, for example, the collection of rights monies for other publishers and the generation of revenue from their own distribution service. This not only allows the other publishers to share costs and save time, but also leaves them free to concentrate on core business issues. The company's full service model is shown in Figure 9.16.

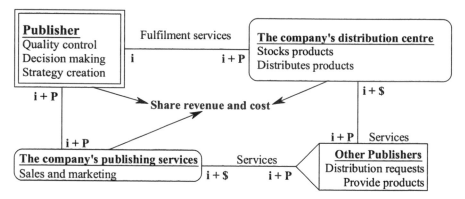

Figure 9.16   Full service business model for a trade publisher

Stage 3: Printers (all outsourced) produce the physical copy

Publishers digitize the content and develop eBooks (some of which are developed in-house, but most of which are developed in cooperation with third parties). POD or aggregated models can be linked with this stage. For the case company concerned, the aggregation here entails collaboration between the company and an Indian partner (who also works with third parties). This accounts for all of the company's printing operations and eBook development. The company's aggregated model of eBook creation is shown in Figure 9.17.

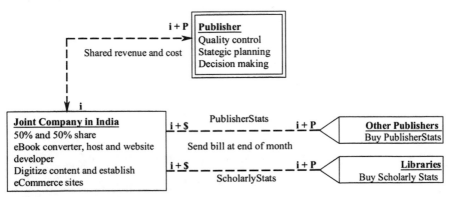

Figure 9.17   Aggregated model of eBook creation for a trade publisher

Stage 4: Market through various channels

Trade publishers generally aim for minimal sales from their own websites, fearing channel conflict and the likelihood of upsetting booksellers. The company uses both traditional and electronic channels to sell its products. The business model used in this stage is a multi-channel distribution model. It can be modified to suit various products. Other models which the company can link with this stage are the direct to customer model, the publisher's representatives selling to booksellers model, the online-to-customer and online-to-retailer models, the site licences model, and the subscription model. A combined model of subscription, site licensing and data licensing is shown in Figure 9.18.

Stage 5: Archive content in digital repositories, allowing for content reprints or reuse in the future

An example linked to this stage is the collaborative model (shown in Figure 9.19), which is closely aligned to the TitlePage industry-run price information and availability service.

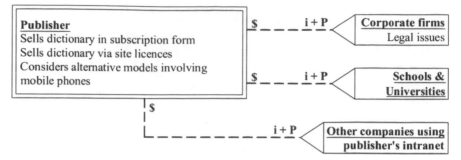

Figure 9.18   Subscription, site licence and data licensing model

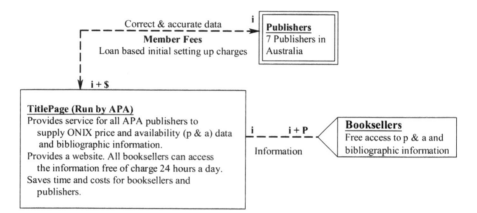

Figure 9.19   Collaborative model for a trade publisher

The company's revenue streams are derived from services provided to third parties and from sales through its distribution channels, with the most lucrative being those of traditional hard-copy books based upon long-run models.

* * *

As emphasized repeatedly, no one model is appropriate for all companies, as they all have their own strategies, products and customer segments, which will require modifications to models. There is, however, a growing trend towards the creation of collaborative customer-focused models. This trend is discussed in the next chapter.

Freemium models

As indicated in Chapter 8, freemium models involve the provision of free access to certain types of content, while providing a higher level of service to those willing to pay for it. Osterwalder and Pigneur (2009) explain that such arrangements are possible because of the low marginal cost of serving additional free users. These models are mainly web-based and the products and services concerned are in digital form. Although freemium models did not feature to any significant extent in the work of our 14 case companies, they are an important development and, as such, are covered in the final chapter of this book.

Meanwhile, another free-to-user model, the Open Access publishing model, continues to operate in certain areas of publishing. Although our research did not specifically address the issue of Open Access publishing models (which we viewed as being more relevant to journal than to book publishing), the matter was raised during interviews. None of the case study companies believed that open access models posed a threat to the book publishing industry, either at that time or in the foreseeable future. Indeed, the overwhelming consensus among book publishers was that, while potentially useful in terms of relationship building, Open Access did not make much sense, as what it actually amounts to is publishers giving their product away for nothing.

An explicit interest in business models among book publishers in Australia is a relatively recent phenomenon. Until quite recently, the nature of book publishing did not allow for much variation in the range of activities and transactions involved. However, globalization, the threat of competition from non-traditional as well as traditional sources and the hyperbole that inevitably surrounds advances in technology have all led publishers to revisit fundamental issues of value and profit and of how these might be modelled. It is safe to say that, in general, the need to consider new, more appropriate business models in a context of growing digitization is now widely acknowledged by book publishers. They also understand that the business environment is volatile and that there can be no single model to suit all circumstances.

Depending on their products and services, their distribution channels, their customers and business strategies, publishers will need to design business models for each stage of their value chains. This activity will undoubtedly reflect the growing importance of customer choice and of multi-channel distribution facilities.

Despite some variation in the level of commitment to digitization, all the case study companies were keen to develop business models suitable for operation in both the old and the new business environments. Traditional players continue to operate familiar and profitable business models, while implementing or participating in hybrids which allow for the activities of additional players and the impact of digital technologies. More recent entrants into the market, notably among specialist publishers, are already moving into largely digital operating environments.

Chapter 10
The Future of Book Publishing

Introduction

The previous chapter provided an overview of traditional and current business models in Australian-based book publishing. Owing both to their Australian provenance and to their limited number, these models are best regarded as being indicative rather than comprehensive, both in coverage and in application. That said, the majority of the companies involved were Australian offshoots of global publishing empires, and all of them were engaged in tackling the challenges posed by changes in markets and technologies. Furthermore, all publishers today, whatever their location, categorization and target markets, face the common challenge of designing business models against a background of digitization, unrelenting competition and the growing power of customers.

Our research confirms that familiar and profitable book publishing business models are continuing to operate, alongside experimental and hybrid models which allow for the activities of additional players and the impact of digital technologies. In many cases this involves participation by various stakeholders as both providers and recipients of value within these arrangements. This chapter begins by looking at a range of alternative business models which, while located outside the traditional book publishing domain, are of real significance to its current and future operations. It then considers a number of emergent business models within book publishing. Finally, it abstracts from all these developments in order to anticipate what the near future is likely to hold for global book publishing.

Anybody Can be a Publisher: Alternative Publishing Models

The internet and the World Wide Web have enabled major improvements in the storage and delivery of all forms of content. The ability to reproduce perfect copies of content assets and to use compression technologies for distribution has opened up new horizons for content distribution and exploitation. Although such developments have been welcomed by publishers, they have also brought the threat of new and increased competition in an environment within which it seems anybody can become a publisher.

As a consequence of such developments there is now a trend towards the emergence of new kinds of publishing models that do not require the presence of book publishers. As evidence for this trend, Osterwalder and Pigneur (2009) have identified eight publishing models, only one of which involves a traditional publisher. In this section we will consider several alternative models. Although all these models can be seen as posing a threat to traditional book publishing businesses, their growing presence in the market could just as easily help to encourage an innovative and competitive response from mainstream book publishing. The three alternative models described below are all variants on the common theme of author independence and are, respectively, business models for self-publishing, social publishing and community publishing.

Self-publishing models

This kind of model manifests itself in different forms. One such form allows authors to be completely independent, setting up their own website and organizing all the functions of printing and distribution, managing, marketing and promotion. This model is more likely to be aimed at niche markets, and often implemented by established authors with the experience and expertise to monitor the costs and potential benefits. Its greatest potential, however, is as a vehicle for new authors or for those unable to find an outlet for their work through established book publishing channels.

Case study 10.1: Lulu.com

This kind of model manifests itself in different forms. One such form allows authors to be completely independent, setting up their own website and organizing all the functions of printing and distribution, managing, marketing and promotion. This model is more likely to be aimed at niche markets, and often implemented by established authors with the experience and expertise to monitor the costs and potential benefits. Its greatest potential, however, is as a vehicle for new authors or for those unable to find an outlet for their work through established book publishing channels.

Another form of the self-publishing model involves collaboration between authors and a variety of organizations, including marketing companies and online bookshops, as well as those created specifically to serve the self-publishing market. All these companies provide a range of fulfilment services which allow authors the flexibility of choosing from what is available to meet their individual needs. Some of these services are provided free of charge, whereas for others payment is required. Authors are required to meet the printing costs and can choose from a number of format options, including printed books or eBooks, CD and DVD. One very good example of a self-publishing service is that offered by Lulu.com.

Lulu.com epitomizes the potentially disruptive presence of new self-publishing models that challenge the hegemony of traditional industry gatekeepers by providing a facility whereby anyone can publish a book. It offers this service on the basis of a set of relatively simple publishing tools that enable anybody to format and upload digital content. There is also the attraction of gaining access to a potential global marketplace, as Lulu.com has millions of registered users and attracts two million visitors to its site every month. The key activities and services available through Lulu.com include:

- Publishing: the publishing service is user friendly and there are no set-up fees. Lulu also provides a wide range of related services, such as pre-publishing, graphics, translations, marketing and publicity. All these services attract fees on the part of the customer.
- Pricing: the revenue model is particularly attractive from an author point of view, with 80 per cent of royalties going to authors and the rest to Lulu. The author sets the price, with Lulu printing and shipping each item on POD for a 20 per cent commission on each sale.
- Marketing and sales: a range of marketing and selling alternatives is available, including through Lulu Marketplace or by listing on the Google or Yahoo search engines and the Amazon and Barnes & Noble websites.
- Connectivity and contact: the benefits offered to users include access to social networking and the provision of various web tools to help people connect to each other. These include: Forums, Lulu Blog, Newsletters, Lulu Groups, and Events, for example, meetings with authors.

It is hardly surprising that, as the popularity of user-generated content continues to grow, Lulu.com is the leader in the market for self-publishing. Whereas around 280,000 books were published in traditional format in the United States in 2008, during 2009, Lulu.com published over 400,000 titles (Lulu.com 2010). In light of such evidence it would appear that Lulu.com could well turn out to be a serious competitor for the established book publishing houses. Indeed, at the time of writing Lulu.com is reported to be preparing for an Initial Public Offering some time in 2010 (Jones 2010).

Lulu.com is also enhancing its credentials in the world of web-based publishing through a growing range of strategic alliances. In 2008, Lulu.com formed a strategic relationship with the social networking company WeRead, an entity with something in excess of two million registered members via social networking sites such as Facebook, MySpace and Bebo. This agreement seeks to exploit the core capabilities of both companies by combining the functionality of Lulu.com's free self-publishing tools and distribution capabilities with the richness and reach of WeRead's readership communities. To date, WeRead members have contributed more than 1.5 million book reviews to these networks, while also listing their favourite books, providing book recommendations and participating in online discussions. The perceived win-win nature of this alliance is evident in statements made by some of the principals involved. Hence, the President and CEO of Lulu enterprises claimed that, by providing a better match between writers and readers, the agreement would transform publishing by bringing together traditional and self-published works in one marketplace (Andriani 2008). To this, WeRead's co-founder added that the alliance marked the first step towards the democratization of publishing, whereby anyone should be able to write a book and let the marketplace rate it fairly in a way that people could trust (Andriani 2008).

In 2008 Lulu also forged a partnership with the Scribd social document-sharing site. Under this arrangement Lulu adopted the use of Scribd's iPaper viewer to display Lulu's free eBooks online at the Lulu.com website. Lulu also employs a unique feature of Scribd that enables the display of Google's AdSense within iPaper. The arrangement is that Scribd will pay blog owners who embed documents in their blogs using iPaper, with payment based on the number of ad impressions served via Google AdSense. This advertising dimension in effect subsidizes the provision of free content to users.

The iPaper format was designed to operate like a YouTube for PDFs and other standard document formats. With iPaper, publishers can easily upload and share their documents online via the Scribd.com website. The site provides an avenue where document creators can publish and share their files and can email, download or embed documents elsewhere. The document creator can also choose to secure the file by assigning it read-only status. This provides the option to restrict access on the basis of the privacy settings selected by the content owner, with no requirement for DRM. Under this arrangement Scribd is paid a 20 per cent commission for sharing its technology. (This is discussed in greater detail later in this chapter.)

Lulu.com's business model is based on the provision of a forum that will help niche and new authors to bring their work to the marketplace. It has the potential to eliminate such entry barriers as the gate-keeping activities of traditional publishers by providing authors with the tools to complete the full publishing process in an online environment. This is in direct contrast to the traditional model of selecting material that publishers think will appeal to the market. There has been a very positive response from those who have adopted Lulu.com's self-service tools to publish and market their products. In addition to providing access to markets, this can be a very cost-effective affair, as books are only printed subject to demand. This process also provides Lulu.com with the benefits of a no sale, no cost arrangement. Figure 10.1 shows a brief version of Lulu's business model.

The primary costs for Lulu.com involve platform management and development expenses. Lulu.com receives a 20 per cent commission from each sale, with publishing service fees representing the bulk of its revenue stream.

* * *

Social publishing models

Social publishing models are similar to those in the self-publishing category, with the major distinction that they place greater emphasis upon social activities and sharing. By way of example, we will describe the activities of Scribd.com, whose stated aim is to provide an efficient and convenient service to both authors and publishers and to make a wider range of content available to end readers.

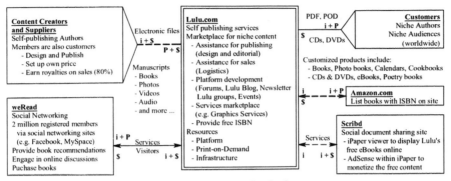

Figure 10.1   Abbreviated business model for Lulu.com

Case study 10.2: Scribd.com

Scribd is now the largest global social publishing company. Its global document-sharing site handles over 50,000 uploads daily and is said to contain approximately 10 times the amount of content of Wikipedia (Pagliarini 2009). Every month millions of people use this site both to publish their own material and to search for original writings and documents. In many ways Scribd epitomizes the knowledge-intensive company, not least through its creative use of technology to provide a novel range of services to its users. This includes its innovative iPaper document-reader technology, which has propelled Scribd to the forefront of an ongoing transformation of the way in which written works are distributed, marketed and shared. The efficient conversion of file formats using iPaper technology means that, for example, PDF, Word, PowerPoint and Excel formats can all be converted into web documents that can be shared globally (scribd.com 2009). Scribd's customers include print and media publishing companies, authors, corporations and organizations.

Following its launch in March 2007, Scribd Inc. focused its attention on two areas of interest, namely, documenting and social interaction.

- **Documenting** The site is now highly ranked in global terms, with more than 35 billion words in its system. It contains a wide variety of digital content, ranging from academic papers and PowerPoint presentations to recipes and electronic books, and all easily accessible for visitors to the site. Hence it has been claimed that as YouTube is to video, and Flickr is to photography, so Scribd is becoming to the written word (Johnson 2009). With Scribd, users can upload documents of any description, before they are converted into a Flash-based reading format (iPaper) or made available for downloading or sharing online.
- **Social interaction** Scribd has been described as being in essence an exercise in the democratization of publishing. This includes the building

of a central hub, called Project Social, from which all its written material –
user-generated and professional – can be made instantly available (Johnson
2009). Scribd.com home and profile pages emphasize the social aspect of
written works and not only allow the site's users to share, download, read
and purchase eBooks, but also make it easier for people to share comments
and to follow (in the social networking context) authors, publishers and
each other (Kinsella 2009). Among the specific social features of the
Scribd.com services are:

- a 'scribble box' enabling the instantaneous publication of user
  comments
- publisher RSS feeds
- a follower/following system
- a one-click publishing widget.

Scribd is currently working on a project that will allow people to create reading
lists to share with others and is cooperating with Twitter and Facebook to interface
with those sites. The goal is for scribd.com to become a truly interactive reading
community.

Scribd has clearly established its position in the digital environment through
provision of a cost-effective service that facilitates the building of business
relationships and enables its users to:

- create profiles: by sharing works, managing documents and creating
  reading lists;
- publish instantly: by uploading content for instantaneous sharing with
  others;
- build communities: by constructing communities of people who share
  common interests and experiences;
- discover new work: by accessing various forums to locate content of
  interest;
- enjoy the benefits of real-time reporting and updating of content: which is
  a real advantage when compared with a lag of a month or so in the case of
  most eBook resellers (Pagliarini 2009).

Scribd opened its first eBook store in May 2009, with several well-known authors
under contract and more than 650 O'Reilly eBooks available for preview and sale.
All included DRM-free PDF downloads with every purchase (Savikas 2009).
Since then the business had developed rapidly and is already having an effect on
the traditional book publishing market. Deals with traditional publishers, including
Simon & Schuster, have subsequently been signed, and in June 2009 Scribd agreed
to sell 5,000 eBooks from Simon & Schuster, bringing bestselling writers including
Stephen King and Dan Brown to the platform (Ha 2009). Savikas (2009) indicates
that Scribd is preparing to add ePub as a format within the near future.

Publishing through Scribd provides an efficient and cost-effective alternative to the use of traditional publishing channels. Nor does publishing in one format preclude publishing in another. Hence, concerned that his novel *The Sower* included so many topical references that it might be dated by the time it was published, author Kemble Scott decided to self-publish the book on Scribd's website, selling it for $2 a copy with 20 per cent of the revenue going to Scribd. However, *The Sower*'s success on Scribd attracted the attention of publisher Numina Press, who, using POD technology, was able to make it available in bookshops in just 29 days. The book became a bestseller within two months (Ha 2009).

In 2009 Scribd agreed to provide its powerful software iPaper to major newspapers such as the *New York Times* and *Los Angeles Times*, with the likelihood that others, including the *Chicago Tribune* and three popular blogs – The Huffington Post, TechCrunch and Mediabistro – would follow suit (Boyd 2009). Web documents from these sources can be shared on Scribd.com or on any website that allows embeds. This can offer the following benefits to news organizations:

- the embedding of documents in news stories and added transparency to the reporting process;
- an increase in the time that people spend in reading each story;
- increased brand recognition on and off their website through reader logos;
- retention of recognition for original document uploads, regardless of where the document travels to on the internet;
- increased traffic through links back to the original story;
- allowing visitors to share the documents on Facebook, Twitter and blogs.

Scribd's initial goal was to build its library of content, with texts that ranged from published paper books to unedited manuscripts. It then contrived to make those texts available to users at random, either to read via computer, buying through the Scribd store or to download to a device of the user's choosing, including the iPhone. From May 2009, authors could choose to forgo copyright protection and publish as an unprotected PDF, which would allow the document to be read on the Kindle and via the Kindle's iPhone application. Saleable texts are processed through a copyright verification system to ensure that users are not scanning copyrighted texts and selling them (iPhone News 2009). However, one area where Scribd is currently at a disadvantage in competing with mainstream publishers is that of sales and marketing, which for Scribd is largely limited to what can be achieved through its website.

Scribd's revenue streams are derived from four main areas:

- Advertising: Scribd attracts high click rates from people engaged in general information-seeking activities or who, having engaged via a search engine are seeking something specific. This influx of visitors makes the site an attractive target for advertisers.

- Scribd store: the store is perhaps the most popular feature of the site, and is highly popular with mainstream publishers, authors and the public. The business logic involved is simple. Content owners charge a fee for access to their online content, paying 20 per cent of this to Scribd in return for its hosting the service.
- Selling eBooks: the Scribd site is emerging as a popular platform for the sale of eBooks, with partners including such prestigious imprints as those of Harvard University Press and Simon & Schuster.
- Sharing its iPaper technology with publishers and news organizations.

The key costs incurred by Scribd are those of technology development and employee salaries. Table 10.1 summarizes the key elements of the Scribd business model.

If the number of companies seeking to do business with it is any guide, Scribd appears to be facing a rosy future. Currently it has a problem in that its technology base is not able to support anything like the demands made upon it by potential clients and thus, the company must be selective as to who it deals with. Nevertheless, this amounts to an impressive list which includes: Harvard University Press, Lonely Planet, O'Reilly Media, Pearson Schools, Random House Publishing Group, Simon & Schuster and the *New York Times*. However, despite its success in this new market, Scribd does not have a monopoly. Currently, Scribd's primary source of income is based on its advanced software, iPaper, which is considered to be superior to that of its competitors. Nevertheless, competitors hot on its heels include DocStoc, Issuu, and Edocr, not to mention Google with its own embeddable doc viewers (Kincaid 2009). A simplified business model for Scribd is shown in Figure 10.2.

Table 10.1   Key elements of the Scribd business model

Element	Brief description
Value propositions	Advanced document-view software: iPaperAttractive social connectivity
Products and services	Provides iPaper software to publishers and news organizations A platform for self-publishing Scribd store for publishing, downloading, purchasing and selling content Selling eBooks for publishers on Scribd store Free online distribution
Stakeholders	Authors: individual creators Publishers News organizations Social networking sites
Intangible resources	Software development knowledge Established brand name Established customer base
Cost structure	Technology development Employee salaries
Revenue models	Advertising model Virtual marketplace: Scribd store Technology sharing with publishers and news organizations
Strategies	Ongoing development of document-view software: iPaper Expansion of their social network Global expansion of Scribd store

Source: www.scribd.com, www.scribd.com/store

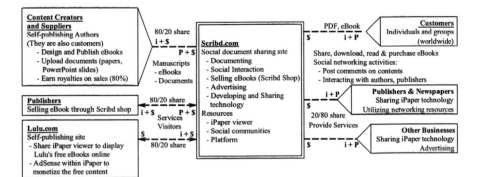

Figure 10.2   Abbreviated business model for Scribd.com

Community publishing models

In view of the growing significance of communities on the web, and specifically on social networks, it was only to be expected that they would emerge as a force in the book publishing arena. As an example of a successful community book publishing project we recount the experience of a group founded by two Swiss-based academics, Alexander Osterwalder and Yves Pigneur.

Case study 10.3: Business Innovation Hub

In pursuit of their long-standing interest in business models, the founders of the Business Innovation Hub succeeded in building up a global community of like-minded people, practitioners as well as academics, reinforced by the inclusion of several key players with specialist expertise in design, creativity and editing. By the end of the project the community consisted of some 470 members in 45 countries and the resulting book, entitled *Business Model Generation*, appeared in September 2009, in both hard-copy and digital form.

Although the project took nine years from conception to publication, the actual writing process began as a blog in 2006. This was achieved largely on the basis of an extremely effective participant engagement and project management process designed for the purpose. This comprised a transparent set of processes and practices to facilitate the injection of chunks of content into the Hub community and to stimulate both feedback and further contributions. Participants paid to be members of this community publishing project, with membership fees located on a sliding scale whereby early joiners paid only a nominal rate and those who joined in midstream paid more. The writing process entailed the submission of contributions from members to any of nine distinct content chunks. As the work progressed, all aspects of the book, including its content, design, illustrations and structure were scrutinized and subject to the feedback of Hub members. The core team acknowledged the feedback and incorporated the input, where practicable, into the book's structure.

Contributors worked to a common view of the key elements of business models which are summarized Table 10.2.

Before the final version of the book was completed, a pre-production draft was presented to a meeting of Hub affiliates in Amsterdam. This meeting was in effect a 'share and compare' exercise, the outcome of which was to be the final version of the book. Attendees reviewed over 200 business models presented in advance by Hub members and watched a video that summarized the entire book-writing process. The result was a number of rewrites of the text and completion of the initial print run of the book.

Table 10.2   Key elements in the business model adopted by the Business Innovation Hub

Element	Brief description
Value propositions	Differentiation: an entirely different format and business model, along with a story that will make the book makes stand out in a crowded market Visual, practical, and beautiful handbook for business model innovators Co-creation of a potential bestseller Personalized books for companies and their customers
Key activities	Anything beyond content creation is outsourced to readily available service providers. Their key activities include: • Content production • Hub management • Guerilla marketing and word of mouth • Logistics and shipping Activities such as design, marketing, and technology are all outsourced
Stakeholders	Individual customers: people with similar interests, and who are described variously as visionaries, game changers, and challengers Group customers: entrepreneurs, executives, consultants, academics and companies Hub members: who are both co-creators and also customers The movement (outsourced design consultants) Ning platform Amazon.com Third-party logistics company Publishers
Intangible resources	Methodology (new way of publishing a book) Blog and visibility on the web Relationship with a powerful network of 470 members (co-creators), most of whom have their own blogs or websites Knowledge from every single member of the network
Cost structure	Design Content production Printing Distribution
Revenue models	Revenue comes from the following sources: • Hub membership fees • Advance and post-publication sales • Royalties from publishers • Customized versions for companies and their clients • Sales from various channels
Strategies	Innovation, communication, collaboration

Source: Osterwalder and Pigneur 2009, www.businessmodelgeneration.com

Much of the effectiveness of this venture can be attributed not only to its process of engagement but also to the approaches and tools used in production of the book. These are summarized in Table 10.3.

Table 10.3   Approaches and tools used during the creation of the book

Key activities	Tools
Strategy	Environmental scanning Business model canvas Customer empathy mapping
Content and R&D	Customer insights Case studies
Open process	Online platform Co-creation Access to unfinished work Commenting and feedback
Design	Open design process Moodboards Paper mockups, visualization, illustration, photography

Source: Osterwalder and Pigneur 2009.

In overall terms, the success of this community publishing project can in large measure be attributed to the common, or at least overlapping, interests of all concerned. The book was produced and launched by a group of people who were at once paying customers and readers and co-creators of content. Also important was the use of a mix of direct and indirect channels and of a phased approach to publication. The community-based approach also lent itself well to viral marketing and word-of-mouth promotion. The channels employed also included Amazon.com, book stores and intermediation through publishers. The co-creators participated not for monetary gain, but for the satisfaction of involvement in the community and the building of relationships which could continue after the book was finished. There seems to be every likelihood that many of these relationships will be maintained through the Hub (businessmodelhub.com) and business model events. Figure 10.3 depicts a simplified version of the community book publishing project business model.

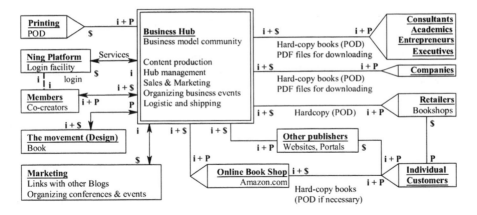

Figure 10.3   Abbreviated business model for the Business Innovation Hub

* * *

These three cases help to reinforce the argument that, in the digital age, just about anybody can be a publisher. Furthermore, the nature and functionality of self-publishing have changed beyond recognition, as compared with the position that existed only a few years ago. Today not only are the processes involved in self-publishing much less complex and cheaper, but also with digitization, the application of Web 2.0 and social technologies has served to reduce distance between content creator and readers. With blogs and social networking sites providing cheap and easy ways to reach thousands of readers, it is likely that the distinction between publishing and self-publishing will become much less meaningful in the foreseeable future (Waxman Literary Agency News 2010).

Emerging Collaborative POD Publishing Models

As explained in Chapter 9, POD offers the prospect of relatively small print runs, while at the same time providing savings to publishers by way of reduced stockholding and warehousing costs. However, as our Australian-based research has revealed, POD technology can be expensive and there are few international standards. Moreover, POD is often less cost-effective than the alternative of large print runs using conventional means. More to the point, however, in-house POD is not, as yet, able to provide the solution to the distribution problems facing book publishers and authors.

In the main, publishers have engaged with this technology by employing the services of specialist POD companies. The presence of these third-party providers of services to authors and publishers is likely to have a substantial impact upon book publishing. To explain the nature and dimensions of this impact, Lightning Source has been chosen as an example of a POD service provider.

Case study 10.4: POD Publishing Model for Lightning Source

Lightning Source is a subsidiary of the Ingram Content Group Inc., which has a history of partnership arrangements with publishers, booksellers and librarians going back more than 40 years. Lightning Source was created to provide printing, distribution and digital fulfilment services, with all responsibilities for rights and the payment of author royalties remaining the responsibility of the publishers concerned. The company specializes in meeting on-demand printing needs in a range of formats, including those of hardcover, trade paperback and colour books. The company also provides short-run and galley printing services. Lightning Source has two primary lines of business:

- An on-demand printing division which prints books to order in a range of formats within two business days, whether the order is for one book or one hundred. Short-run and web-direct distribution orders are printed and fulfilled within 5–10 business days.
- A comprehensive eBook digital fulfilment system which provides a full range of services, from digital rights management to content delivery in multiple formats.

By using Lightning Source's POD system, publishers are said to be able to offer more books to the market, reduce their investment in printing, warehousing and inventory, and fulfil orders punctually. The specific benefits for publishers include:

- Flexibility: print runs can range from the provision of one copy of a book to a reviewer, to 5,000 copies to a warehouse. Offset printing (traditional printing) is available for paperbacks in quantities in excess of 2,000 or for hardbacks in quantities over 750. This offset printing aspect does not represent a component of Print to Order. Traditional printing services are also available for titles requiring large print orders, foreign languages or other versions.
- Control: publishers are able to set the wholesale and retail pricing structure and, if applicable, operate a returns policy. Publishers take orders from booksellers, libraries and, where appropriate, from online consumers, and Lightning Source subsequently processes the orders.

- Cost savings: in particular, those resulting from improved inventory control and reduced overheads (for example, in printing, inventory and warehousing).
- Multiple channel distribution: this can be achieved through a range of distribution channels, including:
  - Ingram Distribution Channel: servicing over 30,000 wholesalers, retailers and booksellers globally, with orders fulfilled and ready for shipment within 12 hours;
  - other distribution channels: these include a comprehensive array of wholesalers and retailers, including booksellers whose decision it is whether or not to stock the titles of individual publishers. Depending on the different contractual agreements between distributors and publishers, paperbacks can be ready to ship within two to five days, with hardbacks available in up to eight days;
  - Lightning Source Distribution Partners: for example, Amazon.com, Baker & Taylor, and Barnes & Noble.

For medium to large publishers, Lightning Source also offers the following assistance:

- Advertising: after the signing of contractual arrangements, Lightning Source will add publishers' titles to its electronic catalogues, reaching a vast network of points of sale.
- Revival of backlist sales: with Lightning print on demand and distribution services, titles are perpetually in print and available, offering the possibility of maximizing sales.
- Complete fulfilment services: publishers can also reduce overheads by authorizing Lightning Source to function as a fulfilment house.
- Minimized returns and pulping: because every book is derived from a request, returns are minimal and the need for pulping is virtually eliminated.

Lightning Source's digital warehouse currently houses 500,000 titles. Typically, 500 titles are added daily to the digital warehouse, and more than 50,000 books have been produced in response to 27,000 orders (lightningsource.com). All these books are printed efficiently and to a high standard, with quality-control checks being completed on each book prior to shipment.

Lightning Source claims to offer a print and distribution model to cover every publishing situation. Five printing models are available for customers to choose from, each vertically integrated and with the complete production process driven by a single communication. These models include:

- **Print to order** This model begins operation when the publisher places an order. After the book is printed, Lightning Source dispatches it through either the publisher's or its own distribution channels. Charging the wholesale price (less printing), it uses ISBNs as identifiers, and provides an inventory activity statement every month. Hence, it is claimed, publishers are being reimbursed for the use of their copyrighted content with virtually no input from themselves.

- **Print to publisher** In this direct-to-publisher model, Lightning Source operates as a partner in order fulfilment. On the receipt of orders, it acts on behalf of the publishers, assuming responsibility for the printing and delivery of books to warehouses, retailers, authors and consumers. As orders are fulfilled using shipping tags embossed with the publisher's logo, it appears to the customer that they have come directly from the publisher. In return, the publishers reimburse Lightning Source for the costs of printing, handling and shipping. Orders in excess of 50 copies receive discounts.

- **Print to warehouse** In this model, publishers are able to integrate Lightning Source's POD service into their supply chain. After a publisher places an order, Lightning Source prints the books and ships them to the publishers' warehouse for cross-docketing with other orders. This allows the publisher to consolidate stocked and non-stocked titles. Depending on the operational requirements at publishers' warehouses, this service is essentially designed for larger publishers who have substantial ordering and cross-docketing capacities. The publishers pay Lightning Source for the costs involved in printing, handling and shipping.

- **Digital print runs** or publishers who prefer to maintain a token inventory on hand, Lightning Source offers volume discounts on larger orders of digitally printed titles. To take advantage of this opportunity, publishers must order minimum quantities of 25 and have them delivered to a single location. Once again, Lightning Source is paid for printing, handling and shipping.

- **Offset print runs** Lightning Source offers an offset printing service when the volume required makes this the most cost-effective approach. A minimum order of 1,500 (paperback) or 750 (hardback) copies is typical for this model. As the life cycle of the title progresses, Lightning Source can easily switch from digital to offset printing – ensuring ready availability and low costs. For this model, Lightning Source collects the wholesale price, deducts print costs and pays publishers the balance. The price for this service is $12.00 per year per title.

Source: www.lightningsource.com

* * *

Rosenthal (2004) analysed a POD book publishing model, showing its underlying cost and benefit structures. This revealed that Ingram normally carries Lightning Source POD books on a short-discount basis (a discount of less than 55 per cent). Rosenthal (2004) argues that this service is attractive not just to publishers, but also to authors interested in self-publishing, because they can earn far greater royalties than the 4 to 7.5 per cent normally accruing on full-price hard-copy paperbacks.

Publishers who are currently partners of Lightning Source (for example Simon & Schuster, Oxford University Press, John Wiley & Sons, and Harcourt Trade Publishers) acknowledge that Lightning Source has proved itself to be an important strategic partner. The Vice President of Strategic Operations of Harcourt Trade Publishers confirmed this position and said that its relationship with Ingram had been pivotal in boosting sales of POD titles. Regarding the immediate future, it seems clear that Lightning Source will play a leading role in shaping the future of integrated digital distribution. Indeed, the Director of Business Development of Oxford University Press stated that without the assistance of Lightning Source's cost-effective package of POD services the company would have struggled to achieve the significant sales revenues that it has reached (www.lightningsource. com/testimonials.aspx).

Emerging eBook Publishing Models

Issues in eBook publishing models

As indicated in Chapter 4, book publishers are well aware that in many respects digitization is a two-edged sword. On the one hand, there are the potential benefits in terms of reduced costs, extended market reach and the longevity of digital content. On the other hand, there are concerns over issues of digital rights and copyright protection, along with potential channel conflict and the alienation of booksellers and distributors. One example was the price war between Amazon and B&N with both pricing eBooks at $9.99 while also offering a range of discounts on hard-copy volumes. In the latter case, the 2009 edition of the *Oxford Atlas of the World*, which had a cover price of $80, was available through Amazon for $27.20. Not only did this amount to a 66 per cent discount but also, it all but guaranteed that Amazon was losing money on each sale (Nawotka 2009b). This situation has already impacted substantially upon publishers as well as on booksellers.

The ambiguity in perception is also present with regard to the specific example of eBooks. Although a majority of our case study companies were optimistic about the future of eBooks, there remains a sense that for many publishers their current commitment to eBooks is as much a matter of insurance as anything else. They are scared of missing the eBook boat, should it eventually come in, but for the time being they are reluctant to commit fully to the costs and the effort required to make a success of this venture.

This caution is all too understandable when seen from the perspective of commentators such as Schnittman (2009), who argues that, as things stand, the current eBook model is not viable, owing to the costs involved. As he points out, despite the absence of manufacturing costs, publishers still have to meet the costs of purchasing the rights to books and paying advances against royalties, while funding those costs necessary for editing, designing and producing the content. Indeed, if anything, the total costs of eBook publication could well exceed those for traditional publishing, not least in view of the emergence of new line item costs for everything from managing and editing digital content to mastering the intricacies of web-based publishing (Schnittman 2009). Furthermore, beyond the specific matter of costs, there is a host of strategic considerations that will need to be addressed, including those to do with metadata and content management, with sales and marketing and with a much wider range of stakeholder interactions. There are opportunities for publishers to promote and sell eBooks direct to their customer base at a relatively low price. However, there is no guarantee that these eBooks will not be processed through the more traditional channels. Under this scenario, it is important for publishers to consider the likelihood that if their eBook price structure is channelled through multiple layers, then a number of stakeholders will share the benefits along with them.

It is clear that in order to respond to such challenges publishers will have to learn new skills, not just in the technical domain, but also in the development of innovative strategies. This is most likely to succeed where the focus switches from issues of rights management and the cost of devices, to those of knowledge sharing and the publishing of free content within communities of readers and writers. Moreover, this must all take place in a context of imaginative digital strategies that take account of the inexorable increase in eBook titles and the growing presence of online booksellers (Wischenbart 2009).

However, it is just as important that, in the process, publishers must maintain a clear focus on their core competencies and capabilities in content acquisition, distribution and management. This is likely to be the best foundation for the creation of business models that reward them for the value they provide through the publication of eBooks, and which ensure that their intellectual property rights in these markets are properly protected. It may well be that success in this regard will require that publishing reaches the same kind of tipping point that occurred in the music industry in the 1990s. There, digitization not only enabled a fundamental shift in focus from the object (the record or CD) to the content (digital music files), but also the removal of hitherto insurmountable obstacles in the shape of file formats and digital rights management (Young 2007). Clearly, there are significant differences in both the status and scale of the activities involved, with, arguably, the activities of reading and of book publishing providing less fertile ground for such breakthroughs. Nevertheless, the ability to access and download digital books from electronic bookstores using intelligent search algorithms on ubiquitous networks could result in a similar transformation of both the climate and the fortunes of the book publishing industry.

In order to reach this tipping point however, there will have to be industry-wide changes, and not least, changes to the culture of book publishing. To people brought up on the belief that their industry was somehow different, and a major element of cultural heritage, the challenges involved in such changes are understandably daunting. Nevertheless, the music industry had to face its own demons, including fears of the destruction of its infrastructure and markets, before it reformed its way to current prosperity.

Developments in eBook publishing models

In building business models for eBooks, more may be at stake for publishers than simply trying to cover new and inflated costs. Much more significant would be the need to respond to existing or potential competitors in eBook publishing and, indeed, beyond. One approach lies in collaboration with third parties such as online retailers and booksellers. This option, too, would involve strategic challenges for all concerned, not least because the most obvious candidates for partnership are companies like Amazon.com, Barnes & Noble, Scribd and Apple, which, with their immense global leverage and market presence, could make uncomfortable bedfellows in any such relationship. Let us look at some of these companies in turn.

Case study 10.5: A Collaborative Approach to eBook Publishing – Amazon

Clearly, Amazon.com is in a very strong position with regard to any approaches from potential partners. It launched its original eBook Store in 2000, which, using the Microsoft Reader format, permitted customers to download titles to a laptop or PC (King 2000). The eBook model utilized during the period 2000 to 2006 is shown in Figure 10.4.

From April 2005, Amazon.com shifted from selling eBooks directly from its website to acquiring a facilitator, Mobipocket.com, as a channel for the sale of eBooks. A simplified version of the resultant business model is illustrated in Figure 10.5

In late 2007, Amazon.com developed its own eReading device, Kindle, a product that has since progressed to Kindle 2 and Kindle DX. Customers can download titles direct to their Kindles from the Kindle store, a facility akin to the Apple iTunes service. These devices provide free access to the internet. From September 2009, Mobipocket.com ceased opening new accounts for publishers who wished to sell titles through the Kindle Store or Mobipocket.com. However,

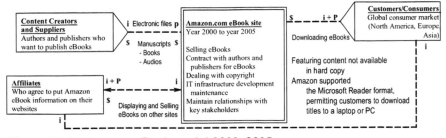

Figure 10.4   Amazon eBook model 2000–2005

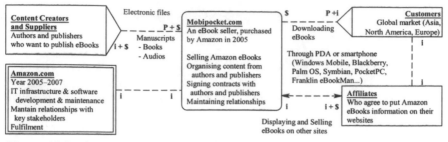

Figure 10.5   Amazon eBook model 2005–2007

Mobipocket.com is still providing services for existing accounts. Publishers, including new entrants to the market, have the opportunity to sell eBooks in the Kindle store via DTP (Digital Text Platform, a vehicle for authors to self-publish directly to the Kindle). However, publishers or authors have to prove that they have ownership over the digital rights to the books (Munarriz 2007). Depending on the quantity of eBooks requested, the authors receive 35 per cent of revenues based on their list price, regardless of discounts by Amazon. However, as will become apparent later in this chapter, these terms subsequently became open to negotiation with, variations emerging according to circumstances (DTP Admin 2010). Amazon's eBook model again underwent reconstruction in 2007 and is shown in Figure 10.6.

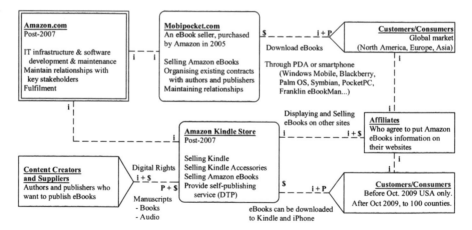

Figure 10.6   Amazon e-book model post-2007

Prior to October 2008, Kindle devices were limited to the American marketplace. At that time an international version of Kindle 2 with a built-in 3G (HSDPA) and EDGE/GSM wireless modem was released into the international marketplace with a price tag of US$ 259 (Biggs 2009). The facility enables wireless downloading of eBooks, newspapers, magazines, blogs and personal documents.

Initially Amazon operated a policy of strict control whereby only material in Mobipocket format was available, and then only on the Kindle (Herrman 2009). The company soon realized, however, that these restrictions were having an adverse effect on the overall sales of eBooks. Accordingly, in 2009 Amazon developed software which opened up access to its full stock of 240,000 eBooks to a wide range of other devices, from the iPhone and iPod Touch to notebooks, PCs and other reading devices (Elgan 2009). This was in recognition of the anticipated complementarity between the Kindle platform and, say, mobile phone users reading digital copy while waiting in grocery lines, or who, once accustomed to buying books online from Amazon, might migrate to purchasing other products and services (Stone 2009).

However, Amazon's future strategy is to make its eBooks available to other mobile and computing devices (Herrman 2009). Jeff Bezos, CEO of Amazon, is on record as saying that Amazon is more interested in selling as many eBooks as possible on its site and collecting the royalties, while strengthening its ties with customers. Its research indicates that many of its customers will buy other products from Amazon once they become interested in buying eBooks. As evidenced, Amazon does not follow Apple's business model approach, which completely excludes media competitors from using its devices to use iTunes content. Amazon is interested in developing the Amazon Kindle to build a platform where others can sell books, and in allowing readers to download eBooks to their iPhone, notebooks, PCs and other eBook readers (Elgan 2009). However, the true extent of Amazon's ambition can be seen in the variety of publishing and self-publishing initiatives that have followed upon the launch of the Kindle. These include the release in 2010 of four titles under its publishing imprint AmazonEncore, all emerging from its Amazon Breakthrough Novel Award contest. The first original manuscripts to be published by Amazon, these are available in print format and as wireless digital downloads from the Kindle Store in less than 60 seconds (Yahoo Finance News 2010). Although emanating from outside the publishing mainstream, it would be dangerous for book publishers to assume that this will be the case for future activities on the part of Amazon.

* * *

On the face of it, much of this recounting of Amazon's success might seem to argue against rather than in favour of attempts on the part of book publishers to seek an alliance. However, the online bookselling giant still does not have everything going its own way. Not only has it still to bring its expanded access strategy to fruition, but also much of the success of its current business model can be attributed to the relatively weak margins on book sales, based on a low-price strategy (Osterwalder and Pigneur 2009). Furthermore, there are plenty of competitors vying for a share of the eBook market, most recently, as will be seen below, Apple, following the launch of its iPad eBook reader. This is not simply a matter of competition for market share but also involves challenges to the well-established wholesale model for eBooks. However, before we discuss the latest developments in business models for eBooks, let us look at another US-based rival to Amazon, Barnes & Noble.

Case study 10.6: A Collaborative Approach to eBook Publishing – Barnes & Noble

The most obvious difference between Amazon.com and Barnes & Noble is that the latter has been long established as a serious player in the US book trade. Currently it has the potential to be, on the one hand, an alliance partner in eBook publishing, and on the other, a competitor with mainstream book publishers. Barnes & Noble operates as a cluster of businesses, including bookshops, an online subsidiary (BN. com) and a self-publishing programme. In July 2009, as part of an overall digital strategy, Barnes & Noble launched its eBookstore. This entry into eBooks also entailed the purchase of online retailer Fictionwise, which became responsible for the ongoing development of the Barnes & Noble eBook reader programme.

In October 2009, Barnes & Noble introduced nook, an eBook reader with a colour screen, 3G and WiFi, and with a US$ 259, a price tag comparable to that of Amazon's Kindle. The company started to ship orders to customers during the first week of December 2009 (Gonsalves 2009). Significantly, nook was compatible with a wide range of competing devices from the start, including Apple's iPhone and iPod Touch, BlackBerry smartphones, and the Plastic Logic eReader, as well as with most Windows environments and Mac laptops, and PCs. Users could download the eReader software for free from an eBook store whose initial 700,000 titles were predicted to grow to over one million within a year of launch. In addition to these titles, many of them new and bestselling works available for purchase at only $9.99, a further 500,000 public domain books could be downloaded for free from Google.

Barnes & Noble is aiming to have its content available on every major platform, and from the start the system has offered the extremely user-friendly feature of allowing readers to lend books to each other. Its strategic partnership with Plastic Logic offers the potential to extend the compatibility of nook to include Sony readers, while providing Plastic Logic users with access to the Barnes & Noble eBookstore (Kendrick 2009). A particularly innovative feature of the eBookstore is that iPhone and iPod Touch users can download their products (books, movies and CDs) from Apple's App Store. This application also allows users to search millions of products simply by snapping a photograph. Using the camera on an iPhone, customers can snap a photo of the front cover of any book and within seconds be supplied with product details, editorial reviews, and customer ratings. Indeed, as the application also includes bestseller lists and book recommendations, and a store locator and events calendar, users can even find and reserve a copy of a book in any store in the B&N chain (Kendrick 2009).

Nor do the facilities offered by Barnes & Noble extend only to the owners of nook and similar reading devices. The company has a policy of working directly with both publishers and authors. In 2001, Barnes & Noble (www.bn.com) announced the creation of Barnes & Noble Digital, an electronic publishing imprint creating a direct link between authors and their readers. The two major features of this arrangement are that authors can expect to receive a greater share of the income from their works (35 per cent royalty on the retail price) and that the retail prices of these books are set lower, in an effort to build up the market for eBooks. Indeed, this facility offers authors a one-stop, direct-to-market service, including online editorial support (Business Wire News 2001). A simplified version of the B&N eBook publishing model is shown in Figure 10.7.

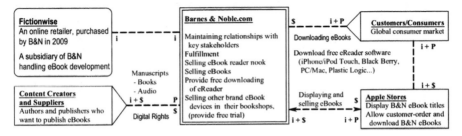

Figure 10.7 B&N eBook model

* * *

Clearly, for book publishers looking for potential partners in the eBook business, an alliance with America's largest bricks-and-mortar bookshop would have quite a lot to recommend it. However, there are other alternatives, including the somewhat different service available from the social publishing site Scribd, which we discussed in a previous section. Savikas (2009) argues that Scribd would be a more attractive partner for publishers than Amazon or B&N because of the arrangement whereby publishers set the sale price and retain 80 per cent of revenues. This compares very favourably with Amazon's (desktop publishing) programme, where the standard terms as set by Amazon allow the publisher only 35 per cent of the *suggested* price. Other attractive features of Scribd are automated pricing and real-time reporting (Savikas 2009). However, this does not necessarily mean that Scribd will win the competitive battle, because both Amazon and B&N occupy powerful market positions and they are continuing to develop their new eBook selling structure in search of competitive advantage.

The agency model: the ideal solution for eBook and future book publishing?

As mentioned in Chapter 4, just as we were completing the writing of this book, Apple introduced its new iPad tablet computer to the market. Not only is this device likely to mount a serious challenge to the market dominance of the Kindle, but also its release has precipitated a barrage of serious questions about business models for eBooks. The principal change expected is a quite radical shift away from the hitherto dominant wholesale model whereby online bookstores like Amazon.com can acquire titles from publishers and sell them at their own price, towards an agency model, which at first sight would appear to operate very much in favour of the publishers (Publishers Lunch Deluxe News 2010b).

Simultaneously with the launch of the iPad came the announcement that five major publishers namely HarperCollins, Penguin, Simon & Schuster, Macmillan and Hachette had entered into an arrangement to sell eBooks on the iPad on terms that offered the publishers a 70 per cent share of any revenues from sales through the iBook store, along with the ability to set higher prices than those at Amazon (Johnson and Arthur 2010). Although not signatories to the agreement with Apple, a number of major textbook publishers, including Pearson, McGraw-Hill and Houghton Harcourt Mifflin, subsequently struck deals with ScrollMotion Inc, a software company experienced in writing applications for Apple's iPhone and iPod Touch. The expectation was that this was in preparation for use of the iPad to access different kinds of instructional material (Trachtenberg and Kane 2010). However, just before the iPad was launched, Amazon had announced its own revised arrangements for eBooks sold via the Kindle platform, once again offering authors and publishers 70 per cent royalties on books priced in the range US\$ 2.99 to US\$ 9.99, net of a delivery charge and sold within the United States (Amazon.com News Release 2010b). While the proposals of both Amazon and Apple could clearly appeal to eBook buyers, they raised a number of issues in regard to the interests of authors and publishers, issues that went right to the heart of the proposed new agency model for eBook publishing.

In the agency model, the publishers retain possession of the goods, that is the eBook files, and pay a commission to authorized selling partners. This would not only allow publishers rather than online book retailers to set the price, but also, in enabling the simultaneous publication of eBook and hard-copy versions, could bring an end to the previous 'windowing' strategy whereby eBook versions were routinely withheld until after the hard-copy edition had been published. The agency model could also provide an opportunity to produce enhanced versions of eBooks at different prices from the original, and thus introduce an element of differentiation into a market that had threatened to become commoditized. Even more significantly, however, its implementation could go some way towards helping publishers to regain control of their content (Publishers Lunch Deluxe News 2010b).

Although the combination of higher royalties and a better deal for consumers on prices is a powerful one, there are even more fundamental issues at stake here for book publishers. First is the issue of control in the market for eBooks. Under the agency model as it currently operates, publishers would actually receive less from the proceeds of eBook sales than they would under the wholesale model. However, for publishers the major drawback with the wholesale model is that it essentially entails the operation of a loss-leading strategy which not only is unsustainable in the long run, but also maintains the dominant position enjoyed by Amazon.

This explains why the initial group of five big publishers was so interested in the deal offered by Apple. As the Hachette Group CEO later explained, adoption of the agency model would allow publishers to make rational decisions on pricing and to abandon the practice of having different release dates for eBooks and for hard-copy versions. It would also enable them to invest in authors and ensure that there was sufficient diversity in book supply to meet the demands of consumers, while assisting in the survival of both retailers and the literary culture (Publishers Lunch Deluxe News 2010h). It also explains why Macmillan subsequently engaged in a minor confrontation with Amazon over the price of eBooks. In the event, Amazon had to back down to the content owner and agree to increasing the price range of Macmillan eBooks sold on the Amazon website from the US$ 9.95 level to somewhere between US$ 12.99 and US$ 14.99 (Wray 2010).

Such concerns also explained why Random House, originally party to the discussions with Apple over the iPad and the agency model, had been reluctant to sign up along with the other five big publishers. Specifically, Random House had concerns over the issue of price control and, indeed, what it regarded as the industry's general lack of experience in setting retail prices. There were also concerns over the implications of the agency model for the future of books with lower commercial expectations, and that any requirement for windowing might adversely affect both sales and future relations with potential eBook readers (Publishers Lunch Deluxe News 2010g). Much more interesting, however, was the concern that, in focusing on eBooks, publishers might lose sight of their core mission and competencies, and specifically the importance of their most valuable asset, their editors. Critically, Random House was looking beyond the immediate issue of eBooks and competing technologies and business models, to the pursuit of strategies that would sustain and realize the real value of book publishing within a digital environment.

These events are of course only the continuation of the ongoing cut-and-thrust between book publishers, device manufacturers and online retailers, albeit with a more explicit knowledge-intensive dimension. Hence, few would regard the initial arrangement between Apple and the five publishers as by any means the definitive conclusion to negotiations over the terms of trade between them. Although the current agreement enables publishers to set book prices, there are concerns that Apple has an evolving position on pricing, not the least being the maximum price for enhanced versions of eBooks, which are those with additional features (Publishers Lunch Deluxe News 2010d).

At this point a number of observations can be made about this pricing issue. First, the ongoing price war in hard-copy bestsellers between Amazon and big retailer chains such as Wal-Mart and Woolworths will still result in their selling titles at way below the price recommended by the publishers. Second, from a consumer and free market perspective, it is hard to feel comfortable with a position where content owners can use their market power to maintain the price of eBooks at an artificially high level. Much depends, of course, on who these content owners are and the continuing nature of their arrangements with retailers. Quite conceivably, small and independent publishers could well seize the opportunity to introduce more flexibility to the pricing of eBooks and, as a result, benefit at the expense of their larger colleagues.

Nor in talking about content owners should the issue of DRM be overlooked. Arguably, it is control over content in the form of DRM that really lies at the heart of this skirmishing between the parties. All the owners of reading devices employ DRM and are encouraged to do so by publishers. This includes Sony and Barnes & Noble, as well as Apple and Amazon. In the case of Sony and Barnes & Noble, this DRM is non-proprietary and is available to any device manufacturer on a non-exclusive basis. However, that employed by Apple and, in particular, by Amazon is proprietary and restrictive (Krozser 2010). Despite the natural desire to protect content from piracy and, indeed, to fend off the competition, it is clear that material that is somehow locked-in is inherently less valuable than that which is more openly available. Nor does it sound plausible to suggest that in, say, 30 years' time, people will still be using the same devices from the same manufacturers as they are today (Tamblyn 2010).

Beyond issues of pricing and content control, however, an even bigger concern for publishers is the all-too-evident opportunity for Apple to follow Amazon by becoming a publisher in its own right. Were Apple to enable users to convert documents and images easily into eBook format, and especially if it exploited the latent self-publishing market using a variant of the agency business model, it could become a serious publishing player in a relatively short time (Nawotka 2010). In the meantime, further concerns have been expressed lest the current iTunes model, seen as restrictive and controlling by open internet enthusiasts, be applied to the iStore, thus inevitably limiting people's options when it comes to setting up and selling books (Johnson 2010c).

However, the introduction of the agency model in the deal between Apple and its five partners is only the start of a much larger process. Already there are concerns that, as it currently stands, the agency model is restrictive in that the iPad does not provide access to applications from other book retailers offering the same new titles at lower prices. The model is also likely to require some adjustment, pending the extension of the original arrangements to other publishers, and especially to smaller publishers. One current suggestion is that this might work best through these smaller publishers partnering with bigger ones more able to represent their interests in negotiation with Apple (Publishers Lunch Deluxe News 2010d).

In the meantime, competition in the eBook market continues to intensify. No sooner had the Apple deal with the five publishers been announced, than Amazon launched a niche market initiative in partnership with Harvard Business Review Press. Aimed at business users seeking to kill time or to relax for short periods, this innovation in the market for eBooks enables users worldwide to download 'short cuts', or summaries of chapters of books, to their Kindles for periods ranging from 10 to 30 minutes (Amazon.com News Release 2010c). Although the relative positions of the partners and the division of costs and benefits are as yet unclear, the assumption has to be that both players expect to make money from the arrangement. The same is likely to be the case for the recently announced joint venture between Amazon and the British Library. Under this arrangement, 19th-century fiction from the library's extensive collections will be made available for downloading free of charge on the Kindle reader. Users wishing to have their own copies can purchase them for delivery via Amazon's POD service (Brindley 2010). There are likely to be many more such initiatives as existing and incoming players compete for domination in this fast-changing and uncertain market. Just as likely is that such innovation will extend beyond models for eBook markets, into the digital marketplace as a whole, as book publishing strives to maintain its integrity in the face of technological and organizational turbulence.

Potential Considerations in Building Future Business Models for Book Publishing

This book has consistently argued the need for changing business models in book publishing in order that the industry might survive and, hopefully, prosper in the face of continued market turbulence, relentless competition and the effects of digitization. Clearly the responses to these challenges will differ from market to market and from publisher to publisher, and there will be no 'one-size-fits-all' solution. Nobody can accurately predict the future for book publishing. However, there is a growing portfolio of potential strategies and solutions, some of which are now discussed.

Collaboration

From what has already been said, it is clear that collaboration is likely to be a major element of any response by book publishers to the challenges outlined in the foregoing paragraph. The essential objective of collaboration is the co-creation and co-extraction of value in different collaborative arrangements. However, if this is to happen, then significant change will be required in the technical and social infrastructures of book publishing. Furthermore, book publishing is no different from any other industry, in that the possibilities for collaboration are many and varied, not least as regards those for collaboration with suppliers, partners and customers. These include:

- Collaboration with suppliers and key customers: this can improve costs and response times, increase sales and marketing opportunities and enhance customer satisfaction. However, if the full benefits are to be obtained, a considerable amount of information sharing will be required, which in regard to certain kinds of information can be problematic. Many firms will share data and information to do with such items as order management, aggregated sales and marketing and sales forecasts. However, they are often reluctant to share that relating to individual customers, to cost structures by product or service, and to financial and other resource allocation. For partners or potential partners to agree to the sharing of these more sensitive forms of data and information will require not only incentives to do so but, even more challenging, the establishment of trust between the parties concerned. Consequently, the practice of collaboration will be found to exist at different levels, depending on the actual business arrangements in place and the nature of the relationships between collaborating parties. At its highest level of development this will entail collaboration in the development and creation of value.
- Collaboration for co-development and creation: as firms move towards co-development, both within the firm and with other firms, the management of shared tasks, joint goals and resource leverage becomes increasingly complex, but the potential to co-create value is much greater. In order for the partners to reach this stage of collaboration, agreement will first have to be reached on issues to do with the ownership of intellectual property, on potential trade-offs between risk and reward, and responsibility for deliverables.

As pointed out in Chapter 9, participation in collaborative activities, even with competitors and potential competitors, makes sense for book publishers. Not only can this provide access to otherwise scarce resources, but also it can help make publishers more competitive, especially in emerging, network-based markets. Indeed, as also discussed in Chapter 9, book publishers are already heavily committed to collaboration in virtually every form of business activity, from R&D to manufacturing, to marketing and sales and service. This includes collaboration with competitors in order to provide a wider range of content choice to customers, including the option to produce their own books from the input of different publishers. The key to and basis for much of this collaborative activity is the networked digital environment.

Collaboration in online communities Although, in a business context, the concept of community goes back at least as far as the Middle Ages, it has attained dramatically new levels of significance in the age of the internet and the World Wide Web. These technologies have brought about hitherto inconceivable forms of interaction. In the process they have obliterated not only barriers of time and distance, but also pre-existing distinctions between the personal and commercial, and the individual and the communal. By creating and engaging in effective online communities, businesses can reach out to new and potential partners and customers, while creating and leveraging the value that leads to competitiveness and profitability. These communities can range from the transactional (where goods and services are bought and sold) to those where people with common interests (say in cooking or a particular genre of literature) come together to discuss and share ideas. They also include those social networks which range over the social and the commercial spectrums, and in some cases converge. As an example of an effective online community it would be hard to beat that of O'Reilly media.

Case study 10.7: Online Community – O'Reilly.com

O'Reilly maintains an extensive global presence through its technology books, online services, magazines, research and technology conferences. Just as important for present purposes, is that Tim O'Reilly, founder of O'Reilly media, was quick to recognize the importance of community. Acknowledging the role of community in its business model, O'Reilly emphasized the importance of acquiring a full understanding of community structures and of the need for collaboration to benefit all concerned (O'Reilly 2009). Indeed, a decade ago O'Reilly (2000) described its business strategy and tactics as follows:

> To become the information provider of choice to the people who are shaping the future of our planet, and to enable change by capturing and transmitting the knowledge of innovators and innovative communities.

So far as publishing is concerned, over the years O'Reilly has followed a strategy of building communities whose participants work with O'Reilly in the creation of books and content contributions. O'Reilly provides platforms where key stakeholders can contribute content, discuss issues and communicate with each other. However, the degree to which O'Reilly lends support to these communities extends beyond online contact, to embrace the active promotion and pursuit of innovation and ideas, including through hosting and participating in conferences around the world. It believes that collaboration with its stakeholders, listening to their opinions, learning from them and adopting their ideas can enhance O'Reilly products and services while adding value to its entire business network.

O'Reilly provides a variety of opportunities for participants to engage with its business processes. These include the opportunity to:

- Join and become a member at no cost. Membership offers the following benefits:
  - 40 per cent discount on new editions of the same book
  - membership discounts on books and events
  - free lifetime updates to electronic formats of books

- multiple eBook formats, DRM free
- participation in the O'Reilly communities
- newsletters
- account management.
- Write book reviews.
- Join O'Reilly forums, as discussed in Chapter 5.
- Comment on blog posts, put forward ideas and comments, share knowledge and receive feedback from others.
- Attend events both online and in person. O'Reilly regularly provides a list of upcoming events where their authors, editors, or staff will be presenting, exhibiting or participating. Some of these events are free, while others involve payment of a fee. They all provide opportunities for people to learn from each other and to share ideas.
- Start a user group: the O'Reilly user group and professional association programme supports their users and professional groups by providing:
  - review copies of O'Reilly products
  - donations of books and other promotional items
  - user group member discount on all O'Reilly books and conferences
  - monthly newsletter
  - O'Reilly speakers.
- Grab a widget for your website: members can construct any O'Reilly book widget on their website, blog or social networking page. These widgets are user friendly and allow copying and pasting of the code onto member websites. They are customizable and flexible as regards changes in their size and style and can add functionality to existing links to Amazon or other affiliates. They are dynamic to the extent that if new books are published, they will be automatically added to the member's widget.
- Ask a question or share an idea: members can ask questions or share ideas through http://getsatisfaction.com/oreilly.

In addition to the foregoing opportunities, O'Reilly also provides flexible avenues for the members of its communities to stay in contact. Hence, members can subscribe to O'Reilly newsletters and RSS services or connect to O'Reilly through YouTube, Twitter, Facebook and Flickr. The combination of all these services and activities is akin to a spider's web that connects and links together all stakeholders engaged in mutual support, knowledge sharing and collaborative activity for better outcomes.

* * *

Collaboration in team publishing   Another example of this type of model is that of the independent publisher Hol Art Books. Greg Albers, founder of Hol Art Books believes that collaboration can help to ensure the future survival of book publishers. To this end the company engages in collaboration during the content creation stage, employing what it terms a 'team publishing model'.

Case study 10.8: Team Publishing Model – Hol Art Books

Hol Art Books is an independent press and a relatively new player in the industry. The company was established in Boston in 2007 by founder Greg Albers. The company's vision is focused on the promotion and publishing of significant writing related to the visual arts. Its range of content extends over classic works of art criticism and history, artistic texts and biographies, translated foreign literature, and contemporary writing. Its primary focus is on the printed book but there is a growing interest in eBooks and other formats.

The company has adopted a team publishing business model which utilizes the internet to establish a community of authors, editors, designers and others with the necessary skills to contribute to the publishing process (Nawotka 2009b). The company claims that this model bridges the technological, cultural and economic gap between traditional book publishing houses and Web 2.0 self-publishing services. Through the Hol service, anyone can search for book projects and write and publish books. There are two core functions of this team model:

- Encouragement of ongoing development and maintenance of a community of users, both online and offline, together with the tools and resources required providing a cohesive work environment that enables the completion of editorials, design, and publicity related to Hol Art Book titles.
- Financing and management of vital areas such as production, distribution, and marketing for all Hol Art Book titles during the developmental stages, involving teams of users (holartbooks.com 2009).

Hol Art Books is open to various project ideas, provided that the scope of the proposal is compatible with its publication requirements. These projects are not solely limited to those conducted in the United States, nor to those in the English language. Authors have autonomy regarding the selection of team members to complete their book project. This would include people with the following attributes:

- experienced book editors, publicists, and cover designers;
- those who have management experience in leading a team that is focused on both the task and schedule;
- persons who work full-time at an independent or museum bookstore.

The key activities include:

- Find a book: particular projects can be searched for Hol Art Book's proposed or current project lists. Alternatively, authors can submit a book proposal and inaugurate a new project.

- Apply to join an existing project or build a team: authors wishing to join or to start a new book project for which approval has been given have a range of options for roles. These include those of project manager, author, editor, publicist, designer, bookstore sponsor, translator, and virtually any other roles that might be considered necessary to the completion of the project.
- Collaborate online: once assembled, the project teams coordinate their activities to present a more formal book proposal. Using a template provided by Hol Art Books, the proposal should include marketing and publicity ideas, an analysis of similar titles already in the marketplace, and sales projections. The proposal should encompass the knowledge and expertise contributed by the individual team members prior to submission for peer review. This entails an evaluation of the proposal by members of other book-publishing project teams. Where the review is favourable, Hol will commit to a contract and instigate the book-publishing process. If the proposal fails to meet the review requirements, it can be resubmitted at a later date.

It costs nothing to work on a project with Hol. However, Hol does not pay advances to authors or up-front fees to team members. Everyone (including Hol), participates on the basis of receiving a percentage of future sales. Everyone shares both the risks and the benefits. Hol's share is based on a sliding scale relative to the number of copies sold. In the case of team members, Hol provides suggestions as to the value of each individual role in the process, but the final say of who gets what remains a team decision. For example:

On a first printing of 3,000 copies of a 336-page paperback with a cover price of $15.95 Hol might estimate the net profit at $8,882. For the initial print run, the publisher's share would be 50 per cent and the author/team's share 50 per cent. For each subsequent 3,000 copies sold, the publisher's share would be reduced by 5 per cent, to a minimum of 35 per cent. Generally, the suggested team share percentages are: author 25 per cent, editor 8 per cent, publicist 8 per cent, designer 6 per cent and project manager 3 per cent.

Although readers are the final audience for all books, a publisher's primary customer often continues to be the bookseller. Indeed, the active participation of booksellers and arts institutions as sponsors is absolutely critical to the success of this publishing venture. These people represent vital stakeholders who provide the teams with encouragement and support, and a sense of purpose and direction in effectively validating their work for sale to the public.

This support and validation remains essential, given that Hol faces strong competition from:

- established publishing houses
- Google, Amazon and other internet contemporaries

- self-publishing companies
- enterprising niche entrepreneurs.

In getting to grips with this kind of competition, Hol employs a number of financial strategies which include:

- minimizing pre-production costs
- utilizing print-on-demand
- increasing staff scalability
- eliminating returns (Hol's business plan 2008).

Figure 10.8 illustrates Hol's team publishing model.

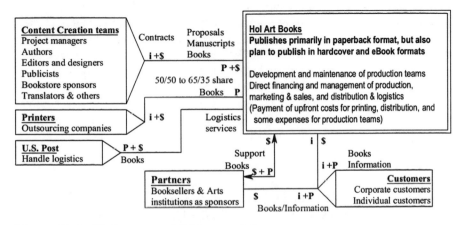

Figure 10.8   Hol's team publishing model

* * *

Collaboration with other publishers and publishing intermediaries   As indicated above, collaboration is already widespread both between book publishers and between them and a range of intermediary companies. For an illustrative example of the kind of collaboration that can operate between publishers we once again turn to O'Reilly Media. In July 2001, O'Reilly Media, Inc. and Pearson Education joined forces to create Safari Books Online. The original purpose was to upload the best technology books from leading authors and publishers to an online database that technology, IT, creative, business and management professionals could access in search of reliable and definitive answers to strategic questions.

The end result is a vast array of technology, creative, digital media, business and management content not available in any other digital library. The service has to date attracted almost one million enquiries from professionals seeking relevant and accurate information in regard to critical issues. In many ways, Safari Books Online has become a benchmark in the information and media businesses.

Having covered the issue of book publisher collaboration with third-party players such as Scribd, Lightning Source, Google, Amazon and Barnes & Noble, we now look at two examples of inter-publisher collaboration from Australia, namely the TitlePage and CoursePack projects.

TitlePage is an industry-sponsored price and availability service operated by the Australian Publishers Association. Regarded within the industry as a showpiece of collaborative effort, TitlePage was initially funded on the basis of a loan advanced by eight publishers, with the use of a subscription model to amortize repayment of the loans. General membership of the scheme is available as part of the fee that publishers pay for membership of the Australian Publishers Association. Membership is free to booksellers, who can access the bibliographic information provided via the TitlePage website. For publishers the scheme offers considerable advantages through obviating the need for them to maintain their own systems, with all that is required of them being the supplying of accurate data to TitlePage. In November 2009 the Australian Publishers Association was preparing to put out a tender for a contract to enhance the functionality of TitlePage by extending its coverage to include the availability of eBooks. Under this new arrangement, publishers would enter into a non-exclusive contract with TitlePage to enable booksellers to supply eBooks to customers through their websites or in-store, in much the same way as they sell printed editions (Sorenson 2009).

The Coursepack System is a project operated in Australia by the Copyright Agency (CAL). The project aims to make content from educational publishers and university presses available, for example, on a single-chapter basis, to universities who can create their own customized copies from the CAL website. The CAL CoursePack model is premised on gaining rights permission from publishers to reprint any amount of their works in course packs (over and above the statutory licence) in return for an agreed level of remuneration. It is also premised on publishers applying DOIs to the electronic source content of their works at an appropriate level of granularity (for example, per chapter or per article) and allowing academics to prepare and print course packs using this content. CAL's research indicated that academics and their students appreciated the convenience of content in a pack but strongly disliked the then available delivery mechanism. Accordingly, CAL set about building a platform for the system, including a search engine. It contacted publishers and suggested that they break their content down into individual electronic chapters and make it available by linking it to the CAL system. CAL's CoursePack value chain model is shown in Figure 10.9 (CAL 2004).

The system is quite straightforward in operation, whereby any institution (including booksellers) or academic that wants access to the material needs to sign a licence agreement. This done, where an institution or academic wishes to create a pack, they log in to the system, search for the desired content, compile

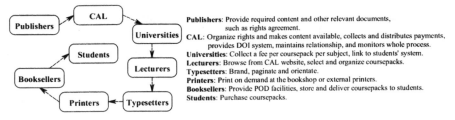

Figure 10.9   CAL's CoursePack value chain model

it online and send it to the students, either electronically or in print form. The academic can store the file and add to it the following year if required. Regarding income collection, booksellers sign a comprehensive copyright agreement which incorporates a membership fee. Universities pay each semester, based on the level of use of the material. During the semester academics can log in to the system and view an abstract of a chapter or print out a preview. They are then advised of the cost. There is no charge if a course pack is not created. If a course pack is created, the user confirms this and the transaction is recorded and billed, after which the user is free to download the material.

Clearly, the nature of collaboration varies widely between the parties concerned, and this is something that is true not just for Australia but for the rest of the world. The following example of a successful case of collaborative publishing, or as it was also termed, participatory ePublishing, was the alliance in the United States of some 20 publishers brought together by *Electric Literature*, the quarterly literary magazine that uses new media and innovative distribution to restore the place of the short story in popular culture, to co-publish a short story on Twitter. The use of the Hotsuite web-based Twitter account management service enabled the tweets to be scheduled and broadcast to all participants, with each tweet published to their feed as their own content rather than appearing as messages from *Electric Literature*. New tweets were issued every 10 minutes over a three-day period in order to maximize the likelihood of contact with the audience. The experiment was not without its problems and the target audience, comprised mainly of publishing professionals, bloggers, booksellers and journalists, was not slow to make this clear. Nevertheless, 90 per cent of the comments from followers were positive and many of the publishers involved were more than happy with the outcome (Hunter 2009b).

All the indications are that collaborative business models will become increasingly important in the near future. However, their success is predicated on the ability of the partners involved to engage in two forms of collaboration. These are collaboration in the matter of revenues, in order to open up and exploit new areas, and collaboration in cost sharing in order to operationalize the benefits to be shared (PriceWaterhouseCoopers 2009). Through their involvement in these kinds of collaborative activities, book publishers are clearly operating within networked and, in many respects, knowledge-intensive markets. In the process they are increasingly exhibiting many of the features of knowledge-intensive organizations. Before turning to a final consideration of this topic, we will look briefly at a class of business model commonly associated with knowledge-intensive operations, namely the freemium model.

Freemium models

One very good example of the operation of a freemium model is that of the advertising component of the Google business model. This is illustrated in case study 10.9.

Case study 10.9: Google's Business Model

The Google advertising model is comprised of three customer segments:

- AdWords: advertisers have the opportunity to pay for display advertisements and sponsored links on Google's search pages. The ads are displayed alongside the results of those using the Google search engine facility. Google maintains editorial control over the search quality and ensures that only relevant results appear.
- Google.com (search engine): a free service with attractive features including Gmail (web-based email), Google maps, and Picasa (an online photo album) and blogs.
- AdSense: this facility enables Google ads to be displayed on non-Google websites in return for a portion of Google's advertising revenue.

As a multi-dimensional platform, Google has a very distinctive revenue model. It earns revenue from one customer segment (advertisers) while subsidizing free offers to two other segments: web surfers and content owners. The Google business model is shown in Figure 10.10.

Already, many book publishers have expressed concern as to the extent of the free options available through Google. However, the company continues to enhance the attractiveness of its site, and this has definite implications for its freemium business model. Just one such implication relates to the proposed Google Book Settlement, which, should it eventually pass legal scrutiny, will result in a fourth customer segment for Google – and one that will definitely not be free. (This matter is considered briefly below, in the next section.)

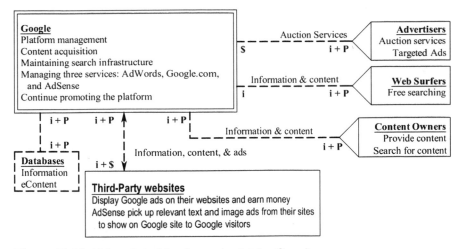

Figure 10.10 Abbreviated business model for Google

* * *

The Google initiative aside, however, freemium models could well have a future in book publishing, as could a new range of models funded by advertisements and underpinned by more targeted, relevant and personalized messages tailored to individual recipients and operating across a number of platforms (PriceWaterhouseCoopers 2009). These and similar developments would all appear to be a logical consequence of the book publishing industry becoming even more knowledge intensive in nature.

The Google Book Settlement

The settlement resulted from a collaborative project between Google and its industry partners that aimed to digitize out-of-print works held in libraries in the United States, some of which turned out to be still in copyright, and to display so-called 'snippets' of these works online. The immediate response to this initiative was a class action brought against Google by the Authors Guild (US) and the Association of American Publishers. This resulted in the announcement of a settlement in October 2008, and its subsequent amendment following criticism from foreign rights holder groups and government agencies, including the U.S. Department of Justice. While there were objections on a number of grounds, a major source of concern was that the settlement had the potential to create a monopoly for Google in respect of so-called 'orphan works', that is, works that are still in copyright but where the rights owner is not known or cannot be found. Other important amendments involved the restriction of revenue models to print-on-demand, file download and subscription, and other changes intended to facilitate competition with Google in online book sales (CAL 2009). The settlement was headed for approval at a final Fairness Hearing in February 2010.

As this book goes to press, the final judgment at the U.S. District Court for the Southern District of New York is still some time away, perhaps extending to a matter of months. Right up until Judge Chin convened the court on 18 February 2010 objections continued to pour in, not only from within the book trade but, significantly, from the U.S. Department of Justice. Apart from concerns over class certification and copyright, the Department was most concerned with a potential abuse of antitrust principles. It argued that, even with current amendments, the agreement still conferred significant and possibly anticompetitive advantages on Google as a single entity, thereby enabling the company to be the only competitor in the digital marketplace, with the rights to distribute and otherwise exploit a vast array of works in multiple formats (Miliot 2010). It is hardly surprising, therefore, that Judge Chin needs more time to arrive at a judgment, something that clearly will not happen before the deadline for submission of this book.

Does the future lie in book publishers becoming knowledge-intensive organizations?

Arguably, in the context of a global, networked economy, it is imperative that any organization seeking to be competitive, let alone to survive, must aim for or enhance its knowledge-intensive credentials. For some industries, this is likely to be harder than for others, although, as has been seen in Chapter 6, even companies operating within the primary sector can succeed in this regard through adoption of the appropriate strategies. This would also be true of book publishing, that unusual combination of manufacturing industry and cultural icon, where knowledge-intensive characteristics, while inherent, are still to some extent unevenly distributed and leveraged. The nature and integrity of these characteristics is already being tested in relation to a range of domains and issues, including:

- Ongoing and radical changes in the business environment: in terms of cost structures, buyer sophistication, consumer acceptance of new products, rights trading, mergers and acquisitions, and the clustering of firms.
- Legislation: particularly that relating to copyright and the protection of intellectual property, to information technology, privacy, data protection and competitiveness, and to the regulation and ownership of media.
- Taxation: particularly as regards levels of taxation of digitized products, with variations between tax regimes carrying implications for competition and the pace of transition from print to electronic media. These variations can also produce distortions in business models through bundling (while potentially stimulating innovation), and can lead to the migration of eContent businesses to more favourable tax regimes.
- Drivers of media spending and use: significantly, the availability of time and money and the effect of changing demographic structures. The ageing

population could be a particular problem for book publishing, with strong indications that the electronic media are more appealing to the younger generation. Consumer reading time is heavily contested by an increasing range of media, and through the proliferation of new activities made possible by digital technology.

- Shortage of human capital and skills: including the core publishing skills of content selection, editing, packaging, marketing and sales, along with business acumen and technical skills.
- Distribution structures: notably the search for efficient supply chains for controlling costs and maintaining profit margins, ensuring that orders are fulfilled speedily and accurately to bookshops, and that stock levels and returns of unsold books are minimized.

As we have tried to show throughout this book, publishers are responding to the challenges of these and other issues in a variety of ways and to different degrees. This has resulted in considerable innovation in organizational structures, practices and management, much of it enabled by developments in technology. Book publishers are utilizing technologies in their supply chains not only to conduct transactions, but also to share information and to improve connectivity with key stakeholders (Innovation+Technology 2007).

As has emerged continually throughout the book, however, technology, while undoubtedly a key enabler, and as such a necessary element in the digitization of book publishing, is not in itself a sufficient determinant of success. For this to happen, the industry must engage in the pursuit of innovation not only in technology adoption, but also across the board in terms of products, services and markets. One area that exemplifies such developments is that of verticals.

Verticals

As we have seen, both specifically in Chapter 3 and in other places throughout the book, the emergence of verticals is already a significant feature of book publishing markets. This is evident, for example, in the distribution services provided by some publishers for others, with the provider having expanded vertically from production to distribution. Although not all publishers will be large enough or sufficiently flexible in their processes and management systems to undertake the pursuit of verticality, this is a development of industry-wide significance. If, as seems likely, the globalization of publishing leads to even greater corporatization and conglomeration, smaller niche publishers surviving on the basis of innovative core competencies and capabilities will in all likelihood be unable to undertake such expansion on their own. They will need the support of partners in collaborative vertical alliances for important aspects of their supply and value chain processes. Nor need this only be an issue for smaller publishers. In the event, however, publishers will have to decide whether or not this kind of arrangement is suitable for them, and in what form. Not for the first time, we turn for an example to the work of O'Reilly Publishing.

Case study 10.10: Vertical Development at O'Reilly

O'Reilly's extensive business interests can be divided into three key areas: publishing, conferencing and online business. Its online business includes four areas as follows:

- O'Reilly.com: which offers in-depth and independent treatment of open and leading edge technologies.
- Safari Books Online (safaribooksonline.com): this joint venture with the Pearson Technology Group offers a searchable reference library of computer books from O'Reilly, Addison-Wesley, Microsoft Press and other publishers. The latest version, Safari Books Online 6.0, promises a new level of ease of use and includes features such as improved interactivity, personalized folders, collaboration and smart folders. New books, videos and articles are being added to Safari Books Online all the time.
- O'Reilly Radar blog (radar.oreilly.com): written by a team of O'Reilly technologists, this presents intelligence about emerging technology and highlights original research conducted by the O'Reilly Research group.
- Conferencing (conferences.oreillynet.com): O'Reilly media entered conferencing after the realization that this could provide a valuable tool for consumer interaction and could also play an important role in their communities. To align with its publishing programme, its conferences focus on practical, in-depth information based on an awareness of technology issues, crystallizing the critical aspects of emerging technologies. One excellent example is its Tools of Change for Publishing (TOC) conference.

At O'Reilly the philosophy for success combines business viability with the pursuit of what is deemed important. Furthermore, the focus is not on the form of the book, but on issues relating to providing value to the customer. It believes that books should encompass features such as teaching, informing and entertaining, with all the available tools being utilized to provide maximum opportunity in assisting its customers to complete their projects successfully.

* * *

Another, less well-known, example of a vertical is that operated by the online Chinese publisher Shanda Literature.

Case study 10.11: Vertical Development at Shanda Literature Ltd

Shanda Literature Ltd. was established in July 2008 and is a subsidiary of Shanda Interactive Entertainment Limited, a leading Chinese media company. Its key businesses areas include:

- Shanda Games: the company is China's leading online game company in terms of revenue and the scale and diversity of its game portfolio, which includes MMORPGs and technically advanced games.
- Haofang: one of the most popular e-sports game platforms in China.
- Hangzhou Bianfeng and Gametea: two of the leading online chess and board game platforms in China.

Shanda Literature Ltd. is China's largest online literature business, focusing on the publication of original, reader-generated literary compositions (PR Newswire 2008). Shanda Literature accounts for 30 per cent of China's top 10 online literature platforms in terms of daily average page views (as of 31 March 2009). These include:

- Qidian.com, which was acquired by the Skanda Group in 2004 and has become China's largest online original literature platform. As of 31 March 2009 it had accumulated approximately 29 million registered accounts. Qidian targets young males and features kung-fu, science fiction, military and general history stories.
- Hongxiu.com, which is attracting an ever-growing audience of young, impressionable females who enjoy immersing themselves in romantic tales. The platform held approximately two million registered accounts as of 31 March 2009.
- Hongxiu, Jjwxc.net, which also focuses on young female romantics, and as at 31 March 2009 had amassed almost three million accounts. Both Honxiu and Jiwxc were acquired by the Shanda group in 2007.

As of March 2009, Shanda Literature's three platforms, in aggregate, averaged in excess of 500 million page views per day (Huang 2009), with Shanda's customers posting more than 50 million words (the equivalent of thousands of books) each day. Depending on levels of user receptiveness to their work, some authors are given contracts whereby they can participate in a revenue-sharing agreement with the company (Shanda Interactive Entertainment Limited 2008).

Shanda Literature has also contracted a number of famous Chinese authors to furnish literary works for publication. The company has formally established 28 partnership arrangements with traditional offline book publishers. This gives these publishers the opportunity to use an online platform for books which previously had only been available through traditional channels in hard copy. Furthermore, any prospective writer can register with Shanda and can post their fictional works on any site of their choosing. Shanda editors are continually searching for titles that have commercial potential, and may subsequently offer publishing contracts to the authors concerned. This includes the possibility of the manuscripts being modified for use in other types of media, such as films, cartoons or games (Huang 2009).

Shanda Literature is one of the few companies in China with the necessary government approval to publish literature either via the internet or through a wireless network. The company generates its revenues by monetizing the copyrights of published literary works. Shanda Literature allows its users free access to most of these literary works, but charges a subscription fee for access to premium content. The CEO, Hou Xiaoqiang, who worked for Sina.com, one of China's largest internet portals, prior to joining Shanda, explained that users accessing these latter sites are able read the first half of a book for free and then must pay a small charge (about 3 cents per one thousand characters) for the remainder (Huang 2009).

Shanda Literature's content also provides opportunities for other businesses to develop alternative interactive entertainment offerings. For example, Shanda Literature has licensed certain intellectual property rights from third parties to Shanda Games, with the aim of developing MMORPGs. The company has also seconded some of its intellectual property rights relating to particular literary works to television producers, movie studios, and traditional offline book publishers.

Shanda Literature's business model is designed to source literary material provided online by authors, which is then made available, for a fee, to users through the company's online portals. After several years of operation, Shanda Literature has established a unique subscription model for online literature in China. Since literature provides a platform for creative content, expectations are that Shanda Literature will achieve potential synergies with the other entertainment content located on Shanda Online's platform. Its mission is to centralize the platform, and decentralize the content by constantly reviewing and improving its integrated services, ultimately achieving an expansion of its already diversified content offerings.

Shanda has established partnership arrangements not only with publishers but also with technology companies, the digital games industry, financial organizations and various other online portals and businesses. Representing the vertical development segment of its business, Shanda's interactive entertainment platform attracts a large and loyal user base. Collectively, Shanda has a database of 2.7 million user-generated titles. This entity provides a beneficial sideline, as many of these users represent some of the 700,000 writers who have contributed to Shanda's sites (Huang 2009). These writers are also their readers.

In 2009, Shanda Literature attended its first Frankfurt Book Fair. It was keen to establish collaborative relationships on a global basis to promote its literature to a worldwide audience (Huang 2009). A simplified overview of the Shanda Group's organizational chart is shown in Figure 10.11.

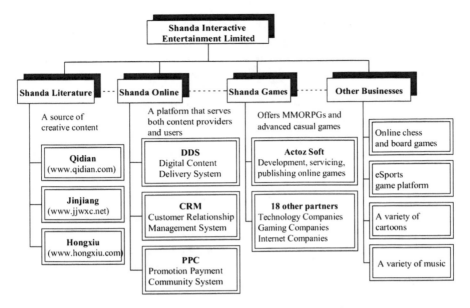

Figure 10.11 Abbreviated organizational chart for Shanda

* * *

The Shanda case illustrates how not just the notion of verticality, but also its uptake and practice by a Chinese book publisher, has already spread to the world's manufacturing heartland. In terms of future developments this could have implications for publishers everywhere. As China has come to dominate manufacturing in everything from automobiles to white goods, who is to say that before too long it could not become the world's publishing centre? With the practice of outsourcing already extending to include some or all editorial functions, it is quite conceivable that many if not most of the activities across value and supply chains could shift from West to East. Whereas it is true that the great Western publishing houses are founded on centuries of expertise and experience and have brand names that in many case epitomize quality and success, this was also once the case for manufacturing icons like Rolls Royce and Aston Martin, which are, sadly, long gone from their original locales. It can be argued that book publishing is different and that the publishing expertise resident in Western conglomerates will ensure that control of the intellectual software remains there, but there are at least some grounds for taking the opposite point of view.

Currently, this is merely a matter of speculation, but as we have suggested, it would be dangerous and perhaps fatal for the book publishing industry not to consider the possibilities of such developments. Arguably, there is a case for greater collaboration in vertical markets across the industry, collaboration which should extend to new players and potential competitors in countries such as China and India.

Already Penguin is testing these waters by having become in 2009 the first international publisher to sign an agreement with a Chinese publisher. Partnering with Beijing-based Apabi, it will make its front and backlists of English titles available using Apabi's proprietary CEB format (Pearson News 2009). This is only one example, and in the broader context of collaboration and competition many issues remain in need of resolution. We can expect to encounter other and perhaps more challenging ones in the near future.

Viewed from the purely commercial perspective, however, and from the standpoint of comparative advantage, it could be argued that, on grounds of cost and efficiency, the fulcrum of the entire book publishing industry should shift eastwards. We are not saying that this should be the case, and clearly there are powerful practical and social reasons why this should not happen, not least in such areas as political control, censorship, cultural and open communication. But few things remain as they are forever, and not least in markets.

In more familiar vein and in terms of the kind of developments that hopefully would help to reinforce and sustain the future of book publishing, major changes are needed to culture, structures and behaviour within the industry. To the extent that these changes result in the emergence of companies that are truly customer focused, and are open to ideas and to sharing these with an extensive range of stakeholders across the web and, indeed, the blogosphere, then the knowledge-intensive paradigm will have been realized. But it is important not to make too much of this topic, or to allow the knowledge-intensive tail to wag the organizational dog. This said, we believe that, in a global, networked economy in which knowledge continues to operate as a significant resource, organizations that demonstrate core knowledge-intensive characteristics and behaviours are likely to be more successful. Furthermore, based on its long history of accommodating to change and innovating for success, we are confident that the book publishing industry is more than capable of rising to and overcoming digitization and other challenges, not least those surrounding the issue of copyright.

Although book publishers are already engaged in building business models for a digital era, total acceptance of the concept remains in the future. This book has not attempted to present any simple answers to the many questions arising from the need to find new business models for book publishing. However, it has sought to provide some of the underlying theory, along with practical evidence in the form of case studies and examples. Together, these should help publishers to reflect upon and amend their business models both for current operation and for the future. The range of examples provided has taken into account the fact that models are imperfect phenomena, and that, despite operational similarities, there will be a wide variation in the structure and content of the business models for different publishers.

The final point which we would like to make is that book publishers must not undervalue themselves in this competitive environment. Competition is fierce but, although some battles will be lost, the war is not over. From these battles, opportunities will emerge for book publishers, and those with the courage to innovate will in all likelihood reap the rewards. Publishers still have a pivotal role to play in the digital world. Their professional experience in areas of creativity, marketing and distribution, their extensive connections within the book trade, and the trust that these engender with other stakeholders, are an impressive foundation upon which to build for the future.

References

Abbott, C. 2009. Do Twitter and blogs really drive book sales? *FollowTheReader Wordpress* [Online: 24 June]. Available at: http://followthereader.wordpress.com/2009/06/24/do-twitter-and-blogs-really-drive-book-sales [Accessed 12 August 2009].

Afuah, A. 2004. Business Models: A Strategic Management Approach. New York: McGraw-Hill Irwin.

Afuah, A. and Tucci, C.L. 2001. *Internet Business Models and Strategies*. Boston, MA: McGraw Hill.

Akkermans, H. 2001, Intelligent e-business: from technology to value. *IEEE Intelligent Systems*, 16(4), 8–10.

Alavi, M., Kayworth, T.R. and Leidner, D.E. 2006. An empirical examination of the influence of organizational culture on knowledge management practices. *Journal of Management Information Systems*, 22(3), 191–224.

Albanese, A., Anderson, C., Friedman, J., and Bilton, N. 2009. Jumping off a cliff: how publishers can succeed where others failed. *Bookexpo America* [Online: 20 July]. Available at: http://bookexpocast.com/2009/07/20/jumping-off-a-cliff [Accessed 31 July 2010].

Allee, V. 2002. *A Value Network Approach for Modeling and Measuring Intangibles*, White Paper, The Transparent Enterprise, The Value of Intangibles. Madrid, 25–26 November 2002. Available at: www.intellectualcapitalcertification.it/pdf/A%20ValueNet%20Work%20Approach.pdf [Accessed 7 March 2008].

Allee, V. 2003. The Future of Knowledge: Increasing Prosperity through Value Networks. Boston: Butterworth Heinemann.

Allen, M. 2005. New thinking at Random House. *Grumpy Old Bookman* [Online: 22 November]. Available at: http://grumpyoldbookman.blogspot.com/2005/11/new-thinking-at-random-house.html [Accessed 21 December 2009].

Amazon News Release 2010a. Amazon Kindle is the most gifted item ever on Amazon.com. *Amazon* [Online: 26 December]. Available at: http://phx.corporate-ir.net/phoenix.zhtml?c=176060&p=irol-newsArticle&ID=1369429&highlight [Accessed 10 January 2010].

Amazon.com News Release 2010b. New 70 per cent royalty option for Kindle digital text platform. *Amazon* [Online: 20 January]. Available at: http://phx.corporate-ir.net/phoenix.zhtml?c=176060&p=irol-newsArticle&ID=1376977&highlight [Accessed 21 January 2010].

Amazon.com News Release 2010c. Harvard Business Review short cuts. *Amazon* [Online: 25 January]. Available at: http://phx.corporate-ir.net/phoenix.

zhtml?c=176060&p=irol-newsArticle&ID=1378404&highlight=# [Accessed 26 January 2010].

Amidon, B. 1997. *The Knowledge Evolution*. Boston, MA: Butterworth Heinemann.

Anderson, C. 2006. *The Long Tail: Why the Future of Business is Selling Less of More*. New York: Hyperion.

Andriani, L. 2008. Lulu teams with weRead, *Publishers Weekly* [Online: 8 June]. Available at: www.publishersweekly.com/article/CA6585164.html?rssid=192 [Accessed 20 October 2009].

Andriole, S.J. 2005. *The 2nd Digital Revolution*. Hershey, PA: IGI Publishing.

Ante, S.E. 2009. Scribd: an e-book upstart with unlikely fans. *Businessweek* [Online: 11 June]. Available at: www.businessweek.com/magazine/content/09_25/b4136054153678.htm [Accessed 10 August 2009].

AOL News 2010. Apple introduces new $499 iPad tablet computer. *AOL* [Online: 28 January]. Available at: www.aol.com.au/news/story/Apple-introduces-new-%24499-iPad-tablet-computer/2116691/index.html [Accessed 28 January 2010].

Applegate, L., Austin, R. and McFarlan, W. 2003. *Corporate Information Strategy and Management: Texts and Cases*. 6th edition. New York: McGraw Hill Irwin.

Arthur, C. 2010. Government to set up own Cloud computing system. *The Guardian* [Online: 27 January]. Available at: www.guardian.co.uk/technology/2010/jan/27/cloud-computing-government-uk [Accessed 28 January 2010].

Atkinson, R.D. 2001. *Revenge of the Disintermediated: How the Middleman is fighting E-Commerce and Hurting Consumers*. Washington, DC: Progressive Policy Institute [Online: 26 January]. Available at: www.ppionline.org/ppi_ci.cfm?contentid=2941&knlgAreaID=140&subsecid=292 [Accessed 5 June 2009].

Auer, C. and Follack, M. 2002. Using action research for gaining competitive advantage out of the internet's impact on existing business models. Proceedings of the 15th Bled Electronic Commerce Conference. Vol. 1: Research, Bled, 17–19 June, pp. 767–84.

Australian Broadcasting Corporation Podcast 2008. Cloud computing. *ABC Radio National* [Online: 14 September]. Available at: www.abc.net.au/rn/backgroundbriefing/stories/2008/2359128.htm [Accessed 3 April 2009].

B & N Press Release 2010. Barnes & Noble reports holiday sales results. *Barnes & Noble Booksellers* [Online: 7 January]. Available at: www.barnesandnobleinc.com/press_releases/2010_jan_7_holiday_sales.html [Accessed 11 January 2010]. Chapter 1

Babalina, P. 2009. An overview of online publishing technology widgets. *Helium* [Online]. Available at: www.helium.com/items/297160-an-overview-of-online-publishing-technology-widgets [Accessed 4 August 2009].

Bagchi, S. and Tulskie, B. 2000. *E-Business Models: Integrating Learning from Strategy Development Experiences and Empirical Research*. 20th Annual

International Conference of the Strategic Management Society, Canada, Vancouver, 15–18 October 2000. Available at: www.cioindex.com/nm/ articlefiles/64078-eBusinessModels.pdf [Accessed 25 August 2008].

Bahrami, H. 1998. The emerging flexible organization: perspectives from Silicon Valley, in *Strategic Human Resource Management*, edited by C. Mabey et al. London: Sage Publications, 185–99.

Baker, S. 2009. Beware Social Media Snake Oil, *Business Week* [Online: 3 December]. Available at: www.businessweek.com/magazine/content/09_50/ b4159048693735.htm [Accessed 18 December 2009].

Bangemann, E. 2005. Major publisher supports digitization – on its own terms. *ARS Technica* [Online: 12 December]. Available at: http://arstechnica.com/old/ content/2005/12/5744.ars [Accessed 14 November 2009].

Baranuik, R. 2006. Open source learning. *TED* [Online: August]. Available at: www. ted.com/talks/richard_baraniuk_on_open_source_learning.html [Accessed 5 November 2009].

Barney, J. 1996. Looking inside for competitive advantage. *Academy of Management Executive*, 9(4), 49–61.

Barrett, M., Capplemann, S., Shoib, G. and Walsham, G. 2004. Learning in knowledge communities. *European Management Journal*, 22(1), 1–11.

Batelle, J. 2005. *The Search: How Google and its Rivals Rewrote the Rules of Business and Transformed Our Culture.* New York: Portfolio.

Battelle, J. and O'Reilly, T. 2009. Web Squared. *O'Reilly Webcasts* [Online: 25 June]. Available at: www.oreillynet.com/pub/e/1358 [Accessed 8 August 2009].

Bergman, M. 2008. New currents in the Deep Web: timelines, semantics and ontologies are coming to the fore. *AI3* [Online: 9 October]. Available at: www. mkbergman.com/458/new-currents-in-the-deep-web/ [Accessed 7 June 2009].

Bergman, M. 2009. 'Must see' SemWeb. *AI3* [Online: 21 June]. Available at: www.mkbergman.com/494/must-see-semweb/ [Accessed 29 June 2009].

Bernoff, J. 2009. Winning in a world transformed by social technologies: interview with Josh Bernoff, *Beyond the Book* [Online: 19 July]. Available at: http:// beyondthebookcast.com/social-media-tools-and-tips [Accessed 2 August 2009].

Biba, P. 2009. Bring the e-books home. *Teleread* [Online: 24 March]. Available at: www.teleread.org/2009/03/24/harper-collins-goes-to-digital-catalogue [Accessed 10 December 2009].

Biggs, J. 2009. Kindle 2 goes to $259, international GSM version coming October 19, *CrunchGear* [Online: 7 October]. Available at: www.crunchgear. com/2009/10/07/kindle-2-goes-to-259-international-gsm-version-coming-october-19/ [Accessed 20 October 2009].

Blankenhorn, D. 2008. Why source matters to SaaS. *ZDNet* [Online: 16 April]. Available at: http://blogs.zdnet.com/open-source/?p=2297 [Accessed 10 July 2009].

Botkin, J. 1999. *Smart Business: How Knowledge Communities can Revolutionize Your Company*. New York: Free Press.

Boyd, D.M. and Ellison, N.B. 2007. Social network sites: definition, history, and scholarship. *Journal of Computer-Mediated Communication*, 13(1), article 11 [Online]. Available at: http://jcmc.indiana.edu/vol13/issue1/boyd.ellison.html [Accessed 1 May 2008].

Boyd, E.B. 2009. Scribd releases branded reader to news organizations, *Baynewser* [Online: 7 October]. Available at: www.mediabistro.com/baynewser/scribd/scribd_releases_branded_reader_to_news_organizations_139550.asp [Accessed 10 November 2009].

Bradley, T. 2009. Sony wireless e-book reader proves Kindle was on target. *PC World* [Online: 25 August]. Available at: www.pcworld.com/businesscenter/article/170780/sony_wireless_ebook_reader_proves_kindle_was_on_target.html [Accessed 10 September 2009].

Breede, M. 2006. Plus ca change: print on demand reverts book publishing to its pre-industrial beginnings, in *The Future of the Book in the Digital Age*, edited by B. Cope and A. Phillips. Oxford: Chandos, 27–46.

Briggs, C. 2009. Web 2.0 business models as decentralized value creation systems, in *Web 2.0 The Business Model*, edited by D. Miltiadis et al. New York: Springer, 37–52.

Brindley, L. 2010. A new global readership for forgotten literary gems. *The Sunday Times* [Online: 7 February]. Available at: http://entertainment.timesonline.co.uk/tol/arts_and_entertainment/books/article7017994.ece [Accessed 9 February 2010].

Brodkin, J. 2009. Survey casts doubt on Cloud adoption, *CIO* [Online: 26 June]. Available at: www.cio.com/article/496136/Survey_casts_doubt_on_Cloud_Adoption?TaxonomyId=1448 [Accessed 28 June 2009].

Brooks, G. 2002. Knowledge-based structures and organizational commitment, *Management Decision*, 40(6), 566–73.

Brousseau, E. and Penard, T. 2007. The economics of digital business models: a framework for analyzing the economics of platforms, *Review of Network Economics*, 6(2), 81–114.

Brown, J.S. and Duguid, P. 2001. Knowledge and organization: a social-practice perspective. *Organization Science*, 12(2), 198–213.

Bulkeley, W.M. 2006. U.K.'s Pearson tests the group dynamic for a 'Wiki' book. *The Wall Street Journal* [Online: 16 November]. Available at: http://online.wsj.com/public/article/SB116365019587024790-8qqS0CnfjGAbgmtiwe1pO8jtJ0s_20071115.html [Accessed 10 July 2009].

Burd, B.A. and Buchanan, L.E. 2004. Teaching the teachers: teaching and learning online. *Reference Services Review*, 32(4), 404–12.

Business Week Media 2005. Random House: digital is our destiny. *BusinessWeek* [Online: 28 November]. Available at: www.businessweek.com/magazine/content/05_48/b3961106.htm [Accessed 10 November 2009].

Business Wire News 2001. Barnes & Noble.com launches ebook publishing programme. *All Business* [Online: 18 October]. Available at: www.allbusiness. com/media-telecommunications/publishing-electronic-publishing/6181323-1.html [Accessed 10 October 2009].

Byrd, J. and Daffron, S. 2009. Applying technology to publishing? Start with the right technical people. *Logical Expressions* [Online: 26 March]. Available at: http://blog.logicalexpressions.com/archive/2009/03/26/applying-technology-to-publishing-start-with-the-right-technical-people.aspx [Accessed 27 June 2009].

Cader, M. 2008. Innovation is iteration: thinking next to the box. *Publishing Research Quarterly*, 24(4), 240–50.

Cairns, M. 2008. Forecasting the future of technology in publishing. *Scribd* [Online: 21 February]. Available at: www.scribd.com/doc/2137299/NYC-Technology [Accessed 10 June 2009].

Cairns, M. 2009. Can curation save publishing? *Personanon Data* [Online: 29 April]. Available at: http://personanondata.blogspot.com/2009/04/can-curation-save-publishing.html [Accessed 29 June 2009].

CAL 2004. *The CAL Digital Object Identifier Coursepack Implementation Project: Lessons Learned.* Sydney: Copyright Agency Limited.

CAL 2009. *Your Guide to the Google Settlement* [Online: 20 May]. Available at: www.copyright.com.au/assets/documents/Google%20Settlement%20Guide% 20-%20May%20update.pdf [Accessed 10 September 2009].

Calabrese, F. 2006. Knowledge-based organizations in context, *The Journal of Information and Knowledge Management Systems*, 36(1), 12–16.

Cameron, K.S. and Quinn, R.E. 1999. Diagnosing and Changing Organizational Culture: Based on the Competing Values Framework. Framlingham, MA: Addison-Wesley Publishing.

Cardoso, M., Carvalho, J.V. and Ramos, I. 2009. Open innovation communities or should it be 'networks'? in *Web 2.0 The Business Model*, edited by M.D. Lytras et al. New York: Springer, 53–74.

Casassus, B. 2010. Nourry urges publishers to join digital platform. *Bookseller* [Online: 19 January]. Available at: www.thebookseller.com/news/109849-nourry-urges-publishers-to-join-digital-platform.html [Accessed 20 January 2010].

Cassidy, J. 2002. *Dot.com: How America Lost Its Mind and Money in the Internet Era.* New York: Harper Collins.

Cellan-Jones, R. 2010. Google unveils Nexus One phone. *BBC News* [Online: 5 January]. Available at: http://news.bbc.co.uk/2/hi/8442205.stm [Accessed 7 January 2010].

Cha, B. 2009. What a Hero: HTC unveils latest Android mobile. *Silicon* [Online: 25 June]. www.silicon.com/technology/mobile/2009/06/25/htc-unveils-latest-android-mobile-39445475 [Accessed 27 June 2009].

Cheng, S.G. 2004. *Modern Publishing Industry Structures and Business Models* [Online: 7 February]. Available at: www.china.org.cn/chinese/zhaunti/2004whbg/504236.htm [Accessed at: 6 February 2008].

Chesbrough, H. and Rosenbloom, R.S. 2000. *The Role of the Business Model in Capturing Value from Innovation: Evidence from XEROX Corporation's Technology Spinoff Companies*. Boston, MA: Harvard Business School.

Chesbrough, H.W. 2007. Why companies should have open business models. *Sloan Management Review*, 48(2), 22–8.

Choo, C.W. 2005. *The Knowing Organization: How Organizations Use Information to Construct Meaning*. Oxford: Oxford University Press.

Christensen, J. 2009. Shortcovers: update on e-reading devices and software. Digital Book Conference, New York, 11–12 May 2009. Available at: www.idpf.org/digitalbook09/Presentations/2%20jchristensen.pdf [Accessed 10 June 2009].

Christensen, T. 2007. Mainstream and alternative book publishing. *Blogrightreading* [Online: 6 November]. Available at: www.rightreading.com/blog/2007/11/06/mainstream-and-alternative-book-publishing [Accessed 9 May 2009].

Cohen, D. and Prusak, L. 2001. *In Good Company*. Boston, MA: Harvard Business School Press.

Cohen, H. 2008. Seven ways to market in a virtual world: Part 1. *Clickz* [Online: 8 May]. Available at: www.clickz.com/3629408 [Accessed 27 July 2009].

Collier, M. 2009. The idea that 'content is king' in blogging is total bullshit. *The Viral Golden* [Online: 4 June]. Available at: http://moblogsmoproblems.blogspot.com/2009/06/idea-that-content-is-king-in-blogging.html [Accessed 3 June 2009].

Collingridge, P. 2009. Content is free but curation is sacred. *Time Semit* [Online: 26 January]. Available at: http://aptstudio.com/timesemit/2009/01/26/content-is-free-but-curation-is-sacred/ [Accessed 7 June 2009].

Conboy, G. 2009. Update on IDPF Standards, ePub 101. IDPF conference, New York, 11–12 May 2009. Available at: www.idpf.org/digitalbook09/Presentations/EPUB%20101.pdf [Accessed 10 June 2009].

Cone, E. 2003. Divide and conquer? AOL Time Warner book group falls to pieces. *Baseline* [Online: 1 February]. Available at: www.baselinemag.com/c/a/Projects-Integration/Divide-Conquer-AOL-Time-Warner-Book-Group-Falls-To-Pieces [Accessed 12 June 2009].

Cope, B. and Gollings, G. 2001. *Multilingual Book Production*. Melbourne: Common Ground Publishing.

Cope, B. and Kalantzis, M. 2006. New text technologies, globalization and the future of the book, in *The Future of the Book in the Digital Age*, edited by B. Cope and A. Phillips. Oxford: Chandos, 191–210.

Cope, B. and Phillips, A. 2006. The future of the book in the Digital Age, in *The Future of the Book in the Digital Age*, edited by B. Cope and A. Phillips. Oxford: Chandos, 1–19.

Corso, M., Martini, M. and Balocco, R. 2008. Enterprise 2.0 what models are emerging? Results from a 70 case based research. *International Journal of Knowledge and Learning*, 4(6), 595–612.

Cox, J. 2008, Why Google GPhone won't kill Apple iPhone. *PC World* [Online: 9 October]. Available at: www.pcworld.com/businesscenter/article/138226/why_google_gphone_wont_kill_apple_iphone.html [Accessed 10 June 2009].

Crum, E. 2007. HarperCollins launches browse inside widget for online book fans. *HarperCollins Publishers Corporate Press Releases* [Online: 26 February]. Available at: www.harpercollins.com/footer/release.aspx?id=522&b=&year=2007 [Accessed 22 December 2009].

Dalgic, T. and Leeuw, M. 1994. Niche marketing revisited: concept, applications and some European cases. *European Journal of Marketing*, 28(4), 34–55.

Daniels, M. 2006. *Brave New World: Digitization of Content: The Opportunities for Booksellers and the Booksellers Association*. London: The Booksellers Association of the United Kingdom & Ireland.

Datamonitor 2009. *Publishing in Asia-Pacific: Industry Profile*. MarketResearch.com, Sydney: Datamonitor Asia Pacific.

Davenport, T.H. and Beck, J.C. 2001. *The Attention Economy: Understanding the New Currency of Business*. Boston, MA: Harvard Business School Press.

Davis, M. and Walter, M. 2004. Next-wave publishing technology – Part 2: Revolutions in process. *Seybold Publications*, 3(20), 3–21.

Dawson, G. 2009. Lit bogs drive purchasing decisions. *Literary License* [Online: 13 February]. Available at: http://litlicense.blogspot.com/2009/02/lit-blogs-drive-purchasing-decisions.html [Accessed 12 August 2009].

Dawson, L. 2008. Beyond the tag cloud. *O'Reilly TOC* [Online: 11 November]. Available at: http://toc.oreilly.com/2008/11/beyond-the-tag-cloud.html [Accessed 20 June 2009].

Deal, T.E. and Kennedy, A. 2000. *The New Corporate Cultures: Revitalizing the Workplace after Downsizing, Mergers and Reengineering*. Cambridge, MA: Perseus Publishing.

De Wit, B. and Meyer, R. 2005. *Strategy Synthesis: Resolving Strategy Paradoxes to Create Competitive Advantage*. London: Thompson Learning.

de la Iglesia, J. and Gayo, J. 2009. Doing business by selling free services, in *Web 2.0 The Business Model*, edited by M.D. Lytras et al. New York: Springer, 89–102.

Dear Author News 2008. Random House looks for profits in digital future. *Dear Author* [Online: 24 November]. Available at: http://dearauthor.com/wordpress/2008/11/24/random-house-looks-for-profits-in-digital-future [Accessed 10 December 2010].

Della Penna, M. 2009. Brands struggle to reach and engage younger gen Y's within social networks. *The PMN Blog* [Online: 4 March]. Available at: http://thepmn.org/BlogRetrieve.aspx?ID+1874&PostID=54641 [Accessed 3 June 2009].

Digital Outlook Report 2009 [Online]. Available at: www.razorfish.com/download//img/content/2009DOR.pdf [Accessed 3 June 2009].

Dignan, L. 2009. Smartphones: the mobile industry is about to get 'blown apart'. *Seekingalpha* [Online: 19 May]. Available at: http://seekingalpha.com/ article/138460-smartphones-the-mobile-industry-is-about-to-get-blown-apart [Accessed 20 August 2009].

Don, S. 2009. Interview with Josh Bernoff of Groundswell on social networking. *Forreste* [Online: 13 March]. Available at: http://blogs.forrester.com/ groundswell/2008/03/audio-interview.html [Accessed 1 August 2009].

Douglas, N. 2008. Penguin Books proves the entire internet can't write a novel. *Gawker* [Online: 6 May]. Available at: http://gawker.com/387731/penguin-books-proves-the-entire-internet-cant-write-a-novel [Accessed 2 June 2009].

Drew, M. 2009. Creating a book is one thing: promoting is quite another. *Web 2.0 Meets Book Publishing 2.0.* San Francisco, CA, 26 June 2009. Available at: www.i-newswire.com/pr300408.html [Accessed 3 August 2009].

Drucker, P.F. 1969. *The Age of Discontinuity: Guidelines to Our Changing Society.* New York: Harper & Row.

DTP Admin 2010. Digital Publication Distribution Agreement. *Digital Text Platform* [Online: 15 January]. Available at: http://forums.digitaltextplatform. com/dtpforums/entry.jspa?externalID=2&categoryID=12 [Accessed 2 February 2010].

Edenius, M. and Styhre, A. 2009. The social embedding of management control in knowledge-intensive firms. *Journal of Human Resource Costing & Accounting*, 13(1), 9–28.

Edvinsson, L. 1997. Developing intellectual capital at Skandia. *Long Range Planning*, 30(3), 366–73.

Edwards, P. 2007. *Managing Wikis in Business* [Online: September]. Available at: http://pennyedwards.files.wordpress.com/2007/10/final-report-september-2007.pdf [Accessed 25 January 2010].

Elgan, M. 2009. Here comes the e-book revolution: six trends are conspiring to drive electronic books into the mainstream. *Computerworld* [Online: 7 February]. Available at: www.computerworld.com/s/article/9127538/Elgan_ Here_comes_the_e_book_revolution?taxonomyId=15&pageNumber=1&taxo nomyName=Mobile%20and%20Wireless [Accessed 12 July 2009].

Encyclopaedia of Global Industries 2007. 4th edition. Book Publishing. Detroit: Gale.

Engelhardt, T. 2008. Tomgram: the time of the book. *TomDispatch* [Online: 17 December]. Available at: www.tomdispatch.com/post/175015/the-time-of-the-book [Accessed 23 May 2009].

Epstein, J. 2002. *Book Business: Publishing, Past, Present and Future.* New York: W.W. Norton & Company Inc.

Erez, M. and Gati, E. 2004. A dynamic, multi-level model of culture: from the micro level of the individual to the macro level of a global culture. *Applied Psychology: An International Review*, 53(4), 583–98.

Euromonitor International 2003. *Country Market Insight: Books and Publishing – Australia.* London: Euromonitor International.

European Commission 2003. *The EU Publishing Industry: An Assessment of Competitiveness*. Luxembourg: Office for Official Publications of the European Communities. 92-894-5165-3.

European Commission 2008. Green Paper on Copyright in the Knowledge Economy, Brussels, *COM 466/7/ 20 p* [Online]. Available at: http://ec.europa. eu/internal_market/copyright/docs/copyright-infso/greenpaper_en.pdf [Accessed 8 June 2009].

Evans, P. and Wurster, T. 2000. *Blown to Bits: How the New Economics of Information Transforms Strategy*. Boston, MA: Harvard Business School Press.

Fahlgren, K. 2009. New on O'Reilly Labs open feedback publishing system. *TOC O'Reilly* [Online: 21 May]. Available at: http://labs.oreilly.com/2009/05/ collaborative-publishing-based-on-community-feedback.html [Accessed 4 July 2009].

Farber, D. 2008. Oracle's Ellison nails cloud computing. *CNET News* [Online: 26 September]. Available at: http://news.cnet.com/8301-13953_3-10052188-80.html [Accessed 24 July 2009].

Feigenbaum, L. 2009. The 2009 Semantic Web Landscape: technologies, tools and projects. *Slideshow* [Online: 12 May]. Available at: http://slideshare.net/ LeeFeigenbaum/semantic-web-landscape-2009 [Accessed 24 June 2009].

Feigenbaum, L., Herman, I., Hongsermeier, T., Neumann, E. and Stephens, S. 2007. The Semantic Web in action. *Scientific American* [Online: December]. Available at: www.scientificamerican.com/article.cfm?id=the-semantic-web-in-action [Accessed 4 June 2009].

Feller, A., Shunk, D. and Callarman, T. 2006. Value chains versus supply chains. *Value Chain Group* [Online: 29 March]. Available at: www.value-chain.org/ en/art/120 [Accessed 7 March 2008].

Flamm, M. 2009. Book sales end the year with a surprise. *Crain's New York Business* [Online: 29 December]. Available at: www.crainsnewyork.com/ article/20091229/FREE/912299989 [Accessed 4 January 2010].

Freiert, M. 2008. February top social networks: make way for the new guys. *Compete* [Online: 7 March]. Available at: http://blog.compete.com/2008/03/07/ top-social-networks-traffic-feb-2008 [Accessed 4 July 2009].

Funk, T. 2009. *Web 2.0 and Beyond: Understanding the New Online Business Models, Trends and Technologies*. Westport, CT: Praeger Publishers.

Galbreath, J. 1999. Customer relationship leadership: A leadership and motivation model for the twenty-first century business. *TQM Magazine*, 11(3), 161–71.

Gallaugher, J. 2002. E-Commerce and the undulating distribution channel. *Communications of the ACM*, 45(7), 89–95.

Giaglis, G.M., Klein, S. and O'Keefe, R.M. 1999. *Disintermediation, Reintermediation, or Cybermediation? The Future of Intermediaries in Electronic Marketplaces*. The 12th International Bled Electronic Commerce Conference, Bled, Slovenia. Available at: http://citeseerx.ist.psu.edu/viewdoc/ summary?doi=10.1.1.39.1793 [Accessed 3 September 2009].

Gilberto, J.P. 2009.10 reasons why cloud computing is the wave of the future. *Laptoplogic.com* [Online: 29 April]. Available at: http://laptoplogic.com/ resources/10-reasons-why-cloud-computing-is-the-wave-of-the-future [Accessed 20 July 2009].

Ginna, P. 2010. 8½ unanswered questions about the future of publishing in the digital era. *Dr. Syntax* [Online: 24 January]. Available at: www.doctorsyntax. net/2010_01_24_archive.html [Accessed 2 February 2010].

Godinez, V. 2010. Texas Instruments getting into e-books. *Dallas Morning News* [Online: 8 January]. Available at: www.dallasnews.com/sharedcontent/dws/ bus/stories/010810dnbustiebooks.54f88252.html [Accessed 20 January 2010].

Gold, A.H., Malhotra, A. and Segars, A. 2001. Knowledge management: an organizational capabilities perspective. *Journal of Management Information Systems*, 18(1), 185–214.

Golden, B. 2008. Who's getting ROI from cloud computing now? *PCWorld* [Online: 17 October]. Available at: www.pcworld.com/businesscenter/article/152429/ whos_getting_roi_from_cloud_computing_now.html [Accessed 30 June 2009].

Golden, B. 2009a. Defining private clouds, Part One: Your guide to public vs private. *CIO* [Online: 22 May]. Available at: www.cio.com.au/article/304190/ defining_private_clouds_part_one [Accessed 24 June 2009].

Golden, B. 2009b. Forrester bucks conventional wisdom on cloud computing. *CIO* [Online: 29 June]. Available at: www.cio.com/article/496213?Forrester_ Bucks_Conventional_Wisdom_on_Cloud_Computing?Source=nlt_insider_ 2009–06–30 [Accessed 30 June 2009].

Gomez, J. 2008. *Print is Dead: Books in Our Digital Age*. New York: Palgrave Macmillan.

Gonsalves, A. 2009. Barnes & Noble to sell Plastic Logic ereader. *InformationWeek* [Online: 28 October]. Available at: www.informationweek.com/news/ hardware/handheld/showArticle.jhtml?articleID=220900807 [Accessed 3 November 2009].

Gordijn, J. and Akkermans, J.M. 2000. Business modeling is not process modeling. *Proceedings of ECOMO 2000*, Salt Lake City, UT [unpaged].

Grant, R.M. 1997. The knowledge-based view of the firm: implications for management practice. *Long Range Planning*, 30(3), 450–4.

Greco, A.N. 2005. *The Book Publishing Industry*. London: Lawrence Erlbaum Associates.

Greenwood, D. 2008. Are research universities knowledge-intensive learning organizations? in *Handbook of Research on Knowledge-Intensive Organizations*, edited by D. Jemielniak and J. Kociatkiewicz. Hershey, PA: IGO-Global, 1–18.

Grey, C. and Sturdy, A. 2009. Historicising knowledge-intensive organizations: the case of Bletchley Park. *Management & Organizational History*, 4(2), 131– 50.

Guardian News 2010. The Apple iPad: reactions. *The Guardian* [Online: 27 January]. Available at: www.guardian.co.uk/technology/2010/jan/27/apple-ipad-tablet-reactions [Accessed 28 January 2010].

Ha, A. 2009. Scribd's ebook store jump-starts the Sower's mainstream success. *DigitalBeat* [Online: 11 September]. Available at: http://digital.venturebeat.com/2009/09/11/scribds-e-book-store-jump-starts-the-sowers-to-mainstream-success/ [Accessed 2 November 2009].

Hagel, J. 2002. *Out of the Box: Strategies for Achieving Profits Today and Growth Tomorrow through Web Services.* Boston, MA: Harvard Business School Press.

Hamel, G. 2007. *The Future of Management.* Boston, MA: Harvard Business School Press.

Hamel, G.C. and Prahalad, C.K. 1994. *Competing for the Future.* Boston, MA: Harvard Business School Press.

Hansen, M. 2009. Is social media worth your time? *Harvard Business Publishing* [Online: 8 December]. Available at: http://blogs.harvardbusiness.org/cs/2009/12/is_social_media_worth_your_tim.html?utm_source=feedburner&utm_medium=feed&utm_campaign=Feed%3A+harvardbusiness+%28HarvardBusiness.org%29 [Accessed 18 December 2009].

Hargadon, A. and Fanelli, A. 2002. Action and possibility: reconciling perspectives of knowledge in organizations. *Organization Science*, 12(3), 290–302.

HarperCollins News 2005. HarperCollins to create digital library. *CBROnline* [Online: 13 December]. Available at: www.cbronline.com/news/harpercollins_to_create_digital_library?print=1 [Accessed 8 December 2009].

Hatch, M.J. 1993. The dynamics of organizational culture. *Academy of Management Review*, 18(4), 657–93.

Hauschildt, J. 1997. *Innovations Management.* Munich: Verlag Vahlen.

Hedberg, B. 2000. The new organizations: managing multiple arenas for knowledge creation, in *Knowledge Horizons: The Present and the Promise of Knowledge Management*, edited by C. Despres and D. Chauvel. Boston, MA: Butterworth Heinemann, 269–86.

Hendrickson, M. 2009. Twitter scorecard for publishers. *TOC O'Reilly* [Online: 21 May]. Available at: http://toc.oreilly.com/mike-hendrickson/2009/05/ [Accessed 23 July 2009].

Herman, E.S. 1999. The threat of globalization. *Global Policy Forum* [Online: April]. Available at: www.globalpolicy.org/component/content/article/162-general/48088-the-threat-of-globalization.html [Accessed 23 May 2009].

Herrman, J. 2009. Jeff Bezos wants Amazon e-Books on more devices. *Gizmodo* [Online: 17 June]. Available at: www.gizmodo.com.au/2009/06/jeff-bezos-wants-amazon-ebooks-on-more-devices-kindle-to-fend-for-itself [Accessed 20 October 2009].

Hill, C., Jones, G., Galvin, P. and Haidar, A. 2007. *Strategic Management: An Integrated Approach.* 2nd Australian edition. Milton, QD: John Wiley & Sons Australia Ltd.

Hinchcliffe, D. 2006. Web 2.0 definition updated and Enterprise 2.0 emerges. *ZDNet* [Online: 5 November]. Available at: http://blogs.zdnet.com/Hinchcliffe/ ?p=71 [Accessed 30 June 2009].

Hofstede, G.H. 2001. *Culture's Consequences: Comparing Values, Behaviours, Institutions and Organizations Across Nations.* Thousand Oaks, CA: Sage Publications.

Hofstede, G.H. and Hofstede, G.J. 2004. *Cultures and Organizations: Software of the Mind.* 2nd edition, revised and expanded. New York: McGraw-Hill.

Hol Art Publishing 2008. *Business Plan* [Online]. Available at: www.holartbooks. com/archivesite [Accessed 7 December 2009].

Huang, W. 2009. Shanda's stunning success. *Publishing Perspectives' Frankfurt Edition* [Online: 16 October]. Available at: http://publishingperspectives.com/ ?p=7027 [Accessed 7 December 2009].

Hulse, L. 2008. *Experiments with Free Digital Content* [Online]. Available at: www.idpf.org/events/presentations/digitalbook08/lHulse08.pdf [Accessed 30 June 2009].

Hunter, A. 2009a. If new media is a giant killer, will independent publishing get the golden eggs? *Publishing Perspectives* [Online: 28 December]. Available on: http://publishingperspectives.com/?p=9739 [Accessed 4 January 2009].

Hunter, A. 2009b. Lessons from the Rick Moody Twitter Project. *Publishing Perspectives* [Online: 24 December]. Available at: http://publishingperspectives. com??p=9581 [Accessed 7 January 2010].

Hurst-Wall, J. 2007. *Digitization* [Online: 31 December]. Available at: http:// hurstassociates.blogspot.com/2007/12/digitization-definition.html [Accessed 5 July 2009].

IBISWorld 2005. *C2423 Book and Other Publishing in Australia.* Melbourne: IBISWorld.

IBISWorld 2006. *C2423 Book and Other Publishing in Australia.* Melbourne: IBISWorld.

IBISWorld 2007. *C2423 Book and Other Publishing in Australia.* Melbourne: IBISWorld.

IBISWorld 2008. *C2423 Book and Other Publishing in Australia.* Melbourne: IBISWorld.

IBISWorld 2009. *C2423 Book and Other Publishing in Australia.* Melbourne: IBISWorld.

IBISWorld 2010. *C2423 Book and Other Publishing in Australia.* Melbourne: IBISWorld.

Innovation +Technology 2007. Digital world: a technology map of the book industry. *Supplement*, April, 14–15.

iPhone News 2009. Scribd morphs into e-book retailer, *iPhone News Updated* [Online: 18 May]. Available at: http://iphone.click2creation.com/2009/05/ scribd-morphs-into-ebook-retailer/ [Accessed 20 October 2009].

Iskold, A. 2007. Random House – widgets and web services done right. *ReadWriteWeb* [Online: 18 June]. Available at: www.readwriteweb.com/

archives/random_house_widgets_and_web_services.php [Accessed 22 December 2009].

Iskold, A. 2008. Semantic Web patterns: a guide to semantic technologies. *ReadWriteWeb* [Online: 25 March]. Available at: www.readwriteweb.com/ archives/semantic_web_patterns.php [Accessed 30 June 2009].

Jansen, W., Steenbakkers, W. and Jagers, H. 2007. *New Business Models for the Knowledge Economy*. Aldershot: Gower.

Johnson, B. 2009. How Scribd made pages pay. *The Guardian* [Online: 22 July]. Available at: www.guardian.co.uk/technology/2009/jul/22/scribd-trip-adler-youtube [Accessed 10 November 2009].

Johnson, B. 2010a. Live from Google's Android phone launch. *The Guardian* [Online: 5 January]. Available at: www.guardian.co.uk/technology/blog/2010/ jan/05/google-android [Accessed 8 January 2010].

Johnson, B. 2010b. Apple iPad will choke innovation, say open internet advocates. *The Guardian* [Online: 1 February]. Available at: www.guardian.co.uk/ technology/2010/feb/01/apple-ipad-choke-innovation [Accessed 2 February 2010].

Johnson, B. 2010c. Apple iPad will choke innovation, say open internet advocates. *All Things Digital* [Online: 2 February]. Available at: http://voices.allthingsd. com/20100202/apple-ipad-will-choke-innovation-say-open-internet-advocates/?mod=ATD_rss [Accessed 3 February 2010].

Johnson, B. and Arthur, C. 2010. Apple iPad: the wait is over – but is it the future of media or an oversized phone? *The Guardian* [Online: 27 January]. Available at: www.guardian.co.uk/technology/2010/jan/27/apple-ipad-tablet-computer-kindle [Accessed 27 January 2010].

Johnson, G., Langley, A., Melin L. and Whittington, R. 2007. *Strategy as Practice: Research Directions and Resources*. Cambridge, UK: Cambridge University Press.

Johnson, H. 2009. Why smart publishers care about tech conferences. *Publishing Perspectives* [Online: 16 December]. Available at: http://publishingperspectives. com/?p=9206 [Accessed 5 January 2010].

Jones, D. 2010. Lulu.com eyes C$50m initial public offering. *The Wall Street Journal* [Online: 6 January]. Available at: http://online.wsj.com/article/BT-CO-20100106-710124.html?mod=WSJ_latestheadlines# [Accessed 7 January 2010].

Jusko, J. 2009. Building a better supply chain. *Industry Week* [Online: 22 July]. Available at: www.industryweek.com/articles/building_a_better_supply_ chain_19610.aspx [Accessed 10 August 2009].

Karena, C. 2007. Working the wiki way. *The Age* [Online 6 March]. Available at: www.theage.com.au/news/biztech/working-the-wiki-way/2007/03/05/117294 3353105.html?page=2 [Accessed 10 August 2009].

Karlsen, J.T. and Gottschalk, P. 2004. Factors affecting knowledge transfer in IT projects. *Engineering Management Journal*, 16(1), 3–10.

Karp, S. 2007. W(h)ither the book? *Publishing2.0* [Online: 18 April]. Available at: http://publishing2.com/2007/04/18/whither-the-book/ [Accessed 24 June 2009].

Karreman, D. and Alvesson, M. 2004. Cages in tandem: management control, social identity and identification in a knowledge-intensive firm. *Organization*, 11(1), 149–75.

Kasdorf, B. 2008. O'Reilly TOC: a wake-up call to publishers. *Society for Scholarly Publishing* [Online: 5 March]. Available at: http://sspnet.org/News/OReilly_TOC__A_Wake-Up_Call_to/news.aspx [Accessed 5 July 2009].

Kasdorf, W.E. 2003. *The Columbia Guide to Digital Publishing*. New York: Columbia University Press.

Kazeniac, A. 2009. Social networks: Facebook takes over top spot, Twitter climbs. *Compete* [Online: 9 February]. Available at: http://blog.compete.com/2009/02/09/facebook-myspace-twitter-social-network [Accessed 4 July 2009].

Keh, H.T. 1998. Evolution of the book publishing industry: structural changes and strategic implications. *Journal of Management History*, 4(2), 104–23.

Kelly, K. 2006. Scan This Book. *New York Times* [Online: 14 May]. Available at: www.nytimes.com/2006/05/14/magazine/14publishing.html?_r=2&oref=slogin [Accessed 7 June 2009].

Kendrick, J. 2009. Exclusive interview with Barnes & Noble: e-book reader on every platform, *jkOnTheRun* [Online: 28 July]. Available at: http://jkontherun.com/2009/07/28/exclusive-interview-with-barnes-noble-e-book-reader-on-every-platform [Accessed 3 November 2009].

Kincaid, J. 2009. Scribd streamlines embedded docs with iPaper 2. *TechCrunch* [Online: 7 October 2009]. Available at: www.techcrunch.com/2009/07/10/scribd-streamlines-embedded-docs-with-ipaper-2/ [Accessed 2 November 2009].

King, C. 2000. Amazon.com launches e-Books Store: the Amazon e-book store boasts content that is not available in print. *InternetNews* [Online: 14 November]. Available at: www.internetnews.com/ec-news/article.php/4_511051 [Accessed 10 October 2009].

Kinsella, B. 2009. Scribd adds social networking. *Publishers Weekly* [Online: 8 October]. Available at: www.publishersweekly.com/article/CA6675544.html?industryid=47152 [Accessed 10 November 2009].

Kirchner, K., Razmerita, L. and Sudzina, F. 2009. New forms of interaction and knowledge sharing on Web 2.0, in *Web 2.0 The Business Model*, edited by M. Lytras et al. New York: Springer, 1–16.

Klein, S. and Loebbecke, C. 2000, The transformation of pricing models on the Web: examples from the airline industry. 13th International Bled Electronic Commerce Conference, Bled, Slovenia, 19–21 June 2000. Available at: https://www-wi.uni-muenster.de/wi/forschen/veroeff/Bled-price-14.pdf [Accessed 25 September 2009].

Kleper, M. 2001. *The State of Digital Publishing*. Englewood Cliffs, NJ: Prentice Hall.

Kotelnikov, V. 2002, *Business Model: Ten3 Business e-Coach* [Online]. Available at: www.kotelnikov.biz [Accessed 20 February 2008].

Kotler, P. 2003. *Marketing Management*. Upper Saddle River, NJ: Prentice-Hall.

Kovac, M. 2008. *Never Mind the Web: Here Comes the Book*. Oxford: Chandos.

Koychev, I., Nikolov, R. and Dicheva, D. 2009. *Smartbook: A Vision for the Future e-Book* [Online]. Available at: http://dse.fmi.uni-sofia.bg/files/smartBook/SmartBook-edu.pdf [Accessed 20 June 2009].

Krill, P. 2009. Semantic Web set for critical mass, *InfoWorld* [Online: 16 June]. Available at: www.infoworld.com/d/applications/semantic-web-set-critical-mass-870 [Accessed 24 June 2009].

Krozser, K. 2010. Amazon, Macmillan, agency models, and quality (oh my). *Booksquare* [Online: 31 January]. Available at: http://booksquare.com/amazon-macmillan-agency-models-and-quality-oh-my [Accessed 1 February 2010].

Kumar, S. and Snavely, T. 2004. Outsourcing and strategic alliances for product development: the case of Banta Digital Group. *Technovation*, 24(12), 1001–10.

Kurosawa, R. 2007. Publishers explore the metaverse. *Booksquare* [Online: 18 June]. Available at: http://booksquare.com/publishers-explore-the-metaverse/ [Accessed 27 July 2009].

Ladegaard, G. and Syversten, C.M. 2005. Value creation in knowledge intensive firms. Discussion Paper DP-04/05 [Online]. Available at: http://orgprints.org/6192/1/DP04–05.pdf [Accessed 4 September, 2009].

Laningham, S. 2006. developerWorks interviews: Tim Berners-Lee. *IBM Developer Works* [Online: 22 August]. Available at: www.ibm.com/developerworks/podcast/dwi/cm-int082206txt.html [Accessed 10 June 2009].

Lawlor, M. 2008, Web 2.0 means business. *Signal Magazine* [Online: May]. Available at: http://www/afcea.org/signal/articles/anmviewer.asp?a=1591&print=yes [Accessed 30 June 2009].

Lawrence, E., Lawrence, J., Newton, S., Dann, S., Corbitt, B. and Thanasankit, T. 2003. *Internet Commerce Digital Models for Business*. 3rd edition. Milton, QD: John Wiley & Sons Australia Ltd.

Lawson, S. 2009. Cloud is Internet's next generation HP executive says. *InfoWorld* [Online: 25 June]. Available at: www.infoworld.com/d/cloud-computing/cloud-internets-next-generation-hp-executive-says-120 [Accessed 30 June 2009].

Lee, C.C. and Yang, J. 2000. Knowledge value chain. *The Journal of Management Development*, 19(9), 783–93.

Leitner, P. and Grechenig, T. 2008. Social networking sphere: a snapshot of trends, functionalities and revenue models. IADIS International Conference on Web Based Communities. Amsterdam, Netherlands, 24–26 July 2008. Available at: www.iadis.net/dl/final_uploads/200810C024.pdf [Accessed 4 November 2009].

Li, C. and Bernoff, J. 2009. *Groundswell: Winning in a World Transformed by Social Technologies*. Boston, MA: Harvard Business Press.

Lichtenberg, J. 2000. Thinking outside the book. *Publishers Weekly*, 247(41), 23.

Lichtenberg, R. 2009.10 Ways social media will change in 2009. *ReadWriteWeb* [Online: 11 December]. Available at: www.readwriteweb.com/archives/10_ways_social_media_will_change_in_2010.php [Accessed 20 December 2009].

Liebowicz, J. 1999. Preface, in *The Knowledge Management Handbook*, edited by J. Liebowicz. Boca Raton: CRC Press.

Liu, M.L. and Rao, B.H. 2005. *Operational Concepts and Changes of Academic Journals in the Digital Age*. ChongQing: ChongQing University Publisher.

Lönnqvist, A. 2001. *Business Performance Measurement for Knowledge-Intensive Organizations*. Tampere: Tampere University of Technology, Institute of Industrial Management [Online]. Available at: www.tut.fi/units/tuta/teta/mittaritiimi/julkaisut/HK.pdf [Accessed 20 August 2009].

Luey, B. 2007. Modernity and print III: the United States 1890–1970, in *A Companion to the History of the Book*, edited by S. Eliot and J. Rose. Oxford: Blackwell Publishing, 366–80.

McAfee, A. 2006. Enterprise 2.0 the dawn of emergent collaboration. *Sloan Management Review*, 47(3), 21–8.

McCann, J.E. and Gilkey, R. 1988. *Joining Forces: Creating and Managing Successful Mergers and Acquisitions*. Englewood Cliffs, NJ: Prentice-Hall

McCloy-Kelley, L. 2009. eBooks and ePub: a year in fast-forward. Digital Book Conference, New York 11–12 May 2009. Available at: www.idpf.org/digitalbook09/Presentations/1%20LMcCloyKelley.pdf [Accessed 30 June 2009].

McElroy, M.W. 2003. *The New Knowledge Management: Complexity, Learning and Sustainable Innovation*. Boston, MA: Butterworth Heinemann.

Magretta, J. 2002. Why business models matter. *Harvard Business Review*, 80(5), 86–92.

Marjanovic, O. and Seethamraju, S. 2008. Understanding Knowledge-intensive, Practice-oriented Business Processes. *Proceedings of the 41st Hawaii International Conference on System Science*, 373–83.

Martin, B. and Tian, X. 2008. Implications of digitization for book publishing in Australia, with particular reference to business models. Report to publishers. Melbourne. [Unpublished].

Maskell, B. 2001. The age of agile manufacturing. *Supply Chain Management*, 6(1), 5–11.

Mayer-Schonberger, V. 2009. Can we reinvent the Internet. *Science*, 325(24), 396–97.

Michaelson, G.A. 1988. Niche marketing in the trenches. *Marketing Communications*, 13(6), 19–24.

Miles, R., Snow, C., Mathews, J., Jones, G. and Coleman, H. 1997. Organizing in the knowledge age: anticipating the cellular form, *Academy of Management Executive*, 11(4), 7–24.

Miliot, J. 2010. Justice Department says it still has problems with revised Google settlement. *Publishers Weekly* [Online: 4 February]. Available at: www. publishersweekly.com/article/ca6717779.html [Accessed 9 February 2010].

Miller, L.J. 2007. *Reluctant Capitalists: Bookselling and the Culture of Consumption*. Chicago: University of Chicago Press.

Miller, P. 2007. Mills Davis talks with Talis about multi-billion dollar markets and the Semantic Wave. *Talis* [Online: 11 July]. Available at: http://blogs.talis. com/nodalities/2007/07/mills_davis_talks_with_talis_a.php [Accessed 20 June 2009].

Mills, E. 2005. Amazon, Random House throw book at Google. *CNET News* [Online: 3 November]. Available at: http://news.cnet.com/2100-1025_3-5931569.html [Accessed 20 December 2009].

Mintzberg, H. and Lampel, J. 1999. Reflecting on the strategy process. *Sloan Management Review*, 40(3), 21–30.

Morrison, J. 2006. *The International Business Environment*. 2nd edition. New York: Palgrave.

Morozov, E. 2009. Why we don't need to reinvent the book for the Web age. *Foreign Policy* [Online: 4 May]. Available at: http://neteffect.foreignpolicy. com/posts/2009/05/04/why_we_dont_have_to_reinvent_the_book_for_the_web_age [Accessed 7 July 2009].

Munarriz, R.A. 2007. Why Kindle will change the world. *The Motley Fool* [Online: 27 November]. Available at: www.fool.com/investing/general/2007/11/27/why-kindle-will-change-the-world.aspx [Accessed 10 October 2009].

Murray, S. 2007. Generating content: book publishing as a component media industry, in *Making books: Contemporary Australian Publishing*, edited by D. Carter and A. Galligan. Brisbane: University of Queensland Press, 35–51.

Musser, J. and O'Reilly, T. 2006. An O'Reilly radar report: Web 2.0 principles and best practices. *O'Reilly Radar* [Online: 7 November]. Available at: http://radar. oreilly.com/esearch/web2-report.html [Accessed 15 June 2009].

Nash, R.E. 2010a. Why publishing cannot be saved (as it is)? *Publishing Perspectives* [Online: 1 January]. Available at: http://publishingperspectives. com/?p=9832 [Accessed 4 January 2010].

Nash, R.E. 2010b. 2020 Vision: publishing predictions for the next decade. *Publishing Perspectives* [Online: 8 January]. Available at: http:// publishingperspectives.com/?p=10087 [Accessed 15 January 2010].

National Endowment for the Arts 2004. *Reading at Risk: A Survey of Literary Reading in America*. Washington DC: National Endowment for the Arts.

Nawotka, E. 2009a. Stein calls for redefinition of book in TOC keynote. *Publishers Weekly* [Online: 2 November]. Available at: www.publishersweekly.com/ article/CA6636609.html [Accessed on: 20 November 2009].

Nawotka, E. 2009b. The bookseller who balked at Black Friday, *Publishing Perspectives* [Online: 30 November]. Available at: http://publishingperspectives. com/?p=8383 [Accessed 7 December 2009].

Nawotka, E. 2010. Apple is up to something publishers may not like. *Publishing Perspectives* [Online: 29 January]. Available at: http://publishingperspectives. com/?p=10936 [Accessed 2 February 2010].

Nelson, M. 2006. The blog phenomenon and the book publishing industry. *Publishing Research Quarterly*, 22(2), 3–26.

Newell, S., Robertson, M., Scarborough, H. and Swan, J. 2002. *Managing Knowledge Work*. London: Palgrave.

Nidumolu, S., Subramani, M. and Aldrich, A. 2001. Situated learning and the situated knowledge web: exploring the ground beneath knowledge management. *Journal of Management Information Systems*, 18(1), 115–50.

Nimetz, J. 2007. Social network benefits to the B2B world. *Marketing Live* [Online: 18 November]. Available at: www.marketing-jive.com/2007/11/jody-nimetz-on-emerging-trends-in-b2b.html [Accessed 6 May 2009].

Nonaka, I. and Takeuchi, H. 1995. *The Knowledge Creating Company: How Japanese Companies Create the Dynamics of Innovation*. Oxford: Oxford University Press.

Normann, R. and Ramirez, R. 1993. From value chain to value constellation: designing interactive strategy. *Harvard Business Review*, 71(4), 65–77.

NAICS (North American Industry Classification System) 2007 Washington, DC: U.S. Census Bureau.

O'Reilly, T. 2000. Giving away free books. *O'Reilly* [Online: 30 November]. Available at: http://tim.oreilly.com/lpt/a/5345 [Accessed 10 November 2009].

O'Reilly, T. 2005. What is Web 2.0 design patterns and business models for the next generation of software. *O'Reilly* [Online: 30 September]. Available at: http://oreilly.com/pub/a/web2/archive/what-is-web-20.html?page=1 [Accessed 8 May 2009].

O'Reilly, T. 2007. What is Web 2.0 design patterns and business models for the next generation of software. *MPRA (Munich Personal RePEc Achive) Paper No. 4580* [Online: 7 November]. Available at: http://mpra.ub.uni-muenchen. de/4580/1/MPRA_paper_4580.pdf [Accessed 20 May 2009].

O'Reilly, T. 2008.21st century writer. *The Futurist* [Online: July-August]. Available at: www.wfs.org/May-June%20files/futurist_interview_tim_oreilly. htm [Accessed 19 June 2009].

O'Reilly, T. 2009. O'Reilly makes the argument for open publishing. *Toccon* [Online: 11 February]. Available at: www.toccon.com/toc2009 [Accessed 25 July 2009].

OECD (Organization for Economic Cooperation and Development) 2005. The knowledge-based economy. *OECD* [Online: 10 November]. Available at: http://stats.oecd.org/glossary/detail.asp?ID=6964 [Accessed 6 June 2009].

Osterwalder, A. 2004. The Business Model Ontology: A Proposition in a Design Science Approach. Doctoral thesis, Switzerland Lausanne: University of Lausanne.

Osterwalder, A. and Pigneur, Y. 2009. *Business Model Generation*. Amsterdam: Self-published.

Osterwalder, A., Pigneur, Y. and Tucci, C.L. 2005. Clarifying business models: origins, present, and future of the concept. *Communications of the Association for Information Systems*, 15, 1–43.

Owyang, J. 2009. The future of the social Web: in five eras. *Web Strategist* [Online: 27 April]. Available at: www.web-strategist.com/blog/2009/04/27/future-of-the-social-web [Accessed 20 July 2009].

Pagliarini, R. 2009. Must use resource: learn for free with Scribd. *CBS Money Watch* [Online: 8 July]. Available at: http://moneywatch.bnet.com/career-advice/blog/other-8-hours/must-use-resource-learn-for-free-with-scribd/423/?tag=content;col1 [Accessed 10 November 2009].

Parrish, E., Cassill, N. and Oxenham, W. 2006. Niche market strategy in the textile and apparel industry. *Journal of Fashion Marketing and Management*, 10(4), 420–32.

Pateli, A.G. and Giaglis, G.M. 2004. A research framework for analyzing business models. *European Journal of Information Systems*, 13(4), 302–14.

Paul, I. 2009a, Plastic Logic demos e-book reader with WIFI, 3G. *PC World* [Online: 28 May]. Available at: www.pcworld.com/article/165636/plastic_logic_demos_ebook_reader_with_wifi_3g_html [Accessed 7 September 2009].

Paul, I. 2009b. Sony to embrace open e-book standard. *Macworld* [Online: 14 August]. Available at: www.macworld.com/article/142281/2009/08 [Accessed 7 September 2009].

Pearson News 2009. Penguin and founder Apabi sign e-book agreement in China. *Pearson Blog* [Online: 21 April]. Available at: www.pearson.com/about-us/consumer-publishing/news/?i=109%5bAccessed [Accessed 19 December 2009].

Petrovic, O. and Kittle, C. 2001. Developing business models for e-Business. International Conference on Electronic Commerce, Vienna, 31 October 31–4 November.

Phillips, A. 2007. Does the book have a future? in *A Companion to the History of the Book*, edited by S. Eliot and J. Rose. Oxford: Oxford University Press, 547–59.

Pilkington, E. 2009. Stephen Covey's digital rights deal with Amazon startles New York publishers. *The Guardian* [Online: 15 December]. Available at: www.guardian.co.uk/books/2009/dec/15/stephen-covey-amazon-ebook-deal [Accessed 10 January 2010].

Piller, F. 2002. Customer interaction and digitizability – a structural approach, in *Moving towards Mass Customization: Information Systems and Management*

Principles, edited by C. hrsg. v. Rautenstrauch et al. New York, Berlin: Springer, 119–38.

PIRA International 2002. *Publishing in the Knowledge Economy: Competitiveness Analysis of the UK Publishing Media Sector*. London: PIRA International.

Plastic Logic Press Release 2010. QUE more than an eReader, QUE means business. *Plastic Logic* [Online: 7 January]. Available at: www.plasticlogic.com/news/pr_introque_jan072010.php [Accessed 10 January 2010]. Chapter 4.

Pool, S.W. 2000. Organizational culture and its relationship between job tension in measuring outcomes among business executives. *Journal of Management Development*, 19(1), 32–49.

Porter, M. 1985. Competitive advantage: creating and sustaining superior performance. New York: The Free Press.

Porter, M. 1996. What is strategy? *Harvard Business Review*. 6(2), 61–78.

Porter, M. 2001. Strategy and the internet. *Harvard Business Review* [Online: March] 79(3), 63–78. Available at: http://hvass.nu/s2/artikler/teori/Misc/porter.pdf [Accessed 7 May 2009].

PR Newswire News Release 2007. HarperCollins and LibreDigital announce strategic alliance to jointly provide digital services for publishing industry. *PRNewswire* [Online: 11 January]. Available at: www.prnewswire.com/news-releases/harpercollins-and-libredigital-announce-strategic-alliance-to-jointly-provide-digital-services-for-publishing-industry-53413257.html [Accessed 8 December 2009].

PR Newswire 2008. Article: Shanda announces establishment of Shanda Literature Limited, *HighBeam Research* [Online: 4 July]. Available at: www.highbeam.com/doc/1G1-180927824.html [Accessed 7 December 2009].

Prahalad, C.K. and Krishnan, M.S. 2008. *The New Age of Innovation: Driving Cocreated Value through Global Networks*. New York: McGraw-Hill.

PriceWaterhouseCoopers 2009. Global entertainment and media outlook 2009–2013. *PriceWaterhouseCoopers Global* [Online]. Available at: www.pwc.com/gx/en/global-entertainment-media-outlook/insights-and-analysis.jhtml [Accessed 26 January 2010].

Publishers Lunch Deluxe News 2009. Penguin launches online videos. *Publisherslunch* [Online: 16 June]. Available at: www.publishersmarketplace.com/lunch/archives/005456.php [Accessed 24 July 2009].

Publishers Lunch Deluxe News 2010a. The last decade in books: the biggest thing that didn't happen. *PublishersMarketplace* [Online: 4 January]. Available at: www.publishersmarketplace.com/lunch/archives/006072.php [Accessed 6 January 2010].

Publishers Lunch Deluxe News 2010b. Big Six negotiate with Apple, ready new business model for ebook. *PublishersMarketplace* [Online: 19 January]. Available at: www.publishersmarketplace.com/lunch/archives/006139.php [Accessed 20 January 2010].

Publishers Lunch Deluxe News 2010c. Harper creates new digital group; S&S realigns Australian division under new M.D. *PublishersLunch Deluxe*

[Online: 19 January]. Available at: www.publishersmarketplace.com/lunch/archives/006138.php [Accessed 21 January 2010].

Publishers Lunch Deluxe News 2010d. It's not the iPad, it's the iModel. *Publishers Marketplace* [Online: 28 January]. Available at: www.publishersmarketplace.com/automat [Accessed 29 January 2010].

Publishers Lunch Deluxe News 2010e. Napack at DBW: piracy stems from pre-pub copies. *Publishers Market Place* [Online: 26 January]. Available at: www.publishersmarketplace.com/lunch/archives/006171.php [Accessed 27 January 2010].

Publishers Lunch Deluxe News 2010f. DBW: new biz models changing the commercial rules of publishing. *Publishers Market Place* [Online: 26 January]. Available at: www.publishersmarketplace.com/lunch/archives/006175.php [Accessed 27 January 2010].

Publishers Lunch Deluxe News 2010g. Publishing execs talk to booksellers about the agency model and more. *Publishers Marketplace* [Online: 3 February]. Available at: www.publishersmarketplace.com/lunch/archives/2010_02_03.php [Accessed 5 February 2010].

Publishers Lunch Deluxe News 2010h. Hachette announces agency model, simultaneous releases; Guild says Macmillan will be at 25%. *Publishers Marketplace* [Online: 4 February]. Available at: www.publishersmarketplace.com/lunch/archives/006219.php [Accessed 6 February 2010].

Quinn, J.B. 1992. *Intelligent Enterprise: A Knowledge and Service Based Paradigm for Industry*. New York: Free Press.

Qvortrup, L. 2003. *The Hypercomplex Society*. New York: Peter Lang.

Radziwill, N. and DuPlain, R. 2009. A model for business innovation in the Web 2.0 world, in *Web 2.0 The Business Model*, edited by M.D. Lytras et al. New York: Springer, 75–88.

Rainbird, M. 2004. Demand and supply chains: the value catalyst. *International Journal of Physical Distribution & Logistics Management*, 34(3/4), 230–50.

Rappa, M. 2001. *Managing the Digital Enterprise: Business Models on the Web*. Raleigh, NC: North Carolina State University.

Rappa, M. 2006. *Business Models on the Web* [Online]. Available at: http://digitalenterprise.org/models/models.pdf [Accessed 20 December, 2006].

Ratzlaff, C. 2009. Social media strategy coaching for authors and publishers. *PublishingTrends* [Online: July]. Available at: www.publishingtrends.com/2009/07/the-social-media-consultant-cindy-ratzlaff [Accessed 4 August 2009].

Reed, J. 2009. Kindle 2 and the publishing revolution. *Publishing Talk* [Online]. Available at: www.publishingtalk.eu/blog/ebooks/kindle-2-and-the-publishing-revolution/ [Accessed 8 July 2009].

Rich, M. 2006. HarperCollins steps up its presence on the Internet. *New York Times* [Online: 3 August]. Available at: www.nytimes.com/2006/08/03/books/03book.html [Accessed 10 December 2009].

Rich, M. 2009. Legal battles over e-book rights to older books. *New York Times* [Online: 12 December]. Available at: www.nytimes.com/2009/12/13/business/media/13ebooks.html?_r=1 [Accessed 21 December 2009].

Robertson, J. 2003. So, what is a CMS? *Step Two Designs* [Online: 3 June]. Available at: www.steptwo.com.au/papers/kmc_what/index.html [Accessed 4 June 2009].

Rohde, M. 2008. Develop+Function+Release=Critical mass for semantic technologies. *DevXtra Editors' Blog* [Online: 23 May]. Available at: http://blog.devx.com/2008/05/develop-function-release-criti.html [Accessed 3 July 2009].

Rose, M.J. 2009. E-Gads, 2009! Publishing e-pocalypse or a new age? *Publishing Perspectives* [Online: 18 December]. Available at: http://publishingperspectives. com/?p=9346 [Accessed 9 January 2010]. Chapter 3.

Rosenthal, M. 2004. *Print on Demand Book Publishing*, USA: Foner Books.

Ross, S. 2010. Digital book world: the piracy, social media, and will publishers ever understand new technology? Conference. *The Huffington Post* [Online: 27 January]. Available at: www.huffingtonpost.com/steve-ross/digital-book-world-the-pi_b_437669.html [Accessed 28 January 2010].

Rothman, D. 2006. Sony's new e-reader is unveiled – along with plans to popularize its eBabel favourite. *TeleRead* [Online: 5 January]. Available at: www.teleread.org/2006/01/05/sonys-new-e-reader-is-unveiled-along-with-plans-to-popularize-its-ebabel-entry [Accessed 24 June 2009].

Safko, L. and Brake, D.K. 2009. *The Social Media Bible: Tactics, Tools and Strategies for Business Success*. Hoboken, NJ: John Wiley & Sons.

Sankar, S. 2009. The future of online social networking. *Seeking Alpha* [Online: 7 May]. Available at: http://seekingalpha.com/article/136185-the-future-of-online-social-networking?source [Accessed 19 June 2009].

Savikas, A. 2009. Scribd store a welcome addition to ebook market. *O'Reilly Radar* [Online: 17 May]. Available at: http://radar.oreilly.com/2009/05/scribd-store-a-welcome-additio.html [Accessed 10 November 2009].

Savin, J.M. 2004. Information technology strategy – managing the dark side. *Cambridge Technology Consulting Group* [Online]. Available at: www.ctcg. com/resources/news_details.asp?news_id=1006 [Accessed 29 November 2008].

Schein, E.H. 1985. How culture forms, develops and changes? in *Gaining Control of the Corporate Culture*, edited by R.H. Kilmann, M. Saxton and R. Serpa. San Francisco: Josey-Bass, 17–43.

Schein, E.H. 1999. *The Corporate Culture Survival Guide*. San Francisco: Josey-Bass. [Accessed 25 July 2009].

Schnittman, E. 2007. Kindle: the Holy Grail or the last gasp of ebooks? *OUP Blog* [Online: 19 November]. Available at: http://blog.oup.com/2007/11/kindle [Accessed 20 July 2009].

Schnittman, E. 2009. There will be disintermediation. *Black Plastic Glasses* [Online: 11 May]. Available at: www.blackplasticglasses.com/2009/05/11/ disintermediation [Accessed 5 June 2009].

Schwartz, E. 2009. What's next for book publishing. *Foreword Magazine* [Online: 6 January]. Available at: www.forewordmagazine.net/blogs/matters/ PermaLink,guid,acbfe704-a9be-4f5d-9011–1ff438229b17.aspx [Accessed 10 September 2009].

Scott-Kemmis, D. 2006. Knowledge intensive business services (KIBS). *Services Australia Org* [Online: July]. Available at: www.servicesaustralia.org.au/ pdfFilesResearch/DITR-KnowledgeServices.pdf [Accessed 30 June 2009].

Seddon, P., Lewis, G., Freeman, P. and Shanks, G. 2004. Business models and their relationship to strategy, in *Value Creation from e-Business Models*, edited by W. Currie, Amsterdam: Elsevier Butterworth Heineman, 11–34.

Shah, A. 2010. Apple tablet due on Wednesday, McGraw-Hill CEO says. *PCWorld* [Online: 26 January]. Available at: http://news.yahoo.com/s/pcworld/20100127/ tc_pcworld/appletabletdueonwednesdaymcgrawhillceosays [Accessed 28 January 2010].

Shanda Interactive Entertainment Limited 2008. *Annual Report*. Shanghai: Shanda.

Shatzkin, M. 2007. Publishing and digital change: the implications for the book business in Australia. *The Idea Logical* [Online: 17 June]. Available at: www. idealog.com/publishing-and-digital-change-the-implications-for-the-book-business-in-Australia [Accessed 9 December 2007].

Shatzkin, M. 2008a. The digital state-of-play in the U.S. *The Idea Logical* [Online: 16 April]. Available at: www.idealog.com/the-digital-state-of-play-in-the-us [Accessed 8 October 2009].

Shatzkin, M. 2008b. Publishing trends on cloud computing and publishers. *Publishing Trends* 15(9) [Online: September]. Available at: www. publishingtrends.com/2008/09/cloud-computing [Accessed 24 June 2009].

Shatzkin, M. 2009a. Stay ahead of the shift: what publishers can do to flourish in a community-centric Web world. *The Idea Logical* [Online: 28 May]. Available at: www.idealog.com/stay-ahead-of-the-shift-what-publishers-can-do-to-flourish-in-a-community-centric-web-world [Accessed 8 June 2009].

Shatzkin M. 2009b. The emerging opportunity for today's publishers. *The Idea Logical* [Online: 17 June]. Available at: www.idealog.com/blog/the-emerging-opportunity-for-todays-publishers [Accessed 23 July 2009].

Shatzkin, M. 2009c. A context in which to evaluate ebook strategies. *The Idea Logical* [Online: 19 July]. Available at: www.idealog.com/blog/a-context-in-which-to-evaluate-ebook-strategies [Accessed 12 September 2009].

Shatzkin, M. 2009d. A baker's dozen predictions for 2010. *The Idea Logical* [Online: 30 December]. Available at: www.idealog.com/blog/a-bakers-dozen-predictions-for-2010 [Accessed 10 January 2010].

Shea, D. 2008. The Web beyond the desktop. *Digital Web* [Online: 1 April]. Available at: www.digital-web.com/articles/web_beyond_the_desktop/[Accessed 24 June 2009].

Silvester, J. and Anderson, N.R. 1999. Organizational culture change, *Journal of Occupational & Organizational Dynamics*, 10(1), 1–24.

Smith, P. 2009. A Facebook for books? Random House does social networking. *Paidcontent* [Online: 21 May]. http://paidcontent.co.uk/article/419-a-facebook-for-books-random-house-does-social-networking [Accessed 12 December 2009].

Sorenson, R. 2009. Publishers try to get into our good e-books. *The Weekend Australian*, 21–22 November, Enquirer, 5.

Spark, D. 2009.14 Successful techniques for building your industry voice with social media. *EntertainmentMedia* [Online: 12 July]. Available at: www.intertainmentmedia.com/docs/14_successful_techniques_with_social_media.pdf [Accessed 3 August 2009].

Stephen, A. 2009. Web 3.0 in plain English. *Stephen's Lighthouse* [Online: 7 June]. Available at: http://stephenslighthouse.sirsidynix.com/archives/2009/06/wb_30_in_plain.html [Accessed 10 July 2009].

Stephens, T. 2009. Empirical analysis of functional Web 2.0 environments, in *Web 2.0 The Business Model*, edited by M.D. Lytras et al. New York: Springer, 1–20.

Stokes, J. 2010. Tablet makers rethinking things in wake of iPad's $499 price [Online: 29 January]. Available at: http://arstechnica.com/apple [Accessed 4 February 2010].

Stone, B. 2009. Amazon to sell e-books for Apple devices. *New York Times* [Online: 4 March]. Available at: www.nytimes.com/2009/03/04/technology/04kindle.html [Accessed 10 October 2009].

Stone, B. 2010. With its tablet, Apple blurs line between devices. *New York Times* [Online: 27 January]. Available at: www.nytimes.com/2010/01/28/technology/companies/28apple.html [Accessed 3 February 2010].

Stone, B. and Rich, M. 2010. Apple courts publishers, while Kindle adds apps. *New York Times* [Online: 20 January]. Available at: www.nytimes.com/2010/01/21/technology/21reader.html [Accessed 3 February 2010].

Straubhaar, J. and LaRose, R. 2006. *Media Now: Understanding Media, Culture, and Technology*. 5th edition. Belmont, CA: Thomson Wadsworth.

Suber, P. 2009. Open access in 2008. *The SPARC Open Access Newsletter* [Online: 2 January]. Available at: www.earlham.edu/~peters/fos/newsletter/01–02–09.htm [Accessed 27 July 2009].

Sutherland, J. 2010. *Will Apple's iPad value-disrupt the market? – Yup* [Online: 1 February]. Available at: http://blog.ennova.ca/business-model/will-apples-ipad-value-disrupt-the-market-yup [Accessed 4 February 2010].

Swan, J., Robertson, M. and Newell, J. 2002. Knowledge management: the human factor, in *Knowledge Management Systems: Theory and Practice*, edited by S. Barnes. London: Thompson Learning, 179–94.

Tamblyn, M. 2010. Agency, pricing and the seven things publishers need to remember. *Kobo* [Online: 1 February]. Available at: http://blog.kobobooks. com/2010/02/01/agency-pricing-and-the-seven-things-publishers-need-to-remember [Accessed 4 February 2010].

The Economist News 2009. The apparatgeist calls. *The Economist* [Online: 30 December]. Available at: www.economist.com/displaystory.cfm?story_ id=15172850 [Accessed 10 January 2010].

The Sydney Morning Herald News 2010. Plastic Logic aims QUE e-reader at business crowd. *SMH* [Online: 8 January]. Available at: www.smh.com. au/digital-life/computers/plastic-logic-aims-que-ereader-at-business-crowd-20100108-lynl.html [Accessed 9 January 2010].

Thompson, B. 2006. Explosive words: at BookExpo America, Publishing's digital wave crashes against a literary pillar. *Washington Post Monday* [Online: 22 May]. Available at: www.washingtonpost.com/wp-dyn/content/ article/2006/05/21/AR2006052101349.html [Accessed 8 June 2009].

Thompson, E. 2009. Define customer relationship management your way. *Gartner* [Online: 23 July]. Available at: www.gartner.com/DisplayDocument?id=1090 116 [Accessed 2 November 2009].

Thompson, J.B. 2005. *Books in the Digital Age*. Cambridge, UK: Polity Press.

Tissen, R., Andriessen, D. and Deprez, F. 2001. *The Knowledge Dividend: Creating High-performance Companies through Value-based Knowledge Management*. London: Financial Times Prentice Hall.

Topolsky, J. 2010. Nexus One review. *Engadget* [Online: 4 January]. Available at: www.engadget.com/2010/01/04/nexus-one-review/ [Accessed 8 January 2010].

Trachtenberg, J.A. and Kane, Y.I. 2010. Textbook firms ink e-deals for iPad. *Wall Street Journal* [Online: 2 February]. Available at: http://online.wsj.com/article/ SB10001424052748703338504575041630390346178.html?mod=WSJ_ Small%20Business_IndustryNews# [Accessed 9 February 2010].

Vaknin, S. 2003. The disintermediation of content. *PromotionWorld* [Online: 23 September]. Available at: www.promotionworld.com/internet/articles/ thedesinter.html [Accessed 8 June 2009].

Vossen, G. and Hagemann, S. 2007. *Unleashing Web 2.0 From Concepts to Creativity*, Burlington, MA: Morgan Kaufmann Publishers.

W3C, World Wide Web Consortium 2007 [Online]. Available at: www.w3.org. [Accessed 24 March, 2008].

Wailgum, T. and Worthen, B. 2007. Logistics log: supply chain management, definition and solutions. *Logistics Log* [Online: 19 March]. Available at: http:// logisticslog.blogspot.com/2009/01/supply-chain-management-definition-and. html [Accessed 10 March 2009].

Waldram, H. 2009. UK publishing companies take up Twitter. *Daily Telegraph* [Online: 16 April]. Available at: www.telegraph.co.uk/scienceandtechnology/ technology/5164953/UK-publishing-companies-take-up-Twitter.html [Accessed 2 July 2009].

Walters, R. 2010. E-readers face risk of saturation. *Financial Times* [Online: 7 January]. Available at: www.ft.com/cms/s/0/6218cefc-fbbf-11de-9c29–00144feab49a.html [Accessed 10 January 2010].

Wang, C.L. and Ahmed, P.K. 2007. Dynamic capabilities: a review and research agenda. *International Journal of Management Reviews*, 9(1), 31–51.

Waxman Literary Agency News 2010. Digital Book World highlights (Jan 26–27, NYC). *Waxman Literary Agency* [Online: 1 February]. Available at: http://waxmanagency.wordpress.com [Accessed 10 February 2010].

Weill, P. and Vitale, M.R. 2001. *Place to Space*. Boston, MA: Harvard Business School Press.

Weinman, S. 2010. Why Apple's iPad won't rescue big publishing. *Daily Finance* [Online: 29 January]. Available at: www.dailyfinance.com/story/company-news/why-apples-ipad-wont-rescue-big-publishing/19335006 [Accessed 29 January 2010].

Weinstein, A. 2009. Bright future for digital books. IDPF conference, New York, 11–12 May. Available at: www.idpf.org/digitalbook09/Presentations/3%20aWeinstein.pdf [Accessed 20 June 2009].

Weissberg, A. 2008. The identification of digital book content, *Publishing Research Quarterly*, 24, 255–60.

Wetsch, L.R. 2008. The 'new' virtual consumer: exploring the experiences of new users. *Journal of Virtual Worlds Research*, 1(2), 1–12.

Wiig, K. 2004. *People-focused Knowledge Management*. Boston, MA: Butterworth-Heinemann.

Wikipedia 2009. Social network service. *Wikipedia* [Online]. Available at: http://en.wikipedia.org/wiki/Social_network_service [Accessed 3 June 2009].

Wilcox, S. 2009. The see-through supply chain. *Supply Chain Management Review* [Online: 1 April]. Available at: www.scmr.com/article/346288-The_See_through_Supply_Chain.php [Accessed 20 August 2009].

Wire, B. 2007. Near-Time and Wrox Press launch partnership to build technology communities. *AllBusiness* [Online: 30 October]. Available at: www.allbusiness.com/media-telecommunications/information-services-online/5301390–1.html [Accessed 30 June 2009].

Wirten, E.H. 2007. The global market 1970–2000: producers, in *A Companion to the History of the Book*, edited by S. Eliot and J. Rose, Oxford: Blackwell Publishing, 394–405.

Wischenbart, R. 2008. Unwrap a book digitally. *Booklab* [Online: 11 February]. Available at: www.wischenbart.com/blog?tag=harper-collins [Accessed 10 April 2009].

Wischenbart, R. 2009. Analyzing the global ranking of publishers, *Publishing Perspectives* [Online: 8 October]. Available at: http://publishingperspectives.com/?p=6675 [Accessed 9 October 2009].

Wolcott, M. 2007. What is Web 2.0, *BNET Briefing* [Online: 15 May]. Available at: www.bnet.com/2403-13241_23-66094.html [Accessed 20 June 2009].

Woudstra, W. 2009. Why book publishers should be on Twitter. *Publishing Central* [Online]. Available at: http://publishingcentral.com/articles/20090427-17-124b.html?si=1 [Accessed 3 July 2009].

Wray, R. 2010. Old media wins battle in ebook war as Amazon raises price to match Apple. *Guardian* [Online: 1 February]. Available at: www.guardian.co.uk/books/2010/feb/01/amazon-macmillan-ebooks-apple [Accessed 2 February 2010].

Wray, R. and Arthur, C. 2010. Vodafone suspends employee after obscene tweet. *Guardian* [Online: 5 February]. Available at: www.guardian.co.uk/technology/2010/feb/05/vodafone-twitter-obscene-tweet [Accessed 6 February 2010].

Wu, Y.J. 2005. Unlocking the value of business model patents in e-commerce. *The Journal of Enterprise Information Management*, 18(1), 113–30.

Yahoo Finance News 2010. AmazonEncore to publish four original manuscript submissions in spring 2010. *Yahoo Finance* [Online: 26 January]. Available at: http://finance.yahoo.com/news/AmazonEncore-to-Publish-Four-bw-2483119069.html?x=0&.v=1 [Accessed 5 February 2010].

Young, S. 2007. *The Book Is Dead: Long Live the Book*, Sydney: University of New South Wales Press.

Zott, C. and Amit, R. 2009. Business model design: an activity system perspective, *ScienceDirect* [Online: 4 July]. Available at: http://sfxprod.aarlin.edu.au:9003/swinburne2?sid=google&auinit=C&aulast=Zott&atitle=Business+Model+Design:+An+Activity+System+Perspective&id=doi:10.1016/j.lrp.2009.07.004 [Accessed 20 October 2009].

Zumbansen, P. 2008. *The Evolution of the Corporation: Organization, Finance, Knowledge and Corporate Social Responsibility*, Working Paper No. 373. Cambridge, UK: Centre for Business Research, University of Cambridge.

Bibliography

Bradbury, D. 2007. Can Amazon wean us off paper? *Guardian* [Online: 22 November]. Available at: www.guardian.co.uk/technology/2007/nov/22/news. gadgets [Accessed: 7 June 2009].

European Commission 2009. Creative content in a European digital single market: challenges for the future. *European Commission* [Online: 22 October]. Available at: http://ec.europa.eu/avpolicy/docs/other_actions/col_2009/reflection_paper. pdf [Accessed: 10 December 2009].

Fichtner, B. 2009. Cool hunting: Plastic Logic reader. *Cool Hunting* [Online]. Available at: www.coolhunting.com/archives/2009/02/plastic_logic_r.php [Accessed: 24 June 2009].

García, J.M., Geuna, A. and Steinmueller, W.E. 2008. The future evolution of the creative content industries – three discussion papers. *European Commission* [Online: December]. Available at: http://ipts.jrc.ec.europa.eu/publications/pub. cfm?id=1920 [Accessed: 9 December 2009].

Giaglis, G., Klein, S. and O'Keefe, R.M. 2002. The role of intermediaries in electronic marketplaces: developing a contingency model. *Information Systems Journal*, 12(3), 231–46.

Martin, B. 2008. Knowledge management. *Annual Review of Information Science and Technology*, 42, 371–424.

Martin, B., Deng, H. and Tian, X. 2007. Expectation and reality in digital publishing: some Australian perspectives. *Proceedings ELPUB2007 Conference on Electronic Publishing*, Vienna, Austria, 8–12 June.

Martin, B., Deng, H., Tian, X. and Byrne, J. 2006. Knowledge management and publishing: the role of intangibles in digital supply chain, *Proceedings of the International Conference on Business Knowledge Management*, Macao, 24–26 October.

Martin, B., Tian, X. and Deng, H. 2007. E-commerce in digital publishing: some indicators from a research project. *Proceedings of the IADIS International Conference e Commerce*, Algarve, Portugal, 7–9 December.

Martin, B., Tian, X. and Deng, H. 2007. Technology and publishing: developments in digital publishing in Australia. *Proceedings of the IASK International Conference E Activity and Leading Technologies*, Oporto, Portugal, 3–6 December.

Schnittman, E. 2008. Do I believe in ebooks? Part two. *OUP Blog* [Online: 11 February] Available at: http://blog.oup.com/2008/02/free_ebooks/ [Accessed 20 July 2009].

Schroeder, R. 2008. Defining virtual worlds and virtual environments. *Journal of Virtual Worlds Research*, 1(1), 1–4.

Shanda Literature's digital publishing model well received at the Frankfurt Book Fair 2009. [Online: 19 October]. Available at: http://ir1.snda.com/releasedetail. cfm?ReleaseID=424748 [Accessed: 25 October 2009].

Sherwood, J. 2009. Roll-out e-book reader development hinges of funding, but next-gen Readius is also on the cards. *Reg Hardward* [Online: 23 April]. Available at: www.reghardware.co.uk/2009/04/23/readius_update [Accessed: 23 June 2009].

Stokes, J. 2009. The future of scholarship? Harvard goes digital with Scribd. *Ars Technica* [Online]. Available at: http://arstechnica.com/media/news/2009/07/ the-future-of-scholarship-harvard-goes-digital-with-scribd.ars [Accessed 15 October 2009].

Tian, X. 2008. Book Publishing in Australia: The Potential Impact of Digital Technologies on Business Models. Thesis, Melbourne: RMIT.

Tian, X. and Martin, B. 2008. Value chains and e-business models in Australian book publishing. *Proceedings of IADIS International Conference on e-Commerce*, Amsterdam, Netherlands, 25–27 July.

Tian, X. and Martin, B. 2009. Business models in digital book publishing: some insights from Australia. *Publishing Research Quarterly*, 25(2), 73–88.

Tian, X. and Martin, B. 2009. Implications of digital technologies for book publishing. *Proceedings of IEEE CONINFO'09 The 4th International Conference on Cooperation and Promotion of Information Resources in Science and Technology*, Beijing, China, 21–23 November.

Tian, X., Martin, B. and Deng, H. 2008. The impact of digitization on business models for publishing: some indicators from a research project. *Journal of Systems and Information Technology*, 10(3), 232–50.

Websites

Amazon.com: www.amazon.com
Barnes & Noble.com: www.bn.com
Books and Publishing: http://booksandpublishing.com/books
Business Model Generation: www.businessmodelgeneration.com
Common Ground Publishing: www.commongroundpublishing.com
Common Ground Publishing Learning Online: http://newlearningonline.com
Digital Text Platform: http://dtp.amazon.com
Hol Art Book: www.holartbooks.com
Ingram Content Group: www.ingramcontent.com/default.aspx
iResearch Consulting Group, China leading Internet research group: http://english. iresearch.com.cn
Lightning Source: www.lightningsource.com
Lightning Source Testimonials: www.lightningsource.com/testimonials.aspx

Mobile & Online Business Innovation Lab (MOB) Wiki project: http://mob-labs.com/casestudies/warners.html
O'Reilly Conferencing: www.conferences.oreillynet.com
O'Reilly Media: www.oreilly.com
O'Reilly Media Community: http://getsatisfaction.com/oreilly
O'Reilly Radar Blog: www.radar.oreilly.com
Safari Books Online: www.safaribooksonline.com
Scribd online store: www.scribd.com/store
Selfpublishing Lulu.com: www.lulu.com
Shanda Interactive Entertainment Limited: http://ir1.snda.com
Shanda Literature, Hongxiu: www.hongxiu.com
Shanda Literature, Jinjiang Yuanchuang: www.jjwxc.net
Shanda Literature, Qidian: www.qidian.com
Social publishing site Scribd.com: www.scribd.com
The International Journal of the Book: http://booksandpublishing.com/journal

Index

Page numbers in **bold** refer to figures; page numbers in *italic* refer to tables; page numbers followed by a star* refer to a mini-case study.

CPSIA information can be obtained
at www.ICGtesting.com
Printed in the USA
LVOW10*2302270318
571423LV00007B/64/P